W9-CZR-404

The Changing of the Guard

The Changing of the Guard

President Clinton and the Security of Taiwan

Martin L. Lasater

Westview Press

BOULDER • SAN FRANCISCO • OXFORD

Copyright © 1995 by Westview Press, Inc.

Published in 1995 in the United States of America by Westview Press, Inc., 5500 Central Avenue, Boulder, Colorado 80301-2877, and in the United Kingdom by Westview Press, 12 Hid's Copse Road, Cumnor Hill, Oxford OX2 9JJ

A CIP catalog record for this book is available from the Library of Congress.
ISBN 0-8133-8806-6

Printed and bound in the United States of America

The paper used in this publication meets the requirements
of the American National Standard for Permanence of Paper
for Printed Library Materials Z39.48-1984.

10   9   8   7   6   5   4   3   2   1

To Chi

Contents

1

Introduction

The end of the Cold War has brought many changes to U.S. policy in Asia, but one area of continuity is the continued U.S. interest in peace and stability in the Taiwan Strait. From the outbreak of the Korean War in June 1950 through 1994, successive U.S. administrations determined it would be against American interests if the Republic of China (ROC) on Taiwan fell victim to aggression from the People's Republic of China (PRC) on mainland China.[1] As this book will demonstrate, the PRC threat to Taiwan remains, necessitating continued U.S. involvement in Taiwan's security.

One purpose of this book is to suggest ways the Clinton administration can manage the issue of Taiwan's security within the context of Sino-American (PRC-U.S.) relations. As such, the book concentrates on major factors influencing the security of Taiwan in the 1990s; it does not provide an historical overview of the issue, for which the reader is referred to the bibliography. Factors discussed in this book include President Bill Clinton's foreign policies toward the Asian Pacific region, current U.S. policies toward both China and Taiwan, systemic reforms on Taiwan since 1986, the policy implications of the "new" Taiwan to the United States, the many elements comprising Taiwan's security environment, and the present PRC military threat to Taiwan. Also discussed are the various U.S. interests in Taiwan's security and the policy challenges faced by the Clinton administration over Taiwan in U.S. relations with the PRC.

The main conclusion of the book is that President Clinton should view Taiwan's security as a matter of continued importance to the United

States. As will be discussed in detail, U.S. interests related to Taiwan's security include maintenance of peace and stability in East Asia, protection of a favorable balance of power in the region, protection of market democracies from authoritarian aggression, economic development and political stability in Asia, protection of human rights in China and Taiwan, and the avoidance of a U.S. war with the PRC.

Most of these interests have been important factors in U.S. policy toward China for decades. But in the 1990s there are significant changes in Taiwan's security environment which may require some adjustment of U.S. China policy. Of special concern in this regard are the policy implications of the modernization of the People's Liberation Army (PLA), increased calls on Taiwan for the island's independence, and the concentration of the American people on domestic issues rather than national security affairs.

It is important to keep in mind that the purpose of U.S. policy is not to divide China, but to persuade Beijing not to use force against Taiwan. This requires a delicate balance in U.S. policy so that the myriad U.S. interests in both China and Taiwan can be protected and served. While preserving this balance is in the U.S. interest, doing so has become increasingly difficult.

Areas of Inquiry

In large part, U.S. interests in the security of Taiwan hinge on the relationship between Beijing and Taipei. The United States has a strategic interest in a peaceful resolution of the future of Taiwan, the so-called "Taiwan issue." President George Bush in his 1991 statement of national security strategy expressed this interest as follows: "The United States maintains strong, unofficial, substantive relations with Taiwan where rapid economic and political change is underway. One of our goals is to foster an environment in which Taiwan and the People's Republic of China can pursue a constructive and peaceful interchange across the Taiwan Strait."[2] The U.S. interest in a peaceful resolution of the Taiwan issue was reiterated in July 1993 by Ambassador Natale H. Bellocchi, chairman of the American Institute in Taiwan, who said, "American policy toward Taiwan has remained firmly rooted in our fundamental view that the issue between the PRC and Taiwan must be settled by the people on both sides of the Straits themselves. Our abiding interest is that the issue be resolved peacefully."[3]

To protect its interests in peace in the Taiwan Strait, the United States encourages Beijing and Taipei to work out their differences without the use of force. To help ensure that this will be the case, the United States is deeply involved in both military and non-military aspects of Taiwan's security.

Taiwan's security is a very complex subject. It involves not only the military capabilities of the PRC and ROC, but also more intangible factors such as Beijing's intentions to use force in the Taiwan Strait, the political evolution underway in the "two Chinas," the reaction of other Asian countries, and the likelihood of U.S. military intervention in the event of hostilities between Taipei and Beijing. Answers to specific questions must be sought:

1. Does the PRC intend to use force against Taiwan? If so, under what circumstances? What, precisely, are PRC political objectives in regards to Taiwan?
2. Does the PRC have the military capability to use force against Taiwan? In what ways? How effective would those uses of force be in achieving Beijing's political objectives?
3. What is the U.S. role in the defense of Taiwan? In what ways, if any, should that role change in the post-Cold War period?

The Taiwan issue is clouded by history and ambiguity. The Kuomintang (KMT) and the Chinese Communist Party (CCP) have engaged in fierce political struggle over the right to rule China since the mid-1920s. Today, that struggle continues in the minds of many Chinese on both sides of the Taiwan Strait. For the United States, the Taiwan issue has been one of the most persistent and difficult controversies in Sino-American relations. Ambiguity characterizes the Taiwan issue, resulting in vastly different assessments of key issues such as the nature of the PRC threat to Taiwan, the ability of the ROC to defend itself, and the likelihood of U.S. assistance to Taiwan in case of war. Much of this ambiguity is deliberately cultivated, part of the strategies of Beijing, Taipei, and Washington to confuse the other parties and to manage effectively the politically sensitive issue of Taiwan's future.

Where possible, an assessment of Taiwan's security should include at least three generic Chinese perspectives: the PRC, ROC, and the Taiwanese people.[4] All three parties want to avoid war in the Taiwan Strait, but each has quite different interests in the future of Taiwan. An effort must be made to understand these viewpoints and their complex interaction.

From the perspective of the PRC, for example, the reunification of China is a fundamental national objective held since the founding of the People's Republic in October 1949. But how is reunification to be achieved? Many analysts believe that if the PRC elects to use force to achieve reunification, it must succeed quickly. Otherwise, Taiwan might gain international support for its defense and, possibly, for its independence as a separate nation-state. On the other hand, if the PRC uses peaceful means to achieve reunification, then Beijing must find a way to convince the people of Taiwan that their interests are best served by unifying with the mainland. This may require fundamental political and economic reform by the Chinese Communist Party and more generous terms for reunification than those offered thus far by PRC leaders.

From the perspective of the ROC, China's reunification is also a long-term national goal. But the ROC vision of a united China differs from that of the PRC. The Nationalists envision a united China under a democratic central government instead of a united China under a communist authoritarian government. Largely independent of these conflicting visions of a reunited China are a host of pragmatic exchanges taking place across the Taiwan Strait that seem to be integrating Taiwan and Hong Kong economically with mainland China in a new entity often referred to as "Greater China."

Greatly complicating relations between the PRC and ROC over the future of Taiwan is a powerful new player: the Taiwanese people. Since the introduction of true democracy on Taiwan since 1986, the people of Taiwan have become an influential force in determining their own future. The political power of the Taiwanese is reflected in the growing strength of the Democratic Progressive Party (DPP), the principal opposition to the ruling Kuomintang and a consistent advocate of Taiwan independence, and in the rise of Taiwanese control of the KMT itself, now about 80 percent Taiwanese and led by Taiwan-born President Lee Teng-hui. The democratization and Taiwanization of Taiwan politics are compelling Taipei to modify its policies toward mainland China and the international community in ways unthinkable a decade ago.

Although not directly involved in the complex interaction between the three Chinese parties, the United States does play a crucial role in the future of Taiwan. It would be difficult for the PRC successfully to use force against Taiwan if Washington intervened on Taipei's behalf. Conversely, it would be difficult for Taiwan to achieve wide diplomatic recognition as an independent country without U.S. political support. The influential role played by the United States in Taiwan's future, the broad U.S. interests in Taiwan's security, and the rapidly changing relationships across the Taiwan Strait combine to create a major policy challenge for the United States that needs to be carefully addressed by the Clinton administration.⌋ 5

US ⊂B to Taiwan

Organization of Book

The book is organized into nine chapters. The introduction explains the purpose and focus of the study and provides a summary of major conclusions.

Chapter Two, "Foreign Policy Under President Clinton," discusses Clinton administration foreign policy principles and its policies toward Asia in general. Chapter Three, "Clinton's China Policy," reviews U.S. policy toward China from 1990 through mid-1994. Both chapters are written primarily for background purposes and are intended to place Taiwan policy in a broader context.

Chapter Four, "The New Taiwan," describes the transformation of the Republic of China since 1986. Areas discussed include Taiwan's rapid democratization, its more liberalized economy, ROC flexible diplomacy, and Taiwan's expanding contacts across the Taiwan Strait.

Chapter Five, "Clinton's Taiwan Policy," examines U.S. policy toward Taiwan during the first two years of the Clinton administration. The chapter speculates on how fundamental changes on Taiwan might affect U.S. interests and American policies toward the "two Chinas."

Chapter Six, "Taiwan's Security Environment," outlines the major factors influencing Taiwan's security in the post-Cold War period. Factors examined include geography, major international trends, the international community's attitude toward Taiwan, political and economic conditions on Taiwan, relations across the Taiwan Strait, U.S.-PRC-ROC triangular relations, the intentions of PRC leaders toward Taiwan, the capabilities of the PLA, and the capabilities and intentions of the United States to assist Taiwan in the event of a crisis in the Taiwan Strait.

Chapter Seven, "The PRC Threat to Taiwan," analyzes the complex nature of Beijing's threat to Taipei in the 1990s. Topics discussed include the military capabilities of the ROC armed forces, Taiwan's war-fighting strategy, the ROC formula for comprehensive deterrence, and various scenarios for the possible use of force in the Taiwan Strait.

Chapter Eight, "U.S. Interests in the Security of Taiwan," examines the broad U.S. interests in Taiwan's security in the post-Cold War period. These interests range from preserving the balance of power in East Asia to enhancing the prospects of China evolving into a market democracy. The many roles played by the United States in Taiwan's deterrence are also analyzed.

The final chapter summarizes the main points of the study and offers recommendations for U.S. policy toward Taiwan and China during the remainder of the Clinton administration.

Principal Conclusions

Several major conclusions should be highlighted at the outset.

First, the United States has a wide range of interests in the "new" Taiwan. Since 1986 the Republic of China on Taiwan has introduced major reforms that have changed Taiwan into a new political entity characterized by democratic, free market, fair trade, and equitable social institutions. Taiwan is becoming more valuable to the United States in terms of helping Washington to achieve U.S. objectives, interests, and policies in the Asian Pacific region.

The wide range of U.S. interests in Taiwan can be seen from the perspective of the foreign policy priorities established by the Clinton administration. These priorities include:

- removing barriers to U.S. trade
- reducing trade deficits with major U.S. trading partners
- limiting the proliferation of nuclear weapons and missile delivery systems
- promoting democracy
- promoting greater respect for human rights
- ensuring security through cooperative efforts with friends and allies to reduce defense costs to the American taxpayer.

Few nations in Asia further these goals as much as the Republic of China on Taiwan. For example, Taiwan has

- systematically dismantled most of its trade barriers to U.S. goods and services
- reduced dramatically its trade surplus with the United States and formally agreed to reduce that surplus even further in progressive stages

- supported U.S. nonproliferation efforts
- established a multiparty democracy and sought to expand the community of market democracies in Asia and the world
- lifted martial law, removed restrictions on civil liberties, and respected human rights at a level equivalent to Western democracies
- sought to work with the United States and other nations to enhance collective security in the Western Pacific
- supported U.S. leadership in the Asian Pacific region and welcomed President Clinton's proposals to create a new Pacific community.

Second, Taiwan is especially valuable as an agent for positive change on mainland China. A fundamental foreign policy assumption of the Clinton administration is that "political relaxation, tolerance of opposition, a freer press, the rule of law and other democratic elements are inescapably linked with economic development."[5] Since the collapse of the Soviet Union, the United States has been especially concerned with encouraging the remaining socialist countries to adopt more democratic and free market institutions. China, as the world's largest and most powerful communist state, has received special attention from the Clinton administration in this area.

Taiwan's experiences with a free market economy and multiparty democracy provide relevant examples for the PRC. For its own interests, Taiwan is taking practical steps to encourage the PRC to liberalize its economic and political systems. These steps include:

- allowing large Taiwan investments in the Chinese economy, especially in southern and eastern coastal provinces where the free market has taken firm root
- allowing trade across the Taiwan Strait to expand rapidly
- encouraging China to become fully integrated into the global trading system
- expanding peaceful contact across the Taiwan Strait to reduce tensions with Beijing
- working with other countries to urge political reform and greater respect for human rights in the PRC.

Third, developments on Taiwan have important policy implications for the United States. For much of the 1970s and early 1980s, China's strategic value to the United States as a counterweight to the Soviet Union was thought to outweigh most U.S. interests in Taiwan. However, when the PRC adopted an "independent" foreign policy in late 1982 (including a stated willingness to have cordial relations with Moscow), U.S. policy toward the PRC and Taiwan became much more balanced. The Ronald Reagan administration adopted a "dual-track" China policy predicated on the principle that official U.S. relations with Beijing would not sacrifice friendly unofficial relations with Taipei.

To date, the "dual-track" U.S. China policy has been very successful. In all likelihood the Clinton administration will continue the policy. At the same time, it is widely recognized that U.S. interests in Taiwan have increased in recent years because of at least three key factors:

1. As it becomes more powerful, the PRC is showing signs of becoming a regional hegemon, thereby bringing into potential conflict a wide range of American and Chinese interests.
2. ROC political, economic, and social goals are much more closely aligned with those of the United States than are those of the PRC.
3. Unlike Beijing, Taipei seeks to cooperate with the United States to achieve democratic and free market objectives in the Asian Pacific region.

Reflecting these developments, the United States began to adjust its policy toward Taiwan during the George Bush administration. The two most prominent examples were President Bush's announcement in September 1992 to sell Taiwan 150 F-16 fighters and the December 1992 visit to Taipei by the Cabinet-level U.S. Trade Representative Carla Hills. Both of these actions were strongly protested by Beijing as violations of previous Sino-American agreements on the Taiwan issue.

Adjustments in U.S. policy toward Taiwan have continued under the Clinton administration. These adjustments should not cause too much difficulty in Sino-American relations as long as certain, well established principles are observed by the concerned governments:

1. Both Beijing and Washington should continue to honor the Sino-American joint communique of January 1979, marking the normalization of U.S.-PRC relations.
2. The PRC should continue its policy of resolving the Taiwan issue through peaceful means.
3. Beijing should continue its policy of openness to the outside world and of economic and political reform.
4. The ROC, PRC, and U.S. governments should continue to adhere to the principle of "one China," that is, an acknowledgment that there is but one China and Taiwan is part of China.

5. The United States should not support a specific outcome of the Taiwan issue, but it should support a peaceful resolution of the issue between the two sides of the Taiwan Strait.
6. The United States should not become a mediator between Beijing and Taipei.
7. The United States should not pressure Taiwan to accept PRC proposals for reunification.
8. The people of Taiwan should not be forced against their will to unify with the mainland.

These principles serve the basic interests of the four parties directly involved in the Taiwan issue. The United States needs to have continued peace and stability in East Asia and to avoid a conflict with the PRC; the ROC needs to be free from attack by the PRC so that time can resolve the long-standing differences between the KMT and CCP; the PRC needs to be assured that China's national sovereignty and territorial integrity with respect to Taiwan will not be violated; and the people of Taiwan need to have a voice in the determination of their future and to be free from coercion.

Fourth, the greatest threat to Taiwan's security in the 1990s may come from a PRC attack provoked by those who seek Taiwan's independence. As will be shown in this study, ROC deterrence against an unprovoked PRC attack is fairly effective. Beijing is serious about using force against Taiwan, however, if Taipei formally moves in the direction of independence. Any effort by Taiwan to become a nation-state separate from China would likely lead to a war in the Taiwan Strait, possibly involving the United States. In such a conflict, the United States might not suffer many casualties, but damage to the coastal areas of China could be substantial and the costs of the war to Taiwan could be enormous. Whether, at the end of the military confrontation, Taiwan would be recognized as an independent country is dependent upon many variables, most of which are impossible to measure accurately beforehand. Whether the gains of national independence would be worth the costs of fighting the PRC is something the people of Taiwan and their government will have to decide.

From the perspective of U.S. interests, it is difficult to justify the costs of war in the Taiwan Strait with the benefits received by Taiwan independence. An independent Taiwan probably would not bring the United States greater trade or investment opportunities; it probably would not contribute more to peace and stability in East Asia; democracy and human rights probably would not improve markedly on Taiwan or mainland China; the controversy over Taiwan's diplomatic participation in international affairs probably would not disappear; and Sino-American relations probably would not improve.

The costs to the United States of a war in the Taiwan Strait are more tangible. These include a possible military confrontation with the PRC, disruption of trade and investment patterns with both Taiwan and mainland China, a threat to the balance of power in East Asia, and the undermining of peace and stability in the Asian Pacific region. Such a conflict might also separate the United States from its Japanese and Korean allies and might weaken U.S. prestige in Asia.

Other than legitimate American sympathies for the principle of national self-determination, it makes little sense for the United States to encourage or support Taiwan independence. Indeed, it seems wise to be extremely cautious about any move toward Taiwan independence. Washington should not interfere in Taiwan's domestic political process nor withhold arms sales or commitments to the security of Taiwan, but it is appropriate for the United States to inform public audiences about the potential dangers of Taiwan independence. Nonetheless, in the final analysis, the future of Taiwan rightfully belongs to the people of Taiwan.

Fifth, in the 1990s there may be increased possibility of a military confrontation between the United States and China over Taiwan. Neither country wants such a confrontation, but the policies of both nations are based on strongly conflicting interests. For its part, the PRC is deeply concerned that Taiwan may move in the direction of independence. No strong central Chinese government could tolerate Taiwan's secession. Barring the dissolution of the Chinese state, Beijing would almost certainly use force -- if necessary -- to prevent the division of China. The modernization of the PLA is increasing the capability of the PRC to take military action in the Taiwan Strait.

At the same time that the PRC is strengthening its military forces, the people of Taiwan are considering more seriously the advantages of seeking independence from China. Domestic pressure on Taiwan for a dramatic diplomatic breakthrough is building very rapidly. Many Taiwan residents believe the PRC would not attack if Taiwan declared independence, or, if the attack did occur, that Taiwan could withstand PRC aggression with or without U.S. assistance. Even within the KMT, there are deepening divisions over the wisdom of adhering to the ROC's traditional "one China" policy.

While the United States does not seek Taiwan independence, there is a strong possibility Washington would be drawn into a conflict in the

Taiwan Strait -- even if Taiwan provoked the attack by declaring independence. Such a conflict would place the United States in a policy crisis it neither wants nor needs. The executive branch of the U.S. government would no doubt look carefully at the circumstances behind any PRC use of force. But it is far less likely that the Congress or the American people would so closely examine the cause of a conflict in the Taiwan Strait. The public would see on the screens of their televisions and the front pages of their newspapers vivid images of a direct attack by the PRC on a much smaller, democratic Taiwan. Under these circumstances, a popular sense of moral outrage might be more important in deciding whether the United States should intervene than bureaucratic arguments regarding the origins of the struggle or principles found in Sino-American communiques. 10-11

Another determining factor is the availability of U.S. military options. Unlike the situations in Bosnia or Somalia, the United States has the capability in the Western Pacific to intervene decisively on Taiwan's behalf with limited risk to American lives. The potential deployment of one or more aircraft carriers and advanced antisubmarine warfare assets, for example, would give the White House politically acceptable options for intervention in the Taiwan Strait. The probability is high of a decisive involvement by U.S. air and naval forces; American ground forces would not have to be deployed. These conditions -- authoritarian aggression against a friendly democratic country, American public outrage and demand for intervention on Taiwan's behalf, and the high probability of decisive results quickly obtained at minimal loss of American lives -- provide a conducive environment for U.S. military intervention in the 1990s.

Sixth, there is reason for optimism that Beijing and Taipei can peacefully resolve their differences over the future of Taiwan. In recent years one of the most encouraging developments in the Taiwan issue is the increased contact between the people of mainland China and the people of Taiwan. These largely personal contacts hold great promise for creating a favorable environment for peaceful management or equitable resolution of the Taiwan issue.

But it is important for the United States not to lose sight of an opposing reality. The fundamental differences between the CCP, KMT, and DPP are not easily compromised or even successfully managed. A peaceful resolution of the Taiwan issue is indeed possible, but it would be a grievous error to dismiss the risk of force being used in the Taiwan Strait due to incompatible differences.

US will get drawn into PRC-ROC war

US will use military to help Taiwan

Given the possibility of either a peaceful or forceful resolution of the Taiwan issue, it is imperative that the Clinton administration continue to help deter the PRC from using force in the Taiwan Strait. An effective deterrent requires, at minimum, a strong self-defense force on Taiwan, a sufficiently strong U.S. military force in the Western Pacific to intervene if necessary, and a credible commitment from Washington to come to Taiwan's aid if it is attacked.

The maintenance of this minimal deterrence is the greatest contribution the United States can make to a peaceful outcome of Chinese differences over Taiwan's future. By helping to sustain a peaceful environment in the Taiwan Strait, the United States gives time to the various parties to interact and work out their disagreements. Through this gradual process, peace can perhaps be made permanent.

U.S. Policy Dilemma

For the past twenty-five years the United States has sought to balance its interests in both Chinas, an effort which no doubt will continue under the Clinton administration. Clearly, it is in the U.S. interest to maintain this balanced policy. The difficulty that Washington faces is that the balance is becoming increasingly hard to maintain, or even to define with a high degree of consensus. The modalities of U.S. policy toward Taiwan are becoming outdated and dysfunctional in some instances, largely due to circumstances beyond the control of the United States, and perhaps beyond the control of China and Taiwan. Accordingly, U.S. policy toward Taiwan is receiving -- once again -- intense scrutiny.[6]

One point of view argues that the Clinton administration must weigh U.S. interests in Taiwan against U.S. interests in the PRC, particularly as they relate to the future regional security environment in Asia. China plays a major role in counterbalancing Russia, Japan, Vietnam, and India. Taiwan does not have this first magnitude geopolitical importance. Also, the PRC plays a more vital role in immediate issues such as Korea and arms control. Beijing does not always follow parallel policies with the United States, it is argued, but Washington can ill afford to make an enemy out of China over the Taiwan issue. This is especially true if one considers that there are circumstances (e.g., a resurgent Russia or militant Japan) under which China might become less hostile to the United States and more of a true ally. Why sacrifice current and potential U.S. benefits stemming from a positive relationship with China for U.S. support of

Taiwan, which has limited strategic importance to the United States? Moreover, although Beijing, largely because of domestic constraints, cannot now call the United States to task over its support to Taiwan, these constraints might not always exist. In the future a stronger China might penalize the United States for its arms sales to Taiwan and for other actions seen as interference in China's domestic affairs. Are U.S. interests in Taiwan's security worth the cost in terms of adversely affected U.S. interests in China?

These are legitimate questions, and they seem to place the United States in a dilemma in regards to its policies toward Taiwan. But there are other ways to view the issue. From another perspective there is no policy dilemma. It can be argued that U.S. interests in Taiwan are sufficient to stand on their own merits; they should not be held hostage to the whims of Beijing. These interests range from the geopolitical (constraining China's hegemonic ambitions) to the moral (supporting the people the United States has befriended for half a century). From this point of view, trying not to offend the PRC over the Taiwan issue gives Beijing too much influence over U.S. policy, the control of which should be exercised by Americans themselves in defense of U.S. interests. Those interests require the United States to seek good relations with both Beijing and Taipei. If the PRC wants to threaten relations with the United States, so be it. There is no reason why Washington should forfeit its interests in Taiwan because of PRC protests or retaliatory acts. Moreover, it is argued, PRC leaders are pragmatic enough not to seek to damage relations with the United States over Taiwan -- as long as Washington does not attempt to separate Taiwan from Chinese sovereignty.

This view argues that if, in the future, China does becomes strong enough to challenge the United States over Taiwan, then Beijing will be strong enough to challenge the United States over other issues where Chinese and American interests collide. These include the South China Sea, the level of American military forces in Asia, PLA power projection capabilities, trade issues, and advanced arms sales to countries such as Iran. It is natural that major nations have confrontations over conflicting interests. And it is naive, in this view, to think that China would forgo its interests in key areas simply because the United States elects to forfeit its interests in Taiwan. Such forfeiture would only strengthen Beijing by helping it to become the central government of a united China. In exchange for the demonstration of its good intentions, Washington would have created, not an ally in China, but a more formidable opponent to U.S. interests in Asia.

My own viewpoint falls somewhere between these two perspectives. It seems to me that since both Chinese societies are undergoing systemic change, the most important U.S. goal is to maintain sufficient flexibility to further U.S. interests in both sides of the Taiwan Strait. Of fundamental importance in preserving this flexibility is the continued security of Taiwan, a policy issue which is becoming more pressing due to increased calls for Taiwan independence, the modernization of the PLA, political uncertainty in Beijing, and Chinese perceptions of a weakening American commitment to Taiwan. A central theme of this book is that, while pursuing a balanced China policy is not an impossible task, it is becoming more challenging. Closer attention needs to be paid to the Taiwan issue.

In sum, until the issue of Taiwan's future is finally settled, the United States will have to remain concerned with Taiwan's security. This concern will almost certainly be part of the Asian policies of President Bill Clinton and probably will continue well into the twenty-first century.

Notes

1. Throughout the text, the terms "ROC," "Taiwan" and "Taipei" will be used interchangeably, as will the terms "PRC," "China," the "mainland" and "Beijing". Such usage is not intended to convey the author's agreement or disagreement with the concepts of "one China," "two Chinas," or "one China, one Taiwan." The significance of these concepts will be explained in later chapters.

2. George Bush, *National Security Strategy of the United States* (Washington, D.C.: The White House, 1991), p. 9.

3. Natale H. Bellocchi, "Speech to Chinese American Academic and Professional Convention," Chicago, Illinois, July 3, 1993, ms.

4. Within each of these three Chinese perspectives -- PRC, ROC, and Taiwanese -- are a host of different viewpoints. While understanding this to be true, it is nonetheless impossible to analyze these myriad points of view in a study of this size. Out of necessity, therefore, a "black box" approach of generic Chinese perspectives has been adopted in most cases, much like generalizations of policies and perceptions coming from the United States.

5. Winston Lord, "A New Pacific Community: Ten Goals for American Policy," opening statement at confirmation hearings for Assistant Secretary of State for East Asian and Pacific Affairs, U.S. Senate, Committee on Foreign Relations, March 31, 1993, ms.

6. The author is grateful to Ronald N. Montaperto of the U.S. National Defense University for his valuable comments and suggestions on this and other sections of the book.

2

Foreign Policy Under President Clinton

U.S. policies toward Taiwan and its security do not occur in a vacuum. Washington's global and regional policies greatly influence U.S.-ROC relations, as do American policies toward the People's Republic of China. The current chapter places Taiwan's security in this broader context by briefly reviewing the basic principles of Clinton foreign policy and the administration's goal of creating a "new Pacific community." The next chapter discusses the major elements of Clinton's China policy through mid-1994. Since both chapters are intended to provide background information and not substantive analysis, readers familiar with these subjects may want to review them rapidly or move on to Chapter Four.

Principles of Clinton Foreign Policy

In December 1992 President-elect Bill Clinton described his foreign policy strategy as one of "American engagement" in the world. He said his administration would pursue three main objectives:

1. the restructuring of U.S. military forces to reduce the cost of defense to the American people
2. cooperation with U.S. allies to encourage the spread and consolidation of democracy and free markets worldwide

3. reestablishment of American economic leadership to stimulate global growth and prosperity.[1]

These overall objectives were encapsulated by Secretary of State-designate Warren Christopher during his confirmation hearings before the Senate Foreign Relations Committee on January 13, 1993. Christopher said the administration would base its foreign policy on "three pillars": economic growth, military strength, and support for democracy.[2]

Christopher further explained the "three pillars" in a speech to the Chicago Council on Foreign Relations in March 1993.[3] First, the secretary said, foreign policy should serve the economic needs of the United States. The U.S. government should ensure that foreign markets are open to American goods, services, and investments. Washington should "fight unfair competition against U.S. business and labor," and it should press other wealthy nations to do their part to stimulate global economic growth. Second, the armed forces of the United States must be modernized even while they are being reduced and their budgets shrunk. The Clinton administration, Christopher said, is "taking steps to make our military more agile, mobile, flexible and smart." Third, democracy and respect for human rights must be encouraged abroad. The secretary of state observed: "History has shown that a world of more democracies is a safer world, is a world that will devote more to human development and less to human destruction."

The administration's foreign policy strategy was outlined in September 1993 by national security adviser Anthony Lake. In a speech at John Hopkins University, Lake said the United States would adopt a strategy of "enlargement" to replace the Cold War strategy of containment.[4]

U.S. engagement in international affairs throughout the twentieth century, he explained, "was animated both by calculations of power and by this belief: to the extent democracy and market economics hold sway in other nations, our own nation will be more secure, prosperous and influential, while the broader world will be more humane and peaceful." The essence of U.S. foreign policy, he said, is that "we must promote democracy and market economics in the world -- because it protects our interests and security; and because it reflects values that are both American and universal."

Lake noted that during the Cold War the United States "contained a global threat to market democracies." Now, he said, "the successor to a doctrine of containment must be a strategy of enlargement -- enlargement of the world's free community of market democracies." There were four "components" of the new strategy.

First, Lake said, "we should strengthen the community of major market democracies -- including our own -- which constitutes the core from which enlargement is proceeding." In this, "renewal starts at home." Americans must be strong domestically before they have the will or capacity to engage in commitments abroad. In addition, it was vitally important that the United States renew "the bonds among our key democratic allies," especially Europe, Canada, and Japan.

The second imperative of the strategy, "must be to help democracy and markets expand and survive in other places where we have the strongest security concerns and where we can make the greatest difference." Lake assured his audience: "This is not a democratic crusade; it is a pragmatic commitment to see freedom take hold where that will help us most." In terms of priorities, "we must target our effort to assist states that affect our strategic interests, such as those with large economies, critical locations, nuclear weapons or the potential to generate refugee flows into our own nation or into key friends and allies." Further, "We must focus our efforts where we have the most leverage. And our efforts must be demand-driven -- they must focus on nations whose people are pushing for reform or have already secured it." Lake noted that "pursuing enlargement in the Asian Pacific" is of strategic importance to the United States.

The third element of the strategy of enlargement, Lake said, is "to minimize the ability of states outside the circle of democracies and markets to threaten it." Observing that "democracy and market economics have always been subversive ideas to those who rule without consent," he warned, "we should expect the advance of democracy and markets to trigger forceful reactions from those whose power is not popularly derived."

In the case of these "backlash states," Lake said U.S. policy "must seek to isolate them diplomatically, militarily, economically and technologically....When the actions of such states directly threaten our people, our forces, or our vital interests, we clearly must be prepared to strike back decisively and unilaterally....We must always maintain the military power necessary to deter, or if necessary defeat, aggression by these regimes. Because the source of such threats will be diverse and unpredictable, we must seek to ensure that our forces are increasingly ready, mobile, flexible and smart."

"Other anti-democratic states," Lake predicted, "will opt to pursue greater wealth by liberalizing their economic rules. Sooner or later, however, these states confront the need to liberalize the flow of information into and within their nations, and to tolerate the rise of an entrepreneurial middle-class. Both developments weaken despotic rule and lead over time to rising demands for democracy." Lake said, "We cannot impose democracy on regimes that appear to be opting for liberalization, but we may be able to help steer some of them down that path, while providing penalties that raise the costs of repression and aggressive behavior." As an example, Lake pointed to China:

> These efforts have special meaning for our relations with China. That relationship is one of the most important in the world, for China will increasingly be a major world power, and along with our ties to Japan and Korea, our relationship with China will strongly shape both our security and economic interests in Asia. It is in the interest of both our nations for China to continue its economic liberalization while respecting the human rights of its people and international norms regarding weapons sales....We seek a stronger relationship with China that reflects both our values and our interests.

The fourth part of a strategy of enlargement, Lake said, "involves our humanitarian goals, which play an important supporting role in our efforts to expand democracy and markets." Lake noted that public pressure may drive U.S. humanitarian engagement but that other more pragmatic factors must be considered as well, including "cost; feasibility; the permanence of the improvement our assistance will bring; the willingness of regional and international bodies to do their part; and the likelihood that our actions will generate broader security benefits for the people and the region in question." These considerations, Lake observed, "suggest there will be relatively few intra-national ethnic conflicts that justify our military intervention."

Regarding the debate over multilateralism, Lake said: "only one overriding factor can determine whether the US should act multilaterally or unilaterally, and that is America's interests. We should act multilaterally where doing so advances our interests -- and we should act unilaterally when that will serve our purpose. The simple question in each instance is this: what works best?"

President Clinton further defined his foreign policy in a speech to the United Nations General Assembly on September 27, 1993.[5] The United States, the president said, "occupies a unique position in world affairs today." It intends to "remain engaged and to lead," and while "we cannot solve every problem...we must and will serve as a fulcrum for change and a pivot point for peace."

Clinton described his foreign policy strategy as one of enlargement, saying: "our overriding purpose must be to expand and strengthen the world's community of market-based democracies. During the Cold War we sought to contain a threat to survival of free institutions. Now we seek to enlarge the circle of nations that live under those free institutions."

The president listed several U.S. policy guidelines deriving from this strategy:

- "Throughout the world...there is an enormous yearning among people who wish to be the masters of their own economic and political lives. Where it matters most and where we can make the greatest difference, we will...patiently and firmly align ourselves with that yearning."
- "We will work to strengthen the free market democracies, by revitalizing our economy here at home, by opening world trade through the GATT, the North American Free Trade Agreement and other accords, and by updating our shared institutions."
- "We will support the consolidation of market democracy where it is taking new root."
- "We will work to reduce the threat from regimes that are hostile to democracies and to support liberalization of nondemocratic states when they are willing to live in peace with the rest of us."
- "We will often work in partnership with others and through multilateral institutions such as the United Nations. It is in our national interest to do so. But we must not hesitate to act unilaterally when there is a threat to our core interests or to those of our allies."

President Clinton observed: "The United States believes that an expanded community of market democracies not only serves our own security interests, it also advances the goals enshrined in this body's charter and its Universal Declaration of Human Rights." He said, "Democracies rarely wage war on one another. They make more reliable partners in trade, in diplomacy, and in the stewardship of our global environment. And democracies with the rule of law and respect for political, religious, and cultural minorities are more responsive to their own people and to the protection of human rights."

Clinton said that "nonproliferation, conflict resolution, and sustainable development" were the principal security challenges to the democratic world. In regards to proliferation, Clinton declared: "One of our most urgent priorities must be attacking the proliferation of weapons of mass destruction, whether they are nuclear, chemical, or biological; and the ballistic missiles that can rain them down on populations hundreds of miles away....I have made nonproliferation one of our nation's highest priorities. We intend to weave it more deeply into the fabric of all of our relationships....We seek to build a world of increasing pressures for nonproliferation, but increasingly open trade and technology for those states that live by accepted international rules."[6]

As to conflict resolution, the president noted: "As we work to keep the world's most destructive weapons out of conflict, we must also strengthen the international community's ability to address those conflicts themselves....U.N. peacekeeping holds the promise to resolve many of this era's conflicts. The reason we have supported such missions is not...to subcontract American foreign policy, but to strengthen our security, protect our interests, and to share among nations the costs and effort of pursuing peace. Peacekeeping cannot be a substitute for our own national defense efforts, but it can strongly supplement them." But Clinton warned the General Assembly: "The United Nations simply cannot become engaged in every one of the world's conflicts. If the American people are to say yes to U.N. peacckeeping, the United Nations must know when to say no."[7]

One of the most important characteristics of Clinton's foreign policy was its close linkage to domestic concerns. President Clinton told the *Washington Post* on October 15, 1993, "it's simply not possible for the United States to become the ultimate resolver of every problem in the world." Although the United States must remain engaged in the world for its own security, economic, and humanitarian interests, "we've simply got to focus on rebuilding America." He noted that the American people had voted for him instead of George Bush precisely because they wanted their president to concentrate on domestic issues at this time.[8]

The foreign policy priorities of the Clinton administration were summarized in early November 1993 by Secretary of State Warren Christopher. He told the Senate Foreign Relations Committee that "our national security is inseparable from our economic security." Priority administration goals included opening Japan's markets, passage of the North American Free Trade Agreement (NAFTA), successful completion of the GATT talks on reducing tariffs, and the integration of East Asian and Pacific economies with that of the United States. Christopher said that successful reform in Russia was the "highest foreign policy priority" of the United States, followed by a desire to preserve and expand NATO and to establish a new Pacific community. Other priorities included reinforcement of the Israeli-Palesti nian peace agreement and other Middle Eastern issues, as well as nuclear nonproliferation. He described the spread of nuclear weapons as "the most serious threat" to the United States in the post-Cold War era. None of the issues for which the administration received most criticism -- Bosnia-Herzegovina, Somalia, and Haiti -- were listed by the secretary as foreign policy priorities.[9]

Foreign Policies Toward Asia

The presidential transition between George Bush and Bill Clinton was accompanied by the widespread belief that the United States was entering a new era. With the end of Cold War, Americans were confronted with the necessity of focusing on domestic problems held in limbo because of communist threats to national security. The perceived need to turn inward compelled the Clinton administration to redefine the U.S. role in world affairs, a reassessment that many Americans interpreted as meaning a declining role.[10]

Because of the U.S. focus on domestic economic issues, few Asian governments believed the United States would remain the dominant power in the Pacific, although most expected the adjustment to be gradual. While there was hope the United States would play a role in maintaining the balance of power, many Asian leaders concluded that U.S. commitments could no longer be taken for granted These views were strengthened by rising sentiments of nationalism due to the dynamic economies of most Asian countries and steady progress toward democratization. Asian powers were convinced that the United States would be around for a long time, but that it might weaken over the longer term. This process of reevaluating the U.S. presence in Asia began under President Bush and intensified with the election of President Clinton. There was a feeling in Asian countries that the United States had lost the edge and that its national power was declining. At the same time, however, most Asian governments realized that the United States could not and would not withdraw from the region.

Many in the Clinton administration realized that Asian perceptions of the United States as a declining power were harmful to U.S. interests. A weakening U.S. influence would fuel Asian anxieties over the hegemonic ambitions of countries like China, Japan, India, and Indonesia. Such anxiety might lead to a reordering of security, political, and economic relations excluding the United States or, at minimum, further weakening American influence. This unfavorable shift in the balance of power would occur precisely at the time when U.S. interests in the Asian Pacific were increasing, especially in the critical areas of trade and other forms of economic interdependence.

To counter perceptions of declining U.S. power, the new administration quickly reaffirmed U.S. leadership in the region. Most significantly, President Clinton placed a higher priority on Asian policy than had previous administrations. This reflected economic realities (in 1992 Asia bought $128 billion worth of American products while Europe purchased $111 billion), and it signalled a cultural change in Washington where the foreign policy establishment traditionally had been Eurocentric in outlook.

The most complete, early statement of Clinton foreign policy toward Asia was given by Winston Lord, former U.S. Ambassador to China, who was appointed Assistant Secretary of State for East Asian and Pacific Affairs. His March 31, 1993, confirmation statement before the Senate Foreign Relations Committee outlined the new administration's goals and general policies toward Asia.[11] Lord said the United States would remain engaged in Asia because of "our overriding national interests." The ambassador set ten goals that the Clinton administration would pursue to achieve its vision of building a "new Pacific community":

1. Forging a revitalized global partnership with Japan that reflected a more mature balance of responsibilities.
2. Erasing the nuclear threat and moving toward peaceful reconciliation on the Korean peninsula.
3. Restoring firm foundations for cooperation with China while pursuing greater political openness and economic reform.
4. Deepening ties with the Association of Southeast Asian Nations (ASEAN) as it broadens its membership and scope.
5. Obtaining the fullest possible accounting of U.S. missing in action as Washington moves to normalize relations with Vietnam.
6. Securing a peaceful, independent, and democratic Cambodia.
7. Strengthening the Asia-Pacific Economic Cooperation (APEC) process as the cornerstone of economic cooperation in the Pacific.
8. Developing multilateral forums for security consultations while maintaining U.S. alliances.
9. Spurring regional cooperation on global challenges like the environment, refugees, health, narcotics, nonproliferation, and arms sales.
10. Promoting democracy and human rights.

Lord stressed the role of economics in the foreign policy of the Clinton administration, saying, "no region is more central for American economic interests than the world's most dynamic one -- Asia." Lord noted that the Asia-Pacific region is the world's largest consumer market and the biggest export market for the United States. Lord said U.S. policy would confront Asian economic challenges and opportunities on several levels. First, "foreign policy begins at home -- strengthening our competitiveness is a *sine qua non* for an effective policy." Second, "the successful completion of the Uruguay Round [of GATT] is the most urgent multilateral task." Third, "bilaterally we must continue to pry open Asian markets, particularly in those nations running large surpluses with us."

In addition to these steps, "greater regional cooperation is required." Lord said the most promising vehicle in this regard was the Asia-Pacific Economic Cooperation (APEC) forum, whose members comprised half of the world's GNP.[12] The Clinton administration would work to strengthen APEC "at the top of our agenda."

In the area of security, Lord said: "By virtue of history and geography the United States is the one major power in Asia not viewed as a threat. Virtually every country wants us to maintain our security presence. While balance-of-power considerations have declined in the wake of the Cold War, they remain relevant as Asian-Pacific nations contemplate their fates. Each ones harbors apprehensions about one or more of its neighbors. A precipitous American military withdrawal would magnify these concerns. Add the increasing resources available for weapons purchases in the rapidly growing Asian nations and there is a recipe for escalating arms races and future confrontations that could threaten U.S. interests."

There were several dimensions of Clinton security policy toward Asia: a "reaffirmation of our treaty alliances with Japan, Korea, Australia, Thailand, and the Philippines"; "military arrangements under the Compact of Free Association"; "the maintenance of a substantial military presence"; and "prudent modifications" of the U.S. military presence after consultation with allies. Lord emphasized that U.S. allies in the region "can and must assume a growing share of the security burden."

Lord noted that "crises in Asia do not dominate the headlines," although several serious security problems exist. These included Cambodia and Korea, both remnants from the Cold War and both being addressed "by appropriate groupings of nations," and bilateral issues such as the lingering Northern Territories (southern Kuril islands occupied by Moscow since the end of World War II) dispute between Russia and Japan. Lord also introduced a new element in U.S. security policy toward Asia: multilateral security discussions involving almost all regional powers.

> we must develop new mechanisms to manage or prevent other emerging concerns. We welcome increased security consultations in the framework of the ASEAN Post Ministerial Conference. This process can usefully encourage nations to share information, convey intentions, ease tensions, resolve disputes and foster confidence. The United States will fully participate.
>
> For the first time in this century, there are no adversarial fault lines among the great powers in Northeast Asia: the United States, Japan, Russia and China. The post-Cold War period invites dialogue to prevent arms races, the forging of competing alignments, and efforts by one power or group of powers to dominate this strategic region. Our voice will be crucial. In close concert with our Pacific allies, we could engage Russia, China and others inside and outside Northeast Asia.

Lord said the United States did not seek a formal security pact in the Pacific. "We do not envisage a formal CSCE-type [Conference on Security and Cooperation in Europe] structure. But it is time to step up regional discussions on future security issues." He promised the administration would work closely with other countries "to explore new Asian-Pacific paths toward security."

Lord mentioned several important global issues that were of concern to the Clinton administration in Asia, especially the proliferation of dangerous weapons, which "now poses the greatest threat to our security." Lord said the "North Korean programs currently dramatize this challenge." In terms of democracy and human rights, he said, "History is on the side of freedom....For the first time ever a majority of the world's nations are governed by some form of democracy." Noting that "promoting democracy must be one of the central pillars of our foreign policy," Lord said the "spread of liberty not only affirms American values but also serves our interests [because] open societies do not attack one another. They make better trading partners. They press for environmental reform. They do not practice terrorism. They do not produce refugees." Lord cautioned that the pursuit of democracy "cannot be our only foreign goal; we must weigh geopolitical, economic and other factors." He assured Asian governments, "Nor do we seek to impose an

American model; each nation must find its own way in its own cultural and historical contexts. But universal principles of freedom and human rights belong to all, the peoples of Asia no less than others."

The New Pacific Community

President Clinton explained his concept of the "new Pacific community" during a trip to Japan in July 1993 to take part in the annual Group of Seven (G-7) meeting of the heads of government of the United States, Japan, Canada, Great Britain, France, Germany, and Italy. Following the summit, Clinton travelled to the Republic of Korea and visited the DMZ (demilitarized zone separating North and South Korea). The trip to Asia was Clinton's first overseas trip as president, and the administration used the occasion to elaborate on its policy toward Asia in two important policy speeches. At Tokyo's Waseda University on July 7 Clinton discussed the "economic essentials" for the new Pacific community. The president outlined U.S. security policy in an address to the Korean National Assembly in Seoul on July 10.

In his Tokyo speech Clinton said the new Pacific community would rest upon five building blocks:[13]

1. "a revived partnership between the United States and Japan"
2. "progress toward more open economies and greater trade"
3. "support for democracy"
4. "the firm and continuing commitment of the United States to maintain its treaty alliances"
5. the U.S. commitment to maintain "its forward military presence in Japan and Korea and throughout this region."

Clinton emphasized Asia's growing economic importance to the United States in an era of a more integrated global economy. Trade, he said, accounted for well over half of the new jobs in the United States in the late 1980s. Over 40 percent of American trade was with Asia, and in 1992 "over 2.3 million American jobs were related to the $120 billion we exported to Asia." The president said that Asia's imports of $2 trillion were creating "a tripolar world, driven by the Americas, by Europe, and by Asia."

For the United States, "our first international economic priority must be to create a new and stronger partnership between the United States and Japan. Our relationship with Japan is the centerpiece of our policy toward the Pacific community." He noted that the two countries produce nearly 40 percent of the world's output, but that "neither of us could thrive without the other."

Although the security and political aspects of the U.S.-Japan relationship are sound, "our economic relationship is not in balance" due to the persistently high trade deficit in manufacturing products that the United States experiences with Japan. "It is clear that our markets are more open to your products and your investments than yours are to ours," the president observed. "Our people understand when our nation has a huge trade deficit with an emerging economy like China. The same was true just a few years ago with Korea and Taiwan. But both those nations have moved closer to trade balance with the U.S. as they have become more prosperous. The same has not happened with Japan." The president emphasized, "What the United States seeks is not managed trade or so-called trade by the numbers, but better results from better rules of trade."

The second building bloc for the new Pacific community was "a more open regional and global economy." This meant resistance against protectionist pressures, the successful completion of the Uruguay Round of the GATT negotiations, and the reduction of regional trade barriers. The president said that the North American Free Trade Agreement (NAFTA) would not close North America to the rest of the world but open it up. He also raised the possibility that "perhaps we should consider Asian-Pacific trading areas as well." The president said, "the most promising economic forum we have for debating a lot of these issues in the new Pacific community is the Organization for Asia-Pacific Economic Cooperation, APEC."

The third priority in building a new Pacific community, Clinton noted, is "to support the wave of democratic reform sweeping across this region." The president said economic growth, combined with the information age, had made people's craving for freedom irresistible. "This spread of democracy is one of the best guarantees of regional peace and prosperity and stability that we could ever have in this region." Furthermore, "the movement toward democracy is the best guarantor of human rights." Clinton rejected the concept of moral relativism, saying:

> It is not Western urging or Western imperialism, but the aspiration of Asian peoples themselves that explain the growing number of democracies and democratic movements in this region....Each of our Pacific nations must pursue progress while maintaining the best of their unique cultures. But there is no cultural justification for torture or tyranny. We refuse to let

repression cloak itself in moral relativism. For democracy and human rights are not Occidental yearnings; they are universal yearnings.

Clinton's address to the Korean National Assembly on July 10 outlined "the fundamentals of security for that new Pacific community and the role the United States intends to play."[14] At the time, the United States had 84,000 troops in Asia, down from 109,000 in 1990. The planned reduction of 6,500 troops from South Korea by 1995 was put on hold because of the North Korean nuclear weapons program.

The president told the Korean National Assembly, "we must always remember that security comes first." He assured his audience that "the United States intends to remain actively engaged in this region. America is, after all, a Pacific nation. We have many peoples from all over Asia now making their home in America, including more than 1 million Koreans. We have fought three wars here in this century. We must not squander that investment." Clinton said, "The best way for us to deter regional aggression, perpetuate the region's robust economic growth, and secure our own maritime and other interests is to be an active presence. We must and we will continue to lead."

The president said there were four priorities for the security of the new Pacific community: "a continued American military commitment to this region"; "stronger efforts to combat the proliferation of weapons of mass destruction"; "new regional dialogues on the full range of our common security challenges"; and "support for democracy and more open societies throughout this region."

In discussing the first priority, Clinton said, "The bedrock of America's security role in the Asian Pacific must be a continued military presence. In a period of change, we need to preserve what has been reliable....we, therefore, affirm our five bilateral security agreements with Korea, with Japan, with Australia, with the Philippines and with Thailand." The president noted that these agreements serve mutual interests. "They enable the U.S. Armed Forces to maintain a substantial forward presence. At the same time they have enabled Asia to focus less energy on an arms race and more energy on the peaceful race toward economic development and opportunity for the peoples of this region." He emphasized, "Our commitment to an active military presence remains....We have deployed to Japan the Belleau Wood Amphibious Group and the U.S.S. Independence Battle Group, the largest and most modern in the world. These are not signs of disengagement. These are signs that America intends to stay."

"The second security priority for our new Pacific community," the president said, "is to combat the spread of weapons of mass destruction and their means of delivery. We cannot let the expanding threat of these deadly weapons replace the Cold War nightmare of nuclear annihilation." Clinton specifically cited North Korea's "indiscriminate sales of the SCUD missiles" as an example of the proliferation threat, noting that Pyongyang now is developing a longer ranged missile of 600 miles that could threaten Osaka from North Korea or Tel Aviv from Iran. The president added, "We have serious concerns as well about China's compliance with international standards against missile proliferation."

Turning to his third security priority, Clinton noted that the end of the Cold War had brought a host of changes, including the disappearance of "the dominant unitary threat of Soviet aggression." In its place other threats had emerged, such as "ancient ethnic rivalries, regional tensions, flows of refugees and the trafficking of deadly weapons and dangerous drugs." The president said that in Europe the United States and its allies were able to adjust the functions of NATO to meet the new security challenges. In Asia, however, no such institution existed. "The challenge for the Asian Pacific in this decade...is to develop multiple new arrangements to meet multiple threats and opportunities. These arrangements can function like overlapping plates of armor individually providing protection and together covering the full body of our common security concerns." Clinton cited as examples of such multiple arrangements "groups of nations confronting immediate problems" such as North Korea's nuclear program, "peacekeeping" operations such as the U.N.-sponsored mission to Cambodia, and "confidence-building measures to head off regional or subregional disputes."

In addition to these arrangements, "we also need new regional security dialogues." The president mentioned ASEAN's post-ministerial conference and the possibility of a Northeast Asian security forum as cases in point. Regional economic organizations like APEC could also play a role in easing regional tensions. "The goal of all these efforts," he said, "is to integrate, not isolate, the region's powers." Clinton said the United States was attempting to convince Beijing to be a responsible member of the international community while at the same time to involve China in regional security, political, and economic affairs. Clinton assured his audience that new U.S. support for multilateral security forums did not mean American disengagement from the region, but rather should be seen "as a way to supplement our alliances and forward military presence, not to supplant them."

As his fourth security priority for Asia, President Clinton emphasized contributions to peace made by democratic progress:

> Ultimately, the guarantee of our security must rest in the character and the intentions of the region's nations themselves. That is why our final security priority must be to support the spread of democracy throughout the Asian Pacific. Democracies not only are more likely to meet the needs and respect the rights of their people, they also make better neighbors. They do not wage war on each other, practice terrorism, generate refugees or traffick in drugs and outlaw weapons. They make more reliable partners in trade and in the kind of dialogues we announced today.

Secretary of State Christopher further explained U.S. security policy toward Asia during his visit to Singapore in July 24-27, 1993, to take part in the annual ASEAN post-ministerial conference. Upon arriving in Singapore, Christopher said, "In my presentations here I will make it clear that the Clinton Administration has a determination to remain fully engaged on all issues in Southeast Asia -- and across the whole Asian-Pacific region."[15] The secretary commented:

> This continued engagement is especially important with regard to our security presence in Asia. President Clinton has made it clear, and I will make it clear in talking with each of the Asian leaders that I meet here, the United States will maintain a strong security presence in Asia. We will maintain our bilateral security alliances. We will continue our substantial forward military presence. We are not reducing our forces in this region. In fact, we are making them more effective.
> On these foundations we will work with the Asia-Pacific nations to develop regional security dialogues and forums. These dialogues will build upon, but they will not supplant, our alliances and our forward military presence.
> We hope that a central accomplishment of this conference will be to begin integrating a number of other key nations -- including Russia and China -- into this regional security forum.

In his speech to the post-ministerial conference on July 26 Christopher said the most important security issue in the region was "the need for strong international efforts to combat the spread of weapons of mass destruction and their means of delivery."[16] He stressed that the United States was "committed to tough and effective global rules to halt the spread of nuclear weapons." In this regard, "North Korea's adherence to the Non-Proliferation Treaty and its full compliance with its IAEA

[International Atomic Energy Agency] safeguards obligations and the North-South [Korean] Denuclearization Declaration are essential. The United States is determined to see a non-nuclear Korean peninsula."

The secretary said a second major challenge was the proliferation of chemical and biological weapons of mass destruction and the missiles that can deliver them. This was a growing problem for Asia because regional economic and technological development permitted the production of chemicals, sophisticated electronics, and other products and services denied in Europe and the United States. "Asia is at the stage when its participation in international agreements and establishment of export control regimes are most important."

Christopher also discussed the new U.S. policies toward regional security forums:

> At the regional level, the post Cold War dynamic has produced radical shifts in old balances of power. A new Pacific community must create a new regional balance that promotes stability, regional arms control and the peaceful resolution of disputes. As ASEAN has recognized, and the United States has fully supported, we need new regional security dialogues to meet common challenges. This forum [ASEAN's post-ministerial conference] is most promising in this regard. Asia is not Europe. The 1990s are not the Cold War. Thus together we envision not the building of blocs against a common threat but rather intensified discussions among nations which may harbor apprehensions about others' intentions.
>
> Underlining a change in U.S. policy, President Clinton announced at the Korean National Assembly earlier this month that we will participate actively in regional security dialogues in Asia. We believe such discussions can complement our bilateral relationships, help reduce tensions, enhance openness and transparency and prevent destabilizing arms races. These dialogues should therefore be inclusive: the U.S. welcomes the progressive integration of China and Russia, as well as others, in this ASEAN-PMC framework....Let me emphasize, however, that regional security dialogues in no way supplant America's alliances or forward military presence in Asia. Rather, they are supplements to ensure a peaceful and stable Asia in the post-Cold War era.

APEC Meeting in Seattle

The administration's emphasis on the economic aspects of U.S. policy toward Asia could be seen in President Clinton's participation in the Asia-Pacific Economic Cooperation (APEC) forum held in Seattle in

November 1993. APEC was established in November 1989 by the governments in the region for the purpose of promoting trade and investment in the Pacific Basin. In 1993 the United States was chairman of APEC, hosting its fifth annual ministerial meeting in Seattle, Washington, on November 17-19. During the meeting, Mexico and Papua New Guinea were added to the membership, then comprised of Australia, New Zealand, the six ASEAN states, Japan, Korea, China, Taiwan, Hong Kong, Canada, and the United States.

The administration placed high priority on expanding the role of APEC because of the economic importance of its members to the U.S. economy. In 1992 the fifteen APEC members had a combined gross regional product of more than $14 trillion, while their share of world trade approached 35 percent, or $2.3 trillion. In 1992 U.S. exports to other APEC members totalled $219 billion, or 49 percent of total U.S. exports. U.S. imports from other APEC members totalled $313 billion, or 59 percent of U.S. imports. Total U.S. trade with APEC constituted 54 percent of U.S. global trade, compared to 24 percent with Europe and the former Soviet Union.[17]

APEC brought the United States into a collaborative relationship with many of the world's fastest-growing economies. The Clinton administration believed APEC could serve several U.S. interests, including increased economic stability in the Asian Pacific region, economic interdependence among APEC members, and regional trade liberalization. APEC could also be used to apply multinational pressure on countries like Japan and China to open their markets and to make additional trade concessions. Further, APEC provided bargaining leverage over the European Community in the Uruguay Round of GATT negotiations, which were moving toward final agreement in December 1993 after seven years of discussion.

President Clinton explained U.S. support for APEC in a speech in Seattle on November 19.[18] He noted that, with the collapse of communism and the Soviet threat, U.S. security "depends upon enlarging the world's community of market democracies because democracies are more peaceful and constructive partners." Most of the economic growth in the United States since the mid-1980s had been tied to exports. The United States had "no alternative," he said, but to take steps to expand world trade. Clinton noted, "For decades, our foreign policy focused on containment of communism, a cause led by the United States and our European allies....Europe remains at the core of our alliances. It is a central partner for the United States in security, in foreign policy, and in commerce. But as our concern shifts to economic challenges that are genuinely global, we must look across the Pacific as well as the Atlantic."

Clinton pointed out that the United States had a trade deficit with almost all of the Asian Pacific countries; the "trade imbalances with Japan and China alone account for more than two-thirds of our total trade deficit." At the same time, U.S. exports to each of the Asian Pacific nations had increased by at least 50 percent over the past five years. The president emphasized: "We do not intend to bear the cost of our military presence in Asia and the burdens of regional leadership only to be shut out of the benefits of growth that stability brings....we must use every means available in the Pacific, as elsewhere, to promote a more open world economy through global agreements, regional efforts and negotiations with individual countries."

It was necessary, according to the president, to "develop new institutional arrangements that support our national economic and security interests internationally." This endeavor included "working to build a prosperous and peaceful Asian Pacific region through our work here with APEC." The president said, "The mission of [APEC] is not to create a bureaucracy that can frustrate economic growth, but to help build connections among economies to promote economic growth."

Immediately following the ministerial conference, President Clinton hosted the first-ever meeting of APEC leaders at Blake Island near Seattle. In a press conference on November 20 he said that APEC leaders held a "shared view of a regional economy characterized by openness, cooperation, dynamic growth, expanded trade, improved transportation and communications and high-skilled, high-paying jobs."[19] In comments which reflected a more modest expectation of what constituted the new Pacific community, Clinton said, "With today's meeting, we're helping the Asian Pacific to become a genuine community; not a formal, legal structure, but rather a community of shared interests, shared goals and shared commitment to mutual beneficial cooperation."

No substantive agreements were reached at the informal gathering of regional leaders, and the accomplishments of the APEC meeting were modest.[20] Nonetheless, the meetings symbolized a process of economic integration underway in the Asian Pacific region, despite diverse cultures, different political and economic systems, historical animosities and suspicions, even competing regional organizations.

Conclusion

As Clinton suggested in Seattle, he wanted nothing less than to create a new world order in which nations would find security, not in arms, but in stability brought by democracy, free trade, and economic prosperity. From the point of view of many in the administration, no region in the world had greater potential to realize this aspiration than the Pacific Basin. The new Pacific community was intended to be a community of market democracies led by the United States. The next chapter explains why many of Clinton's foreign policy goals were in conflict with the goals and interests of the People's Republic of China. Beijing had its own vision of a new international order. Moreover, many Chinese leaders tended to doubt whether U.S. rhetoric about its continued leadership in Asia could be matched by American capabilities.

Notes

1. Clinton's foreign policy strategy was summarized by Senator Alan Cranston in his keynote speech before the Sixteenth Joint Conference of the ROC-USA and USA-ROC Economic Councils, Taipei, Taiwan, December 1992, ms.

2. *Washington Post*, January 14, 1993, p. A12.

3. *Washington Post*, March 23, 1993, p. A1.

4. Anthony Lake, "From Containment to Enlargement," speech delivered to the John Hopkins University School of Advanced International Studies, Washington, D.C., September 21, 1993, ms.

5. "Address by the President to the 48th Session of the United Nations General Assembly" (New York: The White House, Office of the Press Secretary, September 27, 1993).

6. As the president was speaking to the United Nations, the White House released new guidelines for his policy on nonproliferation. See "Fact Sheet: Nonproliferation and Export Control Policy" (Washington, D.C.: The White House, Office of the Press Secretary, September 27, 1993).

7. A few days before the president's speech to the U.N., Ambassador Madeleine K. Albright told the U.S. National War College: "This administration believes that...young men and women should not be sent in harm's way without a clear mission, competent commanders, sensible rules of engagement and the means required to get the job done." Before deciding to support future U.N. peacekeeping or peace enforcement operations, Albright said, the administration wants answers to the following questions: Does the mission have clear, definable objectives? Is a cease-fire in place, and have the parties agreed to a

U.N. presence? Are the necessary financial and human resources available? Can an "end point" to U.N. participation be identified? For a summary of Albright's remarks, see *Washington Post*, September 24, 1993, p. A19.

8. Excerpts from the interview can be found in *Washington Post*, October 17, 1993, p. A28. Clinton was largely correct in his assessment of American public opinion. A *Washington Post* poll conducted in mid-January 1994 found that 67 percent of the public were satisfied with Clinton's handling of foreign affairs. When asked about their major concerns for 1994, only 3 percent noted foreign policy as the area in which the president should work hardest to solve. Listed above foreign policy were, in order of priority: dealing with violent crime, reforming the nation's health care system, creating jobs, strengthening the nation's economy, dealing with the illegal drug problem, reducing the federal budget deficit, and reforming the welfare system. The only public policy issue ranked less important than handling foreign affairs was bringing needed change to government. See *Washington Post*, January 23, 1994, p. A9.

9. *Washington Post*, November 5, 1993, p. A29.

10. In a background statement to reporters in May 1993 a high-ranking State Department official reportedly said that, because of its limited resources, the United States would focus on domestic economic issues and withdraw from much of its leadership role in world affairs. The remarks were quickly repudiated by Secretary of State Christopher. See *Washington Post*, May 26, 1993, p. A1, and May 28, 1993, p. A34.

11. Winston Lord, "A New Pacific Community: Ten Goals for American Policy," opening statement at confirmation hearings for Assistant Secretary of State, Bureau of East Asian and Pacific Affairs, Senate Foreign Relations Committee, March 31, 1993, ms.

12. As of November 1993, APEC had seventeen members: Australia, Brunei Darussalam, Canada, the People's Republic of China, Hong Kong, Indonesia, Japan, the Republic of Korea, Malaysia, Mexico, New Zealand, Papua New Guinea, the Republic of the Philippines, Singapore, Chinese Taipei (Taiwan's official designation in APEC), Thailand, and the United States of America.

13. "Remarks by the President to Students and Faculty of Waseda University" (Tokyo, Japan: The White House, Office of the Press Secretary, July 7, 1993).

14. "Remarks by the President in Address to the National Assembly of the Republic of Korea" (Seoul, Korea: The White House, Office of the Press Secretary, July 10, 1993).

15. "Arrival Statement by U.S. Secretary of State Warren Christopher" (Singapore: U.S. Department of State, Office of the Spokesman, July 24, 1993).

16. "Statement of Secretary of State Warren Christopher at the ASEAN Post Ministerial Conference, Six-plus-Seven Open Session" (Singapore: U.S. Department of State, Office of the Spokesman, July 26, 1993).

17. Raphael Cung, "The United States and The Asia-Pacific Economic Cooperation Forum (APEC)," *Business America*, Vol. 114, No. 7 (April 5, 1993), pp. 2-4.

18. "Remarks by the President to Seattle APEC Host Committee" (Seattle, Washington: The White House, Office of the Press Secretary, November 19, 1993).

19. "Remarks by the President in Statement Regarding APEC Leader Meeting, Blake Island, Washington" (Seattle, Washington: The White House, Office of the Press Secretary, November 20, 1993).

20. See "Joint Statement of the Asia-Pacific Economic Cooperation Ministerial Meeting, November 17-19, 1993, Seattle, Washington." The report highlighted the "new web of human and commercial relationships" that were being formed within Asia and the Pacific; reaffirmed a commitment to "the central value of a strengthened open multilateral trading system to continued growth in APEC economies"; noted that "growing interdependence within the region is producing shared goals and aspirations and fostering a spirit of common purpose and of community among APEC members"; "confirmed trade and investment liberalization as the cornerstone of APEC's identity and activity"; affirmed the central APEC objectives of "strengthening the multilateral trading system, expanding regional and global trade and improving investment rules and procedures in a GATT-consistent manner"; noted that "APEC's role in sustaining regional growth and development derives from growing intraregional economic interdependence"; and stated that "APEC is an open and evolving process."

3

Clinton's China Policy

Like his predecessor, who pursued a policy of "constructive engagement" with the People's Republic of China, President Clinton understood that it was necessary to deal pragmatically with Beijing. But pragmatism could not obscure the many fundamental differences in national interests between the United States and China. At the root of many of these conflicting interests are differences in American and Chinese perceptions of the new international order that each country is trying to construct and in their view of how relations between states should be conducted in the post-Cold War period.

The U.S. version of the "new world order" is based on democratic values and the free market system. China's vision of the "new international order" is based on the Five Principles of Peaceful Coexistence made famous by Zhou Enlai in the mid-1950s: mutual respect for sovereignty and territorial integrity, mutual nonaggression, noninterference in each other's internal affairs, equality and mutual benefit, and peaceful coexistence. In many respects the two world views are contradictory: the American vision assumes acceptance of universal norms of democracy and freedom; the Chinese vision assumes that each country should determine its own values without outside interference.

One crucial Chinese assumption about the post-Cold War international order is that the United States is a power in relative decline, primarily because of U.S. domestic factors, but also reflected in the reduction of its forward deployed military forces, especially in areas outside the Asian Pacific theater. Initially, there was concern in China that the United States, the world's only superpower and overwhelming victor in the

Persian Gulf War, would attempt to dominate the world in a form of Pax Americana.

According to later Chinese analysis, this would not be the case. PRC scholar Zi Zhongyun concluded: "the world situation in the post-Cold War period will be more complicated. The bipolar world has collapsed, and a multipolar world has not yet come into existence. The United States is far ahead in overall national power, but is hindered by various global forces as well as by domestic problems. Resulting from the overall balance of the factors mentioned above, the possibility of realizing a `Pax Americana' is weaker, not stronger, than in the Cold War period."[1]

A similar view was expressed by Wang Jisi, who wrote: "Generally speaking, the United States has started a strategic withdrawal as the Soviet threat has faded. While ensuring its capacity for quick responses to major regional conflicts, the United States will substantially reduce its military spending, eliminate outmoded nuclear weapons, and trim its overseas military presence. The role of future U.S. overseas military strength will be to cope with abrupt occurrences like the Gulf crisis, and to guarantee continuing political influence."[2]

According to Chinese analysts, at the same time that the United States is reducing its military forces, it is becoming more aggressive in promoting its vision of a new world order. PRC scholars note several weaknesses in the U.S. plan to create a new world order.[3] These weaknesses include:

1. The United States does not have the strength to fulfill its ambition of leading the new world order.
2. The American people do not support such an activist role for the United States in world affairs in the post-Cold War era.
3. U.S. allies hold different views of the new international order, and they object to the United States assigning to itself the leading role.
4. Future U.S.-Russian relations are unpredictable; to base the new world order on that relationship is not realistic.
5. The new world order stresses U.S. values too much; the rest of the world does not accept U.S. values as universal standards.
6. Democracy, freedom, and human rights are domestic issues -- not universal standards to be imposed by the United States.
7. Since the U.S. vision of the new world order is based on values not accepted by other countries, it is foolhardy to try to build such an order.

In response to the U.S. vision of a "new world order," China proposed a "new international order" more traditionally state-centered.

China's international system would be based on the right of all countries to choose their own ideology, political and economic models, social system, and path of development in view of unique national characteristics. The Chinese argue that differences in these areas are inevitable because of the world's diversity, but they should not impede normal relations and cooperation between nations. International relations should be based solely on mutual interests, not moral values. All countries should have equal rights in discussing and handling world affairs. International disputes should be solved through peaceful negotiations. No country should impose its will upon others nor threaten the use of force in a unilateral way.

According to the PRC, the new international order must include a new economic order as well as a new political order. Beijing considers that the causes of most international problems in the post-Cold War period lie in the economic differences between the developed countries and the developing countries. In the new economic order every country should have the right to choose its own economic system, to control its own resources, and to participate in international economic affairs on an equal basis. No political strings should be attached to economic assistance from the developed world to the developing world.

China also has its own interpretation of what constitutes human rights. These were spelled out in June 1993 by Vice-Foreign Minister Liu Huaqiu, head of the Chinese Delegation to the World Conference on Human Rights held in Vienna.[4]

1. "The international community should give its primary attention to the massive gross violations of human rights resulting from foreign aggression and occupation and continue to support those people still under foreign invasion, colonial rule or apartheid system in their just struggle for national self-determination."

2. "World peace and stability should be enhanced and a favorable international environment created for the attainment of the goals in human rights protection. To this end, countries should establish a new type of international relationship of mutual respect, equality, amicable coexistence and mutual beneficial cooperation in accordance with the UN Charter and the norms of international law. All international disputes should be solved peacefully in a fair and reasonable manner and in the spirit of mutual accommodation and mutual understanding, and consultation on equal footing, instead of resorting to force or threat of force. No country should pursue hegemonism and power politics or engage in aggression, expansion and interference."

3. "The right of developing countries to development should be respected and guaranteed. To create a good international economic environment for the initial economic development of developing countries, the international community should commit itself to the establishment of a fair and rational new international economic order."

4. "The right of each country to formulate its own policies on human rights protection in light of its own conditions should also be respected and guaranteed. Nobody should be allowed to use the human rights issue to exert political and economic pressures on other countries. The human rights issue can be discussed among countries. However, the discussions should be conducted in the spirit of mutual respect and on an equal footing."

In China's view the affairs of each country should be handled by the government and people of that country without foreign interference. This principle is embodied in the U.N. Charter. If the principle is carried out in practice, the United Nations can play a larger role in the future. But the PRC warns that the U.N. cannot be used as an instrument of U.S. or other big power foreign policy.

The differences between the U.S. and Chinese visions of the new world order have profound policy implications for Sino-American relations. President Clinton, for example, wants to build a new Pacific community centered around common values of democracy, freedom, and market economies. The PRC, while it considered itself a member of the Asian Pacific community, cannot accept U.S. leadership or U.S. values. Instead, China supports a multipolar world characterized by noninterference in the internal affairs of other countries. The PRC strongly opposes what it sees as an increased tendency for ideological intervention by the United States in the affairs of sovereign states, especially China.

In another important policy area, the Clinton administration believes U.S. forward deployed forces play an essential role in maintaining a regional balance of power in Asia. While acknowledging that the U.S. military presence enhances stability for now, many Chinese think that Washington greatly overestimates its own importance in this regard. Indeed, a large U.S. military presence in Asia is seen as a threat by many Chinese who want American forces to be reduced much more quickly than planned in Washington.

These views were reflected in Chinese summaries of a May 1992 symposium involving U.S. and PRC national security experts. Chinese participants believed that the justification for the American military presence in Asia was growing weaker. Some Chinese participants suggested that the United States withdraw its forces gradually so as not to upset the balance of power in the region, while others believed that there was no reason for the United States to remain in Southeast Asia and that the United States should "adopt a more circumspect attitude on problems related to the Korean Peninsula." The Chinese side commented, "If Sino-U.S. relations were good, China would not regard the U.S. military presence in Asia as a potential threat to its security."[5]

The Clinton administration believes that communist authoritarianism is collapsing worldwide and that democracy has won the ideological battle for the hearts and minds of the world's people. To further this historic trend, the United States accepts the responsibility to use its national power to promote the cause of freedom. The PRC, on the other hand, refuses to allow a multiparty system in China on the grounds that it would lead to chaos. Beijing's leaders adhere to a system of multiparty cooperation under the leadership of the Chinese Communist Party. PRC leaders believe the United States is engaged in a "soft" strategy of "bourgeois liberalization" and "peaceful evolution" against China. That some Chinese respond to western liberal beliefs is seen as evidence of a continued class struggle for power between the communist party and anti-socialist forces on the mainland being manipulated by foreigners.

As leader of the Free World, the Clinton administration believes the United States has special responsibility to promote and protect human rights. Beijing considers standards of human rights to be a matter for each country to decide in accordance with its own internal conditions. The PRC views U.S. attempts to protect the human rights of Chinese citizens -- whether on the mainland, Hong Kong, Tibet, or Taiwan -- as blatant interference in Chinese internal affairs.

CCP General Secretary Jiang Zemin told the Central Disciplinary Inspection Committee in late August 1993 that the West was pursuing a two-tracked strategy toward China: trying to westernize it by promoting democracy, human rights, and other bourgeois ideals and culture, and trying to weaken China by splitting it through separatism and by promoting the independence of Hong Kong, Taiwan, Xinjiang, and Tibet. Jiang told the committee that the West wanted capitalism to succeed in China but that it did not want China to become a major Pacific power.[6]

To maintain public support for their China policies, both President Bush and President Clinton told the American public that constructive engagement with the PRC would help bring about positive change in China. Having experienced this Western strategy since the sixteenth century, it is not surprising that Chinese leaders believe these statements.[7] In Beijing, the words of American leaders are seen by many as proof that the United States is China's principal enemy in the post-Cold War period.

It is difficult to quantify the impact of these differing perceptions of the new international order on Sino-American relations. But they no doubt contributed to the tension that characterized U.S.-PRC relations during the first two years of President Clinton's term in office. The interplay of moral values and pragmatic concerns -- both in international politics and in U.S. foreign policy -- lend an especially poignant quality to Sino-American relations. This can be seen most readily in the controversies surrounding Taiwan, but it is also apparent in other aspects of U.S. policy toward China such as human rights, trade, and proliferation.

Sino-American Relations After Tiananmen

President Clinton's policy toward China can best be understood in the context of Sino-American relations after the Tiananmen Square massacre in June 1989. The Tiananmen incident brought to a grinding halt most of the positive gains made in Sino-American relations during the Carter, Reagan, and Bush administrations. In the aftermath of Beijing's crackdown on pro-democracy demonstrators and a resurgence of leftist tendencies among Chinese leaders, President George Bush imposed several sanctions on China. These sanctions included the suspension of U.S. military sales to the PRC, the postponement of high-level military exchanges, the postponement of all official exchanges with China above the level of assistant secretary, and U.S. recommendations to international financial institutions to postpone further lending to Beijing. In addition, the United States encouraged its European and Japanese allies to impose similar sanctions.

Although China was harmed to some extent by the sanctions, Beijing skillfully broke out of diplomatic isolation by working closely with the Third World, by exerting her influence in Asia, and by appealing to the pragmatic interests of Japan and Europe in the huge market potential of the PRC. Necessity forced Washington to maintain channels of communication with Beijing. Richard Solomon, Bush's assistant secretary of state for East Asian and Pacific affairs, described the administration's China policy in testimony before the Senate Foreign Relations Committee in June 1990: "Our approach is to try to preserve a key relationship that serves important national interests, while at the same time sending a clear message that Beijing's human rights performance has been -- and remains -- unacceptable, precluding a fully normal relationship."[8]

President Bush justified his policy of constructive engagement with the PRC in a speech at Yale University in May 1991: "If we pursue a policy that cultivates contacts with the Chinese people, promotes commerce to our benefit, we can help create a climate for democratic change. No nation on Earth has discovered a way to import the world's goods and services -- while stopping foreign ideas at the border. Just as the democratic idea has transformed nations on every continent -- so, too, change will inevitably come to China."[9]

In addition to human rights, two of the most pressing issues in Sino-American relations under the Bush administration were a rapidly growing trade imbalance in China's favor and the PRC sale of ballistic missiles and nuclear technology to countries in the Middle East and South Asia. As will be seen, these troublesome issues -- human rights, trade, and proliferation -- persisted under the Clinton administration.

In 1990 China enjoyed a $10.4 billion trade surplus with the United States. In 1991 China's trade surplus was $12.7 billion, the world's second highest with the United States after Japan. In 1992 the surplus grew to $18.2 billion, again, second only to that of Japan. Trade between the United States and China topped $33 billion in 1992, with Chinese exports to the United States totalling $25.8 billion and U.S. exports totalling $7.5 billion. China was the fastest growing export market for U.S. goods in Asia, with American exports increasing by 19 percent. In 1992 the United States absorbed 30 percent ($25 billion) of China's total exports of $85 billion. U.S. business investment in the PRC through the end of 1992 totalled about $6 billion.

In part, the size of the Chinese trade surplus was of concern to the United States because some of it was achieved through unfair trading practices. These practices included failure to honor U.S. intellectual property rights, refusal to remove protectionist barriers against imports from the United States, illegal PRC textile shipments through third countries, and Chinese exports made by political prisoners.

Through intense negotiations with Beijing, the Bush administration was able to secure Chinese agreement in several trade areas. In October 1992 China signed a market access agreement with the United States, promising to phase out 70 to 80 percent of China's non-tariff trade barriers over the next four years. In 1992 the PRC also signed an Intellectual Property Rights agreement, and in August 1992 China signed a Memorandum of Understanding under which U.S. officials could inspect facilities suspected of producing goods for export made with prison labor. China had promised in October 1991 to ban the export of such products.

Beginning in 1990 the focus of debate over China policy in the United States centered on whether the president should extend to the PRC most-favored-nation (MFN) trading status with or without conditions. The debate had its legal basis in the Jackson-Vanik amendment to the trade act of 1974 which stipulated that the president must certify annually that nonmarket economies receiving MFN provide freedom of emigration to their citizens. In the case of China, the Democratic-controlled Congress sought to impose by law various conditions on MFN, while President Bush insisted that MFN be extended without conditions. Every attempt by Congress to attach MFN conditions was vetoed by Bush, and the congressional Democrats were unable to muster the necessary two-thirds majority vote in both houses to override his veto.

Another area of concern to the United States was China's policy toward proliferation issues. PRC missile sales to the Third World were deeply troubling to the United States. U.S. intelligence reported that Beijing was ready to sell M-9 short-range ballistic missiles to Syria and M-11 short-range ballistic missiles to Pakistan. The M-9 had a range of about 370 miles, giving Syria the ability to hit military targets in Israel with great accuracy and reliability. The M-11 could carry an 800-kilogram warhead more than 180 miles to targets in India.[10] Because of the volatile nature of politics in the Middle East and South Asia, Washington saw the missiles sales as destabilizing to international peace and against U.S. interests in nonproliferation. In mid-1991 the United States began pressuring China to adhere to the Missile Technology Control Regime (MTCR), whose twenty members sought to arrest missile proliferation by controlling the export of key missile technologies and equipment.

The Bush administration was also concerned by Chinese shipments of nuclear materials and technology to Pakistan and certain other countries. China had a long history of this practice. According to one study, in 1983 the PRC gave Pakistan the design of a tested nuclear weapon with a yield of about 25 kilotons. Beijing also provide Pakistan with enough weapons-grade uranium for at least two nuclear weapons. Chinese scientists routinely worked in Pakistan's Kahuta complex, where nuclear weapons research took place. In addition, Beijing sold India about 150 tons of heavy water, which is used to make plutonium, uranium to South Africa, uranium and heavy water to Argentina, enriched uranium to Brazil, and a heavy water reactor to Algeria.[11] In view of these practices, the Bush administration orchestrated a great deal of international pressure to convince China to join the Nuclear Non-Proliferation Treaty (NPT).

Again, after intense negotiations with the Chinese, the Bush administration was able to convince Beijing to become party to the major agreements on nonproliferation. China agreed to adhere to the Missile Technology Control Regime guidelines and parameters in February 1992, acceded to the Nuclear Non-Proliferation Treaty in March 1992, and became an original signatory to the Chemical Weapons Convention in January 1993.

In addition to these trade and nonproliferation agreements, China made other efforts to improve its relations with the United States during the last two years of the Bush administration. For example, Beijing did not react too vigorously to the U.S. decision to sell Taiwan 150 F-16 fighters in September 1992 or to the visit of the cabinet-level U.S. trade representative to Taipei in December of that year. Also, in November 1992 China purchased over 1.6 million tons of subsidized American wheat, the largest one-day purchase by any country since the U.S. Export Enhancement program began in 1985.

President Bush responded to these signs of Chinese willingness to improve relations with positive signals of his own. In December 1992 the president sent Commerce Secretary Barbara Franklin to restore Sino-American commercial relations. That same month the administration lifted its ban on sales of military technology to China, allowing the completion of four arms sales stalled in the "pipeline" when the ban on such transactions was imposed in June 1989. The completed weapons transfers included avionics for China's F-8-II fighter, two counter-artillery radars, four antisubmarine torpedoes, and the production of munitions. The equipment was shipped as it was, with no follow-up support, spare parts, training, maintenance, or guarantees by the United States on equipment capability or workability. The administration explained, "We are simply closing out FMS [government-to-government Foreign Military Sales] sales programs that were frozen after Tiananmen. The U.S. has no plans to conduct any new arms sales to China."[12]

Evolution of Clinton's China Policy

Despite the heated presidential-congressional debate over MFN, China policy surfaced only occasionally during the presidential campaign. The 1992 Democratic Party Platform approved the "conditioning of favorable trade terms for China on respect for human rights in China and Tibet, greater market access for U.S. goods, and responsible conduct on weapons proliferation."[13] In the televised campaign debate in St. Louis on October 12, 1992, Clinton was asked how he would exert U.S. power to influence China. He responded with several points.

First, the U.S. relationship with China was important and Beijing should not be isolated. However, it was wrong for President Bush to send national security adviser Brent Scowcroft to China immediately after Tiananmen to toast their leaders. Clinton said it should be recognized that China agreed to stop exporting goods made by prison labor to the United States and to do something about its growing trade surplus with the United States, not because the Bush administration "coddled them," but because of pressure by Congress. Second, Clinton promised he would be firm with China and link continued most-favored-nation status with human rights and a more open society. And third, Clinton said the United States should stand up for its economic and democratic interests in China.[14]

In another campaign speech, Clinton said: "The administration continues to coddle China, despite its continuing crackdown on democratic reforms, its brutal subjugation of Tibet, its irresponsible exports of nuclear and missile technology, its support for the homicidal Khmer Rouge in Cambodia, and its abusive trade practices."[15] He promised to link MFN trading status for China to improvements in its observation of human rights, good trade behavior, and restraint in the export of weapons and defense technology.[16]

When it became apparent that Clinton would win the election, however, he adjusted his position by saying that he, too, would approach China in a pragmatic fashion. At his first news conference as president-elect, Clinton said: "We have a big stake in not isolating China....But I stick by the values that I articulated in the campaign." During a mid-November transition meeting in Washington, Clinton repeated: "We have a big stake in not isolating China....But we also have to insist, I believe, on progress in human rights and human decency. And I think there are indications in the last few months that a firm hand by our government can help to achieve that."[17]

In December 1992 Clinton indicated that he did not think it would be necessary to revoke China's MFN status if the PRC continued its course of economic reform and improvement on human rights. He told participants in his national economic conference in Little Rock, Arkansas: "I don't think we'll have to revoke the MFN status...if we can achieve continued progress along [present] lines." Clinton pointed out that China recently had agreed to stop exporting products made by prison labor to the United States and to open some markets to U.S. goods. This took place after "the Bush administration finally agreed to put a little heat on the Chinese." Clinton said, "I don't want to isolate China for political and economic reasons. I don't want to dislocate any industries here....But I do think in the aftermath of Tiananmen Square...that we have an obligation to at least continue to be consistent about the things in which we believe."[18]

Later that month, Clinton observed that China's large trade surplus with the United States "should give us some ground for serious discussion about what kind of world we want to live in and where we're going to go, the kind of freedom that the people of Hong Kong are going to have, what kind of freedom the people of China are going to have and how we can move forward together." He promised to oppose China's "violations of international arms treaties or the proliferation of weapons of mass destruction for economic or other purposes."[19]

Lord's Statement on U.S. China Policy

The various elements of Clinton's emerging China policy were articulated by his designated assistant secretary of state for East Asian and Pacific affairs, Winston Lord. In his March 1993, confirmation hearing before the Senate Foreign Relations Committee, Lord said that one of administration's goals in building a new Pacific community was "restoring firm foundations for cooperation with a China where political openness catches up with economic reform."[20] Lord said the administration would follow a carefully nuanced policy toward China, attempting to balance U.S. interests in maintaining cooperative relations with the PRC because of its importance, yet seeking improvement in China's record of human rights and the termination of policies harmful to U.S. interests.

Lord stressed China's importance as "an influential member of the international order," and he noted that in recent years "China has opened up to the world, moved toward a market economy, and enjoyed the fastest growth rate in the world." Together with Taiwan and Hong Kong, the mainland comprises a Chinese community that "has become one of the most promising areas for investment and trade."

Nonetheless, Lord said Chinese "leaders cling to an outdated authoritarian system" in which serious human rights and other abuses persist. Lord observed, "The Chinese leaders are gambling that open economics and closed politics will preserve their system of control." But it will prove to be "a gamble that sooner or later will be lost."

Lord said, "Our policy challenge therefore is to reconcile our need to deal with this important nation with our imperatives to promote international values. We will seek cooperation with China on a range of issues. But Americans cannot forget Tiananmen Square." Lord said the United States "should conduct a nuanced policy toward Beijing until a more humane system emerges." He cautioned, "Shunning China is not an alternative. We need both to condemn repression and preserve links with progressive forces which are the foundations for our longer term ties."

Lord defined the fundamental elements of Clinton's policy toward China as being:

- The United States "will continue to be guided by the three Sino-American communiques that have provided a flexible framework for our relations." [The communiques are the U.S.-China joint communique issued at Shanghai on February 28, 1972, at the conclusion of President Richard Nixon's trip to the PRC; the joint communique on the establishment of diplomatic relations between the United States and the People's Republic of China on January 1, 1979; and the joint communique of August 17, 1982, on future U.S. arms sales to Taiwan.]
- "It is up to China and Taiwan to work out their future relationship; we insist only that the process be peaceful."
- "Consistent with our undertakings not to challenge the principle of `one China,' we will continue to build upon our unofficial relations with Taiwan based on the [1979] Taiwan Relations Act."
- "In our diplomacy and through the 1992 U.S.-Hong Kong Policy Act we should make clear our large humanitarian and commercial stakes in the future of Hong Kong."

Having reaffirmed what, in essence, was a continuation of Reagan and Bush policies toward China, Ambassador Lord highlighted several issues in Sino-American relations that needed to be addressed by the new administration:

- widespread human rights violations, including those occurring in Tibet
- Chinese exports of dangerous weapons and technology to volatile areas of the world
- the fastest growing trade deficit of the United States, at $18 billion in 1992 second only to that of Japan
- continuous need for collaboration at the United Nations and on regional conflicts
- emerging challenges like the environment and illegal drugs.

Lord said these and other issues required the United States and China to "work together where our interests converge and bargain hard over differences." Lord promised: "We will press forward with this agenda in a sober, constructive fashion. Our approach will reflect that China is a great nation. In response to positive movement by the Chinese, we are prepared to address their concerns and strengthen our ties."

1993 MFN Policy

The administration's attempt to balance the various U.S. interests in China could be seen in its policy regarding continued MFN trading status for the PRC in 1993. In early March 1993, Secretary of State Warren Christopher indicated that the Clinton administration would renew China's MFN in 1993 without conditions but would tie MFN renewal in 1994 to China's progress in human rights and in certain other areas. Christopher told the House Appropriations Subcommittee on Commerce, State, Judiciary and related agencies: "It is my hope we can go forward with MFN this year, but conditioned on their making very substantial progress....It is not the preferred solution, I think, to isolate China further." Christopher said China's human rights record was "poor" and that its trade surplus with the United States was due to "abusive trade practices." Regarding arms proliferation, the secretary noted, "The situation in China is not one for great admiration."[21]

The Congress, while willing to let Clinton take the lead on MFN, nonetheless warned the president that if he did not meet congressional expectations in areas such as human rights, proliferation and unfair trade practices, it would again press the issue through legislation.[22] In April

Representative Nancy Pelosi (D-California) and Senate Majority Leader George J. Mitchell (D-Maine) introduced identical legislation in the House and Senate extending MFN to China for one more year, but requiring that the president certify "significant progress" in certain areas before MFN would be extended the following year. The White House did not endorse the bills but noted, "The general approach of conditioning MFN to progress towards human rights and democracy is something the president consistently has supported and does support."[23]

On May 28, 1993, President Clinton announced his MFN policy toward China.[24] Stating that the United States must "recognize both the value of China and the values of America," Clinton said that China occupied "an important place in our nation's foreign policy" and that "its future will do much to shape the future of Asia, our security and trade relations in the Pacific, and a host of global issues, from the environment to weapons proliferation." Nonetheless, the United States continued "to harbor profound concerns about a range of practices by China's communist leaders," including:

- the continued imprisonment of Chinese political activists and pro-democracy leaders
- the lack of international access to Chinese prisons
- continued reports of Chinese abuses against the people and culture of Tibet
- the proliferation of dangerous weapons, such as M-11 missiles to Pakistan
- China's $18 billion trade surplus with the United States, accompanied by Chinese practices to block American goods and services.

Despite these areas of concern, Clinton said there were many signs of progress in China. "We take some encouragement from the economic reforms in China....We are hopeful that China's process of development and economic reform will be accompanied by greater political reform....The question we face today is how best to cultivate these hopeful seeds of change in China while expressing our clear disapproval of its repressive policies."

The "core" of his China policy, Clinton said, "will be a resolute insistence upon significant progress on human rights in China....Whether I extend MFN next year, however, will depend upon whether China makes significant progress in implementing its human rights record." The president added, "we will use existing statutes to address our concerns in the areas of trade and arms control." To implement his policy, the president issued an executive order that had the effect of separating MFN from trade and proliferation issues and took the MFN issue out of the hands of Congress.

The president also sent a detailed report to Congress which further explained his China policy.[25] The report stated that China had fulfilled both freedom of emigration and foreign travel requirements under U.S. law, but that "China human rights practices remain repressive and fall far short of internationally-accepted norms. Freedoms of speech, assembly, association, and religion are sharply restricted." In addition, the United States was concerned over Chinese policies toward Tibet.

The report said that MFN renewal in 1994 would be conditioned on "significant progress" in a number of areas, including:

1. Respecting the fundamental human rights recognized in the Universal Declaration of Human Rights.
2. Complying with China's commitment to allow its citizens, regardless of their political views, freedom to emigrate and travel abroad (excepting those who are imprisoned, have criminal proceedings pending against them, or have received court notices concerning civil cases).
3. Providing an acceptable accounting for and release of Chinese citizens imprisoned or detained for the peaceful expression of their political views, including Democracy Wall and Tiananmen activists.
4. Taking effective steps to ensure that forced abortion and sterilization are not used to implement China's family planning policies.
5. Ceasing religious persecution, particularly by releasing leaders and members of religious groups detained or imprisoned for expression of their religious beliefs.
6. Taking effective actions to ensure that prisoners are not being mistreated and are receiving necessary medical treatment, such as by granting access to Chinese prisons by international humanitarian organizations.
7. Seeking to resume dialogue with the Dalai Lama or his representatives, and taking measures to protect Tibet's distinctive religious and cultural heritage.
8. Continuing cooperation concerning U.S. military personnel who are listed as prisoners of war or missing in action.
9. Ceasing the jamming of Voice of America broadcasts.

On nonproliferation issues, the presidential report said the administration would approach China through existing legislation and international agreements. The report noted that China had refrained from selling certain items since joining these international agreements, but that its transfer to Pakistan in November 1992 of MTCR-class M-11 missiles and related equipment had violated China's MTCR commitment.[26] The report said, "Seeking full Chinese compliance with multilateral obligations and support for international nonproliferation goals is a top Administration priority. The U.S. is prepared to employ the resources under U.S. law and executive determination -- including the imposition of sanctions -- if the PRC engages in irresponsible transfers that violate its commitments."

The report said that trade issues would be handled separately from MFN, noting the administration "will continue to press for full and faithful implementation of bilateral agreements with China on market access, intellectual property rights, and prison labor." It warned that "Section 301 of the 1974 Trade Act is a powerful instrument to ensure our interests are protected and advanced in the areas of market access and intellectual property rights." The report assured Congress that the administration will "continue to implement vigorously the provisions of the Tariff Act of 1930 to prevent importation of goods made by forced labor."

Further explanation of President Clinton's MFN policy came on June 8, 1993, when Assistant Secretary of State Winston Lord appeared before the House Ways and Means Committee.[27] Lord said that trying to balance U.S. international goals in maintaining cooperative relations with Beijing with U.S. interests in promoting human rights and democracy in China was no easy task. Many different approaches had been considered to find "the best means to remain engaged with China while pressing Beijing for responsible behavior in core areas of concern."

Lord said the U.S. "policy challenge with China...is to reconcile our need to deal with this important nation with our imperative to promote international values." Above all, Lord said, "The U.S. has a basic national interest in a more open, prosperous, and humane China, which will also be a more peaceful and cooperative member of the world community." The guiding principle of Clinton's policy toward China, according to Lord, was that "The Chinese Government cannot expect to enjoy the full fruits of membership in the international community...unless it abides by universally recognized standards regarding treatment of its citizens, global commerce, and the transfer of weapons of mass destruction and sensitive technology."

Continued Tension in U.S.-PRC Relations

The extension of MFN to China left several issues unresolved in U.S.-PRC trade relations, including market access, standards, prison labor, transshipping textiles, and intellectual property rights. Moreover, there was continued disagreement over Chinese human rights practices. In July 1993 the U.S. House of Representatives adopted a resolution urging the International Olympic Committee (IOC) to reject Beijing's bid to host the Summer Olympic Games in the year 2000 because of China's poor human rights record. In August nearly two-thirds of the Senate signed a letter to all ninety members of the IOC with the same message of opposition.

Viewing the games as vitally important to its international prestige, China sought to improve its human rights image. In mid-September, just a few days before the IOC was to make its final decision, the PRC released Wei Jingsheng, China's most famous political prisoner.[28] But a few days after losing its Olympic bid to Sydney, Australia, Beijing again cracked down on dissidents throughout China. The government also passed regulations restricting the personal use of satellite dishes, pagers, and cordless telephones. PRC leaders reportedly were extremely angry over U.S. opposition to China's hosting the Olympic Games. Many senior political and military leaders were said to demand that China adopt a tougher position in Sino-American relations.[29]

Serious problems also arose in the area of proliferation. The United States determined in August 1993 that the PRC had sold M-11 ballistic missile components to Pakistan in violation of the Missile Technology Control Regime. The MTCR banned the sale of missiles and associated technology with a range of more than 186 miles and payload capabilities over 1,100 pounds. Although the M-11 actually had a range of slightly less than 186 miles, the United States concluded that the Chinese sale of M-11 technology and components violated the MTCR because these could be used by Pakistan to produce longer-ranged missiles capable of carrying nuclear, chemical, or biological warheads.

On August 25, 1993, the Clinton administration announced that it would ban the export of some high-technology goods to China for two years. The U.S. sanctions were mandated by an amendment to the 1990 Arms Export Control Act requiring that if a nonmarket economy violated MTCR guidelines, all U.S. activities affecting the development or production of electronics, space systems or equipment, and military aircraft would be subject to sanctions. In a decision affecting about $1 billion in U.S. sales, the administration prevented American companies from obtaining export licenses to sell China rocket systems and rocket subsystems, avionics equipment, launch-support equipment, software, satellites, and advanced computers.

China reacted strongly to the U.S. sanctions, claiming the American decision "was a wrong judgment based on inaccurate intelligence." Vice-Foreign Minister Liu Huaqiu said on August 27 that China had done nothing to violate its 1992 commitment to the MTCR. By contrast, "in blatant violation of the Sino-U.S. Joint Communique of August 17, the U.S. government decided [in September 1992] to sell 150 F-16s to Taiwan, a move that grossly interfered in China's internal affairs." Liu pointed out that the PRC agreement to act in compliance with the MTCR guidelines and parameters "was predicated on U.S. withdrawal of all its sanctions on China." With the resumption of the sanctions, Liu said, "the Chinese government has no alternative but to reconsider its commitments to MTCR. The U.S. shall be held fully responsible for all the consequences."[30]

Another bitter proliferation issue involved U.S. demands that it be allowed to search the Chinese cargo ship *Yinhe* destined for Iran. U.S. intelligence had determined that the ship carried thiodiglycol for mustard gas and thionyl chloride for nerve gas in violation of the recently negotiated Chemical Weapons Convention scheduled to take effect in 1995. After weeks of heated exchanges, the ship was inspected in the Saudi port of Damman in early September 1993, where it was found that the vessel did not contain the banned chemicals. Embarrassed American officials suspected the chemical containers had been dumped en route or that U.S. agencies had been fed disinformation by Chinese intelligence services.

Taking full advantage of U.S. discomfiture, the Chinese Foreign Ministry said on September 4 that the U.S. action in the *Yinhe* incident was "a show of hegemony and power politics, pure and simple." China demanded the United States make a public apology and compensate China for all its financial loses. The Foreign Ministry said, "China has committed itself publicly not to produce or possess chemical weapons, nor does it export chemical products that may be used for the purpose of making chemical weapons."[31] Other Chinese commentators said: "By interfering in China's normal trade activities on totally unwarranted charges, the United States has once again tried to play the role of 'world cop,' revealing itself to be a hegemonic bully....The wrong-doing of the United States in the *Yinhe* incident has cast a dark shadow over Sino-U.S.

relations and the U.S. government must be held fully responsible for all the consequences arising therefrom."[32]

On September 29, 1993, Foreign Minister Qian Qichen denounced the United States before the United Nations for "hegemonic conduct of a self-styled `world cop' who tramples upon international law and norms of international relations." Referring to the U.S. sale of F-16s to Taiwan and subsequent American sanctions against China for the sale of M-11 components to Pakistan, Qian said China was opposed to the use of sanctions "under the pretext of controlling arms transfers while engaging in massive arms sales of one's own which jeopardize the sovereignty and security of the country concerned." Expressing concern that the United Nations was becoming an instrument of U.S. hegemony in the post-Cold War period, Qian demanded that the U.N. Security Council give China the right of "prior consent and [a] pledge of cooperation" before any peacekeeping operations. The foreign minister added that China strongly opposed "any attempt to impose a particular model" of government on other nations.[33]

Adding fuel to the nonproliferation issue was China's detonation of an underground nuclear weapon in October 1993. The test was carried out despite repeated requests from President Clinton and twenty other nations that Beijing join the world's other nuclear powers in foregoing nuclear testing. The White House said it "deeply regrets" the PRC test and called on Beijing to "refrain from further nuclear tests and to join the other nuclear powers in a global moratorium."[34]

Strategy of Reengagement

Despite persistent problems with China, the United States could not deny the growing importance of the PRC on the world stage. In 1993 the PRC imported goods valued at $104 billion, while its exports totalled $92 billion. China's trade surplus with the United States reached $23 billion, second only to the $50 billion surplus of Japan. About $20 billion in foreign investment poured into China, a demonstration of global business interest in the economic potential of China. The PRC also borrowed heavily; its debt in 1993 was about $73 billion. The PRC economy grew about 9.5 percent for the decade, making China the third largest economy in the world, according to some measurements. Its growth rate in 1993 was around 13 percent, the fastest growing major economy in the world.[35] Many American businessmen complained that the sanctions imposed by the United States since Tiananmen had harmed American commercial interests by excluding U.S. companies from lucrative contracts in the PRC.

The growing importance of China as a trading partner, its status as a major power in Northeast Asia, and the assumed long-term liberalizing influence of the free market on China's political system convinced the Clinton administration that it needed to rescue the rapidly deteriorating Sino-American relationship. By mid-September 1993 Washington began to moderate its policy of confrontation with the PRC and to "reengage" China in an attempt to resolve the growing list of problems that had emerged since 1989.

As part of his strategy of reengagement, Clinton sent several top level officials to Beijing for discussions on a wide range of issues. These included Treasury Secretary Lloyd Bentsen and Agricultural Secretary Mike Espy to discuss trade, State Department Assistant Secretary John Shattuck to discuss human rights, and Assistant Secretary of Defense Charles Freeman to discuss resuming U.S.-PRC military ties. Secretary of State Warren Christopher met Foreign Minister Qian Qichen in New York in September to launch the effort to improve Sino-American relations, while Clinton himself planned to meet China's President Jiang Zemin during the Asia-Pacific Economic Cooperation (APEC) meeting in Seattle in November.

Renewed Sino-American Military Contact

Of special interest was the initiative undertaken by Bill Clinton to reestablish military links with the People's Liberation Army (PLA). Such links were banned by President Bush in 1989 as a result of Tiananmen. Wide consensus existed among American China specialists that it was in the U.S. interest to reopen dialogue with the PLA. Several pragmatic considerations were paramount:

1. The PRC was expanding its power projection capabilities and aspired to be a world power equal to the United States.
2. Senior Chinese military leaders were becoming convinced that the United States was China's principal enemy in the post-Cold War period.
3. The PLA was directly involved in many areas of controversy in Sino-American relations, including proliferation of nuclear weapons technology and ballistic missiles.

4. The PLA exerted strong influence within the conservative wing of the PRC leadership.
5. The military could play a vital role in the future political direction of China.
6. Greater contact with the PLA would enable the United States to learn more about Chinese military thinking and perhaps to influence the PLA in ways beneficial to U.S. interests.

Assistant Secretary of Defense Charles Freeman visited Beijing in early November 1993 to discuss regional security issues, Chinese participation in U.N. peacekeeping operations, the problem of converting defense industries to civilian production, and U.S. concerns about proliferation of weapons of mass destruction. Although the talks were seen as the first step toward reestablishing Sino-American military relations, Freeman reported sharp differences over Chinese missile sales to Pakistan and U.S. weapons sales to Taiwan. He said it was not likely U.S.-PRC military cooperation would return to the level maintained during the Cold War and that there was no talk of weapons sales to China. Other officials said the United States would continue to ban the sell of weapons to Beijing and would not approve manufacturing licenses for military-related goods.[36]

A few weeks later the administration announced that it would approve the sale to China of a Cray supercomputer slated for use in weather prediction. Because of its power, the Cray could also be used to develop nuclear weapons and ballistic missile systems. The computer sale was accompanied by a decision to allow China to launch three of eight communications satellites earlier banned because of the M-11 missile sanctions. In return for the lifting of high-tech sanctions, Washington asked Beijing to make more specific its promise to abide by the requirements of the Missile Control Technology Regime. China continued to deny that it had violated its MTCR pledges in the first place.

Clinton-Jiang Meeting in Seattle

On November 19, 1993, President Bill Clinton and President Jiang Zemin met during the APEC ministerial conference in Seattle. In describing the meeting Clinton told the press he had "reaffirmed the United States support for the three joint communiques as the bedrock of our one China policy."[37] He said, "I emphasized to President Jiang the need for early concrete progress on aspects of China policy and practice that are of deep concern to the American people -- human rights, including Tibet, trade practices, and nonproliferation."

The president elaborated on each of these areas, saying he "especially stressed our concerns in the area of human rights....I mentioned in particular the need for prison access by the ICRC [International Committee of the Red Cross], the question of releasing political prisoners, especially those who are sick. I particularly mentioned the case of Wang Juntao [an arrested leader of the Tiananmen Square demonstrations]. I asked for a dialogue on Tibet with the Dalai Lama or his representatives. And I discussed the question of prison labor and the need for our customs officials to visit other facilities as already called for in our memorandum of understanding." The president also discussed permitting relatives of Chinese dissidents exiled in the United States to emigrate to the United States.

In the area of trade, the president said: "I also emphasized the need for progress on our trade imbalance. We discussed the needs for greater market access and for the protection of intellectual property rights. I think our trade relationships alone indicate that the United States has not attempted to isolate China, but instead has attempted to assist its movement into the global economy. After all, this year we will purchase about a third of the total Chinese exports."

In regards to proliferation, Clinton said: "I also stressed that we look to China to participate fully in international efforts to stem weapons proliferation. We continue to have differences on those issues. But we agreed that we should seek to resolve them through dialogue and negotiation."

The president said Sino-American relations for the remainder of the decade "will be one of the most important in the world." In commenting on the significance of his meeting with Jiang, Clinton said: Our "two countries have been somewhat estranged ever since Tiananmen Square. And the very fact that we talked today I think is a positive sign that both of us are interested in trying to resolve our respective problems." Although he could not point to specific areas of formal agreement, the president said the Chinese leader "did engage and discuss" a number of the issues the United States raised. "I thought we began a dialogue," he said.

Secretary of State Christopher reiterated the importance of dialogue in a press conference following the Clinton-Jiang meeting. Christopher said: "the most significant part of [Jiang's] reaction" to President Clinton's requests in the area of human rights "was that he engaged on them....I don't think it's probably proper for me to tell you in detail what he said, but he did not refuse to engage, and they had a vivid and animated discussion on these human rights issues." Christopher said, "There were no specific commitments coming out of the meeting, but the essence of the meeting, I would say, was in the discussion between the two Presidents, and the frankness, the candidness and the directness of the discussion between them."[38]

The Controversies Remain

Following the summit in Seattle, the United States and China continued to disagree over Korea, trade, and human rights.

In the case of Korea, the United States believed that Beijing had more influence over Pyongyang than did any other country. China maintained a security treaty with North Korea and supplied the Democratic People's Republic of Korea (DPRK) with two-thirds of its oil imports. The PRC also provided the DPRK with rocket motors and guidance systems for its ballistic missiles.

Deeply concerned over North Korea's nuclear weapons program, the United States wanted to use the threat of economic sanctions authorized by the U.N. Security Council to pressure the DPRK into allowing full inspections of its nuclear facilities by the International Atomic Energy Agency (IAEA). China, however, opposed sanctions on the grounds that they would have an effect opposite of that intended and possibly precipitate a military crisis on the peninsula. Beijing argued that direct negotiations between the United States and North Korea were the best way to defuse the situation by ending the DPRK's sense of isolation and fear of U.S. attack. An important common ground between Beijing and Washington was that neither country wanted North Korea's nuclear weapons to cause Japan, South Korea, or Taiwan to develop nuclear weapons of their own. China wanted the Korean peninsula to be free of all nuclear weapons, including those of the United States, and preferred to see the Americans withdraw most of their forces from Korea altogether.

In the area of trade, China and the United States also had policy differences. According to U.S. figures (which included entrepot trade through Hong Kong), in 1993 the United States exported $8.8 billion worth of goods to China, while importing $31.5 billion. The $22.7 billion trade deficit with China was the second largest for the United

States after its deficit with Japan, which totalled $59.3 billion in 1993. According to some calculations, U.S. exports to China provided nearly 170,000 American jobs. The U.S. Commerce Department called China the most promising market for American goods over the next two decades.[39]

After the APEC meeting, U.S.-PRC trade differences focused on textiles.[40] The administration charged China with illegally exporting about $2 billion worth of textiles and apparel to the United States by mislabeling products as being made in other countries. Since the previous five-year U.S.-PRC textile agreement was due to expire at the end of 1993, the United States threatened to impose unilateral reductions of China's textile quotas if the illegal exports were not stopped. After months of haggling, the two sides finally approved a new textile agreement in January 1994. Under the previous agreement, China had been allowed to increase its textile exports to the United States at a rate of 4.4 percent annually. The new agreement limited PRC textile exports to the United States to annual increases of 1 percent in 1995 and 1996. To compensate for previous illegal shipments, China's quota for 1994 was frozen at the 1993 level. The agreement also provided for unannounced inspections by joint U.S.-Chinese teams to ensure that Chinese factories were not mislabeling the country-of-origin tags on their products. In a separate pact the two sides agreed to limit the growth in Chinese silk exports to the United States to 1 percent a year.[41]

In early March 1994 U.S. Trade Representative Mickey Kantor told the House Foreign Affairs Committee that the administration had placed China on a priority watch list for flagrant violation of U.S. intellectual property rights. He said his office was deeply concerned over restrictions on U.S. access to Chinese agricultural markets as well.[42]

Human rights remained an area of constant irritation in Sino-American relations. Within the administration sharp debate was heard over which U.S. interest was most important: commercial interests in interacting with the fastest growing economy in the world, even if Beijing did not improve human rights as fast as the United States would like; or human rights interests in using trade as a tool to pressure China to improve treatment of its citizens.

The debate revolved around whether to extend China's MFN status for 1994. Many were concerned that if the United States did revoke MFN, thereby increasing the average customs duty on goods imported from China to 40 percent from 8 percent, the PRC would retaliate by blocking American business opportunities in China and by refusing to cooperate on issues such as arms proliferation and the Korean peninsula. Others were convinced that China desperately needed trade with the United States and would eventually improve its human rights behavior to maintain favorable access to the U.S. market. Some in the policy debate felt American commitments to moral values were more important than commercial profit when dealing with a repressive government such as the PRC.

A few weeks before the State Department was scheduled to release its annual human rights report, China made efforts to show improvement in human rights. In January 1994 the PRC released two Tibetan political prisoners, a move the State Department called "a step in the right direction" but insufficient to meet the requirements to approve MFN later that year.[43] Also in mid-January, Jiang Zemin told former President George Bush and a congressional delegation led by House Majority Leader Richard A. Gephardt that China would take steps to improve its human rights. No specifics were given, but about the same time productive discussions were begun between the PRC and international Red Cross officials over allowing Red Cross visits to Chinese political prisoners.[44]

During his visit to China in late January, Treasury Secretary Lloyd Bentsen (the highest U.S. official to visit China since 1991) warned PRC leaders that Clinton would revoke China's MFN status unless Beijing improved its human rights practices. While in the PRC, Bentsen announced that the two countries had reactivated a 1992 agreement allowing U.S. customs officials to visit Chinese prisons to ensure that their factories were not producing goods exported to the United States. Bentsen also reconvened the China-United States Joint Economic Committee, a forum designed to work out economic differences between the two countries, which was shut down after the Tiananmen incident.[45]

Secretary of State Warren Christopher and Chinese Foreign Minister Qian Qichen met in Paris a few days after the Bentsen trip to China. Christopher told Qian that China's improvement in human rights has "not in my judgment made enough progress to justify my saying that there has been significant overall progress."[46] Such certification from the secretary of state was necessary if China was to receive MFN by June 1994.

Pressure on China increased in early February when the State Department released its annual report on the status of human rights around the world. Highly critical of the PRC, the report said China's "overall human rights record in 1993 fell far short of internationally accepted norms as it continued to repress domestic critics and failed to control abuses by its own security forces." While acknowledging that some progress had been made in 1993 and early 1994, State Department officials pointed out that China's human rights record to date was not sufficient to justify renewal of MFN later in the year.[47]

1994 MFN Decision

Secretary of State Christopher visited the PRC in March 1994 with a strong message that Clinton intended to link China's MFN status with its human rights conduct and that Beijing's policies to date were not satisfactory. In what he described as "very tough exchanges," the secretary secured from the Chinese:

- a joint declaration to end exports to the United States of goods produced by prison labor
- assurances on inspections of all Chinese facilities suspected of producing such goods
- promises to resolve a few of the outstanding emigration cases
- an agreement to review interference with Voice of America (VOA) radio signals
- a promise to talk with Red Cross officials regarding visits to prisoners of conscience
- information regarding some 235 prisoners specified by the United States
- promises to provide information on 106 Tibetans imprisoned in China.[48]

In spite of these accomplishments, Christopher was severely criticized for his handling of U.S. China policy when he returned to Washington.[49] The sharpest criticism came from those who thought he should have cancelled his trip because of Beijing's harassment of leading dissidents and, from the other side of the spectrum, those who regarded Clinton's policy of linking trade with human rights as unwise and self-defeating.

As debate over China policy continued, the most effective lobbyists for change were American business groups with an interest in trading with the PRC. This group of businessmen and large corporations found strong allies within the administration among those who were responsible for trade and economic policy. As a rule, those officials were highly critical of the State Department's management of China policy, particularly Christopher's giving prominence to human rights issues over U.S. economic interests. Some officials responsible for U.S. security warned that it would harm U.S. interests to allow human rights to undermine Sino-American cooperation on such issues as North Korea. U.S. officials from different departments and agencies contradicted each other in judging whether China had made "significant progress" on human rights and whether MFN would be extended in 1994.[50]

As tension within the administration mounted over China policy -- tension enhanced by the president's ambivalence in deciding which U.S. interests were most important -- the PRC assumed a tough public posture by saying that it could live well even if the United States cut off trade. Foreign Minister Qian Qichen observed that the importance of China's trade with the United States was overrated, insisting that his government would not be pressured by Clinton's attempt to link trade and human rights. According to Qian, the U.S. president had "enmeshed himself in a web of his own spinning" in which "he will only have his own hands and feet bound."[51]

To repair the growing rift in its China policy, the White House held a series of top level meetings immediately after Christopher's return from Beijing. One outcome of these meetings was an increased role in the formulation of China policy by the departments of Treasury and Commerce to ensure greater balance between security, human rights, and commercial interests. The administration also signalled greater conciliation toward China, suggesting that Washington would be willing to end the annual MFN trade-human rights debate if the PRC would adopt minimum human rights standards. The president continued to speak of the goal of improving human rights in China, but clearly a page had been turned. After March 1994 the administration emphasized the necessity of maintaining a positive relationship with China rather than threatening trade as a sanction to pressure Beijing on human rights.[52]

As required by Clinton's May 1993 executive order, the secretary of state submitted a report in May 1994 on China's human rights performance as part of the MFN determination for that year.[53] Christopher noted a mixed Chinese performance. In a positive assessment the report said China complied with two mandatory conditions: the resolution of all pending emigration cases and the ending of exports of prison labor to the United States. On the other hand, China "made gains in human rights but has not achieved the `overall, significant progress' in the five additional areas identified in the 1993 executive order." According to the report:

Despite the several significant prisoner releases, many more dissidents were detained, tried, and sentenced during a nation-wide crackdown on political and religious dissent. New laws were codified which, if enforced, would abridge the political and religious rights of individual Chinese. Negotiations with the ICRC [Red Cross] have not yet resulted in any Chinese commitment to permit access to prisons and prisoners. Tibetans who peacefully protest their support for political and religious independence continue to be jailed. The Chinese ignored conciliatory public statements by the Dalai Lama and refused to enter into a dialogue with him. Some jamming of VOA [Voice of America] continues and the Chinese have strongly protested the establishment of Radio Free Asia.

The report concluded that China's human rights performance fell short of the executive order's "overall, significant progress" standard. Nonetheless, "Our judgment is that revocation of China's MFN status would serve neither the interests of promoting human rights progress in China nor the interests this nation has in maintaining mutually advantageous ties with China....we believe that our human rights objectives may now be best pursued with China without conditioning MFN eligibility."

On May 26, 1994, President Clinton announced that he had accepted the State Department's recommendations: "I have decided that the United States should renew Most Favored Nation trading status toward China. This decision, I believe, offers us the best opportunity to lay the basis for long-term sustainable progress in human rights, and for the advancement of our other interests with China. Extending MFN will avoid isolating China and instead will permit us to engage the Chinese with not only economic contacts but with cultural, educational and other contacts, and with a continuing aggressive effort in human rights -- an approach that I believe will make it more likely that China will play a responsible role, both at home and abroad."[54]

The president went on to say:

I am moving, therefore, to delink human rights from the annual extension of Most Favored Nation trading status for China. That linkage has been constructive during the past year. But I believe, based on our aggressive contacts with the Chinese in the past several months, that we have reached the end of the usefulness of that policy, and it is time to take a new path toward achievement of our constant objectives. We need to place our relationship into a larger and more productive framework....

Echoing the arguments of President Bush before him, Clinton said:

I believe the question, therefore, is not whether we continued to support human rights in China, but how we can best support human rights in China and advance our other very significant issues and interests. I believe we can do it by engaging the Chinese. I believe the course I have chosen gives us the best chance of success on all fronts. We will have more contacts. We will have more trade. We will have more international cooperation. We will have more intense and constant dialogue on human rights issues. We will have that in an atmosphere which gives us the chance to see China evolve as a responsible power, ever-growing not only economically, but growing in political maturity so that human rights can be observed....

I think we have to see our relations with China within the broader context of our policies in the Asian Pacific region....I am determined to see that we maintain an active role in this region, in both its dynamic economic growth, and in its security....The actions I have taken today to advance our security, to advance our prosperity, to advance our ideals I believe are the important and appropriate ones. I believe, in other words, this is in the strategic, economic and political interests of both the United States and China, and I am confident that over the long run this decision will prove to be the correct one.[55]

The president's national security advisor, Anthony Lake, called the new policy "a tactical shift" designed to serve "a very important strategic objective...and that is to build a relationship with China within which we can seriously pursue human rights as well as our other security and economic interests."[56]

The Chinese responded favorably to the new commercial pragmatism in U.S. policy. In contrast to the treatment shown Secretary of State Christopher during his trip to Beijing in March, PRC leaders went out of their way to welcome Secretary of Commerce Ronald H. Brown during his visit to China in late August-early September 1994. Brown was accompanied by twenty-four chief executives of American corporations seeking business in China. Emphasizing U.S. commercial interests in dealing with the PRC and downplaying human rights issues in all public statements, Brown and his entourage were awarded with nearly $5 billion in contracts.[57]

In assessing the importance of President Clinton's 1994 MFN decision, several conclusions stand out. First, the decision marked the end of the period in which Tiananmen dominated Washington's relations with Beijing. Second, the decision reinforced the post-Cold War trend of economics being one of the most important factors in normal (i.e., non-crisis) international relations. Third, the decision proved that supporters of the U.S. role as protector of human rights and democracy were weaker politically than those supporting American commercial interests. Fourth, the decision indicated that U.S. strategic interests in maintaining a cooperative relationship with China overshadowed American abhorrence at Beijing's treatment of its citizens. And fifth, the decision came as a reminder -- reflected in the PRC's cold reception of Secretary Christopher in March 1994 and renewed arrests of dissidents a few weeks before the MFN announcement -- that Beijing does not easily bow to U.S. pressure over matters considered China's internal affairs.

Conclusion

Many of President Clinton's foreign policy goals were opposed by the PRC during his first two years in office. The United States wanted to speed the evolution of authoritarian countries into market democracies; the PRC viewed this as hegemonism and big power politics. The United States sought to limit the expansion of nuclear and conventional forces; the PRC saw at least some of these efforts as designed to maintain a favorable balance of power Washington. The United States encouraged the U.N. to play a wider role in peacekeeping operations; the PRC considered this to be manipulation of the United Nations for U.S. purposes. The United States urged all nations to respect what it perceived as universally valid principles of human rights; the PRC believed standards of human rights were domestic affairs and saw Washington's efforts as infringement on national sovereignty. The United States wanted an open and free trading system in the Asian Pacific and greater economic integration of regional market economies; the PRC wanted a more gradual approach to free trade respecting both its socialist economy and its special status as a developing country.

Both sides held negative assumptions about the other. The United States perceived communist power in China as eroding due to market forces and the demands of the Chinese people for greater personal freedom. U.S. leaders believed they had historical and moral responsibilities to assist the Chinese in this evolution, albeit through peaceful means. That the PRC was gaining military power projection capabilities and reasserting ancient territorial claims were seen as signs of warning that Beijing intended to become a regional hegemon. This was something the United States would try to deflect because of traditional American interests in maintaining a favorable balance of power in East Asia.

The PRC, on the other hand, viewed the United States as a declining power in Asia, but one that continued to interfere in Chinese internal affairs. Since PRC leaders believed that the ultimate U.S. objective was to change China into a market democracy, most American demands were greeted with suspicion from the outset. For China, it was vital to become stronger to resist this new form of imperialism. The challenge for Beijing was to maintain good relations with the United States in order to help modernize China, yet at the same time to protect Chinese independence, sovereignty, and territorial integrity in the case of Taiwan, Hong Kong, and Tibet.

These fundamental differences in policy and perception suggested that relations between the United States and China would continue to be strained, especially if the PRC grew stronger and more resistant to U.S. pressure and if the United States intensified its efforts to create a new world order dominated by market democracies. At the same time, the United States and China recognized each other as powerful nations, separated by the Pacific, whose pragmatic interests dictated that they avoid serious confrontation and seek cooperation in areas of mutual benefit. These areas of cooperation included:

- maintaining peace on the Korean peninsula and containing the North Korean nuclear bomb threat
- counterbalancing the rise of Japan as the dominant power in the Western Pacific
- maintaining an increasingly interdependent trade relationship
- modernizing China's economy and ensuring its smooth integration into regional and global economic systems
- accommodating a strong, modern China in the post-Cold War international political system in a way that stabilized, not destabilized, the new international order.

In view of these fundamental areas of disagreement and cooperation, President Clinton had three basic options for his China policy:

1. The United States could pursue relations with the PRC from the point of view of *Realpolitik*, a relationship largely devoid of moral standards. In essence, that is what Beijing proposed in its Five Principles of Peaceful Coexistence. In China's view, relations between states should be based on common interests, not shared values.

2. The United States could pursue a highly moralistic foreign policy, attempting to change China into a market democracy through the many incentives and disincentives available to the president.

3. The United States could attempt to mix the two approaches, in some cases following amoral national interests and in other cases pursuing American values for the presumed good of the Chinese people.

Early in his administration it became clear that Clinton leaned in the direction of the third alternative, adopting a policy characterized by a high degree of public emphasis on human rights but pragmatism on substantive issues. Inevitably, such an approach led to confusion of objectives and conflicts between national interests which bred domestic and international opposition to U.S. China policy.

Clinton's efforts to "reengage" China in a constructive dialogue after September 1993 was a familiar presidential response to deteriorating Sino-American relations. It was felt that not engaging China would harm U.S. interests by denying Washington important channels of communication to discuss vital issues such as proliferation, regional security problems, and trade. Also, there was evidence that human rights conditions in the PRC and the prospects of China becoming a market democracy were not furthered by isolating or imposing sanctions on Beijing.

In May 1994 Clinton decided to renew China's MFN trade status in spite of U.S. dissatisfaction over the PRC human rights record. The decision reflected a triumph of American economic and security interests over its human rights and moral interests. Sounding very much like President Bush, Clinton argued that imposing trade sanctions on the PRC would only hurt the United States and progressive elements within China. The best U.S. strategy, Clinton reasoned, would be to integrate China into the global community rather than to isolate her. Clinton's decision effectively broke the linkage between human rights and trade, a linkage originally created by the Democratic leadership of the Congress to attack the China policy of President Bush.

Clinton's decision pleased the Chinese, but it did little to resolve practical problems in Sino-American relations. Nor did engaging China result in greatly improved PRC international or domestic behavior. Beijing stubbornly or with principle (depending upon one's perspective) pursued its own agenda and refused to adopt policies preferred by the United States.

As will be seen in the remainder of this book, the dilemmas faced by the United States in its overall China policy were reflected even more vividly in U.S. policy toward the Taiwan issue in Sino-American relations. Again and again, the fundamental question of that policy resurfaces: Is U.S. support of Taiwan worth the cost of damaging U.S. relations with Beijing? Or, phrased another way, how can the United States balance its interests in Taiwan against the possible cost of a longer-term alienation of China as a consequence of favorable policies toward Taiwan?

To begin to answer these questions requires an understanding of the systemic changes currently underway in the Republic of China on Taiwan, the subject of our next chapter.

Notes

1. Zi Zhongyun, "Will a `Pax Americana' Prevail?" *Beijing Review*, May 4-10, 1992, pp. 34-37. Zi was a senior research fellow with the Institute of American Studies, Chinese Academy of Social Sciences (CASS).

2. Wang Jisi, "United States: Formulating New Global Strategy," *Beijing Review*, March 9-15, 1992, pp. 33-35. Wang was a scholar with the Institute of American Studies at CASS.

3. Chinese scholars have written extensively contrasting the U.S. and PRC views of the new international order. See, for example, Han Xu, "New World Order: A Chinese Perspective," *Beijing Review*, September 9-15, 1991, pp. 31-34; Qian Qichen, "Establishing a Just and Equitable New International Order," *Beijing Review*, October 7-13, 1991, pp. 11-16; and Pan Tongwen, "New World Order -- According to Mr. Bush," *Beijing Review*, October 28-November 3, 1991, pp. 12-14.

4. Liu Huaqiu, "Proposals for Human Rights Protection and Promotion," *Beijing Review*, June 28-July 4, 1993, pp. 8-11.

5. Hu Yang, "Summary of Symposium with the U.S. National Defense University," *Beijing Review*, December 14-20, 1992, p. 31-32.

6. Reported in *Far Eastern Economic Review*, October 7, 1993, pp. 12-13.

7. See Jonathan Spence, *To Change China: Western Advisers in China, 1620-1960* (New York: Penguin Books, 1980).

8. Richard H. Solomon, "China and MFN: Engagement, Not Isolation, Is Catalyst for Change," Department of State Current Policy, No. 1282 (June 1990).

9. "Remarks by the President in Commencement Address to Yale University" (Kennebunkport, Maine: The White House, Office of the Press Secretary, May 27, 1991).

10. *Washington Post*, June 11, 1991, p. A14; June 13, 1991, p. A36.

11. Gary Milhollin and Gerald White, "A New China Syndrome: Beijing's Atomic Bazaar," *Washington Post*, May 12, 1991, p. C1.

12. *China Post*, December 24, 1992, p. 2; *China News*, December 25, 1992, p. 1.

13. "The Democratic Party Platform, 1992," p. 14.

14. *China News*, October 13, 1992, p. 7.

15. *China News*, November 24, 1992, p. 7.

16. *Far Eastern Economic Review*, November 12, 1992, pp. 10-11.

17. *China News*, November 24, 1992, p. 7.

18. *China News*, December 16, 1992, p. 1.

19. *China Post*, December 24, 1992, p. 1.

20. Winston Lord, "A New Pacific Community: Ten Goals for American Policy," opening statement at confirmation hearings for Assistant Secretary of State, Bureau of East Asian and Pacific Affairs, Senate Foreign Relations Committee, March 31, 1993, ms.

21. *Washington Post*, March 11, 1993, p. A25.

22. *Far Eastern Economic Review*, April 22, 1993, p. 13.

23. *Washington Post*, April 23, 1993, p. A19.

24. "Statement by the President on Most Favored Nation Status for China" (Washington, D.C.: The White House, Office of the Press Secretary, May 28, 1993).

25. "Report to Congress Concerning Extension of Waiver Authority for the People's Republic of China" (Washington, D.C.: The White House, Office of the Press Secretary, May 28, 1993).

26. Just prior to Clinton's granting of MFN status to Beijing in May 1993, U.S. intelligence officials said that new evidence had surfaced of China's violation of the Missile Technology Control Regime. The violation occurred with the shipment of M-11 ballistic missile components to Pakistan. Mobile launch vehicles for the M-11 were sighted inside of Pakistan in early 1991. China continued to deny violating its pledge to abstain from shipping such missiles. See *Washington Post*, May 18, 1993, p. A9. On a related issue, the U.S. intelligence community released an unclassified report in January 1993 stating, "it is highly probable that China has not eliminated its BW [biological warfare] program" as it agreed to do in 1984. *Washington Post*, February 24, 1993, p. A4.

27. "Assistant Secretary of State Winston Lord, Opening Statement, House Ways and Means Committee, International Trade Subcommittee, June 8, 1993," ms.

28. Active during the 1978-1979 Democracy Wall movement, Wei Jingsheng was sent to jail in 1979 for his anti-government writings and for allegedly passing on state secrets to a foreign journalist. Wei proposed that Deng Xiaoping adopt democracy as the "fifth modernization" to go along with the Four Modernizations in Chinese agriculture, industry, science and technology, and defense. In addition to Wei, China released in late January 1993 two prominent political prisoners, Wang Xizhe, arrested for taking part in the Democracy Wall

Movement, and Gao Shan, an economist jailed in connection with the 1989 Tiananmen Square protests. A few weeks later, China released Wang Dan, a prominent student leader imprisoned after the Tiananmen incident. In mid-1993 China released Xu Wenli, a political activist imprisoned for twelve years in solitary confinement for advocating political reform within the communist system. Other leading dissidents released by China during this period included Han Dongfang, Wang Youcai, Luo Haixing, Xiong Yan, Yang Wei, Wang Zhixin, Zhang Weiguo, Bao Zunxin, and a number of Catholic clergy and lesser known political activists.

29. *Far Eastern Economic Review*, October 7, 1993, pp. 12-13.

30. *Beijing Review*, September 6-12, 1993, pp. 6-7.

31. "Foreign Ministry on `Yinhe' Incident," *Beijing Review*, September 13-19, 1993, p. 4.

32. Tiao Yue, "US Breaches International Law on the `Yinhe' Incident," *Beijing Review*, September, 20-26, 1993, pp. 12-13.

33. *Washington Post*, September 30, 1993, p. A15.

34. China became a nuclear power in 1964. As of October 1993, it had conducted 38 tests, the previous one in September 1992. By way of comparison, the United States had conducted 942 tests, while the combined tests of Russia, France, and Great Britain totalled 969. *Wall Street Journal*, October 6, 1993, p. A12; *Washington Post*, October 6, 1993, p. A1.

35. The term "market-Leninism" was coined to describe China's approach to modernization, in which tight political control remained in the hands of the Communist Party even while individual Chinese were given greater freedom to make personal profit. To a degree, this approach mirrored the experiences of Taiwan, Singapore, and South Korea, where authoritarian governments maintained social stability while allowing the growth of a market economy. See *New York Times*, September 6, 1993, p. 1 and September 7, 1993, p. A1; also The World Bank, *The East Asian Miracle: Economic Growth and Public Policy* (New York: Oxford University Press, 1993).

36. *Washington Post*, November 1, 1993, p. A1 and November 3, 1993, p. A12; *New York Times*, November 3, 1993, p. A13.

37. "Remarks by the President After Meeting with President Jiang of China" (Seattle, Washington: The White House, Office of the Press Secretary, November 19, 1993).

38. "Press Briefing, Secretary of State Warren Christopher, International Media Center" (Seattle, Washington: U.S. Department of State, Office of the Spokesman, November 19, 1993).

39. *New York Times*, March 21, 1994, p. A1. According to Chinese figures (which excluded trade passing through Hong Kong), the PRC exported $17 billion to the United States in 1993 and imported $10.7 billion, leaving China with a $6.3 billion surplus. PRC exports to Hong Kong were $22.1 billion,

while imports were $10.5 billion. Chinese exports to Japan were $15.8 billion and imports were $23.25 billion. *Asian Wall Street Journal*, January 10, 1994.

40. In 1993 China was the largest textile exporter to the United States, accounting for more than 13 percent of total U.S. textile and clothing imports and as much as 25 percent of total textiles sold in the United States. Legal Chinese textile exports to the United States were about $4.7 billion. In addition, some $2.2 billion in Chinese silks were exported to the United States.

41. *Washington Post*, January 18, 1994, p. C1; *Wall Street Journal*, January 18, 1994, p. A3; *New York Times*, January 18, 1994, p. D1.

42. Mickey Kantor's testimony before the U.S. House of Representatives, Committee on Foreign Affairs, March 2, 1994, was televised by C-Span that day.

43. *Washington Post*, January 15, 1994, p. A22.

44. *New York Times*, January 16, 1994, p. 1; January 17, 1994, p. A2.

45. *Washington Post*, January 20, 1994, p. A17; *New York Times*, January 21, 1994, p. A1.

46. *Washington Post*, January 25, 1994, p. A16.

47. *New York Times*, February 2, 1994, p. A8. A few days later, Beijing released three political prisoners held in connection with the Tiananmen demonstrations. Other, more high level political prisoners were still in prison, including Wang Juntao and Bao Tong, a chief aide to former Communist Party chief Zhao Ziyang. In early March the PRC arrested several more political dissidents, including Wei Jingsheng. Wei was soon released after it was rumored that Secretary of State Christopher might cancel his first trip to Beijing, scheduled for later that month, as a result of the arrests. During the same crackdown on dissidents, Chinese police briefly detained Tiananmen student leader Wang Dan and warned him not to spread rumors having a "bad impact on the country." In Australia Christopher said, "It is hard to overstate the strong distaste we all feel for the recent detentions and hostile measures taken by the Chinese. Certainly these actions will have a negative effect on my trip." See *Washington Post*, March 9, 1994, p. A13; March 10, 1994, p. A34.

48. Warren Christopher, "My Trip to Beijing Was Necessary," *Washington Post*, March 22, 1994, p. A17.

49. *New York Times*, March 23, 1994, p. A12.

50. A sense of the cacophony of voices from the administration on China policy can be found in newspaper reports. See, for example, *Washington Post*, March 20, 1994, p. A20 and H1; *Wall Street Journal*, March 22, 1994, p. A1.

51. Quoted in the *New York Times*, March 21, 1994, p. A1.

52. See *New York Times*, March 24, 1994, p. A5; March 25, 1994, p. A12.

53. For the official abridged version, see "China's MFN Status: Summary of the Report and Recommendations of Secretary of State Warren Christopher" (Washington, D.C.: The White House, Office of the Press Secretary, May 26, 1994).

54. "Press Conference of the President" (Washington, D.C.: The White House, Office of the Press Secretary, May 26, 1994). For background on the 1994 MFN decision, see articles in the *New York Times*, May 27, 1994, pp. A1, D1.

55. Clinton's revised human rights policy toward the PRC included the following major elements: (1) renewing China's MFN status; (2) delinking MFN renewal from human rights issues, other than the statutory requirements of the Jackson-Vanik amendment regarding freedom of emigration; (3) banning the import of Chinese munitions (mostly small arms and ammunition), valued at $200 million in 1994; (4) maintaining the existing Tiananmen sanctions, including the denial of participation in the U.S. Trade and Development Assistance Program, Overseas Private Investment Corporation, and the U.S.-Asia Environment Partnership Program; continued U.S. opposition to non-basic human needs loans to China by the World Bank and other multilateral development banks; suspension of weapons deliveries; and denial of licenses for dual-use civilian technology and U.S. munitions list items; and (5) implementing a new human rights strategy for China. The components of that new human rights strategy were: (1) intensifying high-level dialogue with the Chinese on human rights; (2) increasing the number of exchanges between Chinese and American legal specialists, jurists, prison administrators, and human rights organizations; (3) working with the American business community to develop a voluntary set of principles to advance human rights in China; (4) increasing radio and television broadcasts to the Chinese people from the Voice of America; (5) inaugurating Radio Free Asia; (6) increasing multilateral pressure on China to improve its human rights practices through the United Nations and other international forums; (7) working more closely with Chinese and American nongovernmental organizations to improve human rights conditions; and (8) working through international organizations to address Tibet's human rights problems and promoting discussions between the Dalai Lama and the Chinese government. See "Fact Sheet: China MFN Decision" and "Fact Sheet: New Initiatives in U.S. Human Rights Policy for China" (Washington, D.C.: The White House, Office of the Press Secretary, May 26, 1994).

56. "Press Briefing by National Security Advisor Tony Lake, Assistant Secretary of State for Human Rights John Shattuck, Assistant Secretary of State for Asian and Pacific Affairs Winston Lord, and Assistant to the President for Economic Policy Bob Rubin" (Washington, D.C.: The White House, Office of the Press Secretary, May 26, 1994).

57. For reports of Brown's trip to China, see *Washington Post*, September 1, 1994, p. B10; *New York Times*, September 2, 1994, p. D1; *Wall Street Journal*, September 9, 1994, p. A1.

4

The New Taiwan

The United States has very important interests in the People's Republic of China, but since the Korean War these interests have never been so compelling as to cause the United States to abandon its interests in the Republic of China on Taiwan. There are many reasons for this, not the least of which is the moral dimension of supporting old allies, democratic friends, and fellow anticommunists. But this book is less concerned with the morality involved -- as important as that is in defining what makes a nation unique in international politics -- than it is with the pragmatic interests the United States has in Taiwan. As this chapter will demonstrate, U.S. interests in Taiwan are growing more substantial in the post-Cold War period.

One of the most dramatic transformations in international politics over the past decade has been the emergence of a "new" Taiwan since 1986 that is quite distinct from the "old" Republic of China that existed previously. Policy reforms initiated by former ROC President Chiang Ching-kuo and carried forward since 1988 by his successor, President Lee Teng-hui, have brought far-reaching changes to Taiwan's political, economic, and social institutions. Most of these changes have been welcomed by the United States, although some reforms have greatly complicated Sino-American relations.[1]

The democratization of Taiwan politics, greater international economic importance, a more flexible foreign policy, and rapidly expanding contacts across the Taiwan Strait are important factors influencing Taiwan's security in the 1990s -- and continued U.S. support of that security. This chapter examines the systemic change underway in the Republic of China, while the next chapter summarizes U.S. policies toward the "new" Taiwan during the first two years of the Clinton administration.

Political Reform

President Chiang Ching-kuo lifted martial law on Taiwan in July 1987.[2] Since then, the ROC's political system has evolved from an authoritarian one-party system dominated by the Kuomintang (KMT) to a multiparty democracy with a strong and healthy opposition. As of early 1995, only three parties (the ruling Kuomintang, the main opposition Democratic Progressive Party, and the Chinese New Party formed in August 1993 by disgruntled KMT legislators) exercised significant political influence.

When compared to the ROC's rapid economic modernization, political reform on Taiwan evolved slowly until the late 1980s. Brutal and corrupt policies adopted by ROC forces who occupied Taiwan after World War II created a deep sense of alienation between the native-born Taiwanese and the newly arrived mainlanders.[3] The most damaging event in that early period was the February 1947 killing of as many as 18,000 Taiwanese by Nationalist troops after riots broke out in several locations in protest of harsh ROC occupation policies. The "February 28 incident" created political tension between many Taiwanese and mainlanders which continues to this day.

After transferring the seat of the ROC government to Taiwan in 1949, President Chiang Kai-shek and other senior KMT leaders decided that Taiwan should serve as a "bastion" for the eventual recovery of the mainland. This strategy required that major accommodation be reached between the mainlander elite and the Taiwanese. Implicit understandings were reached, whereby mainlanders would dominate national ROC politics and occupy the higher ranks of the military and security forces; Taiwanese were welcomed into the KMT and allowed to run in local elections; Taiwanese could develop their economic status largely without hindrance from the mainlanders; and martial law would be enforced in matters of national security, but the day-to-day lifestyle of the people of Taiwan would not be interfered with.[4] The arrangement was enforced by a pervasive KMT presence in virtually all of the island's political, economic, educational, and social institutions. The KMT used its institutional network and powerful security forces to create an effective control system that tolerated little opposition to ruling party policies.

Having made the strategic decision to make Taiwan a "model province" of the *San Min Chu-i*, or Three Principles of the People (Nationalism, Democracy, and People's Livelihood), the ROC government concentrated on improving the quality of life on Taiwan.[5] The long-term goal was to establish a market democracy on the island to serve as a model for the mainland's economic and political development. In this way, the Nationalists could prove their superiority over the Chinese communists and eventually return to a position of leadership.

The death of Chiang Kai-shek in 1975 led to his son, Chiang Ching-kuo, becoming head of the KMT and president of the ROC. Under the younger Chiang significant policy changes were introduced. Two of the most important reforms were the gradual liberalization of the political system, which paved the way for the lifting of martial law in 1987 and the establishment of a parliamentary democracy, and the Taiwanization of ROC institutions. The process of Taiwanization, whereby Taiwanese were brought into the elite ranks of the ruling party and central government, resulted in the KMT gradually becoming a Taiwanese as well as a mainlander party. Similarly, the ROC government became much more representative of both Taiwanese and mainlander interests.

Elections on Taiwan

ROC political liberalization can be traced through the evolution of elections on Taiwan.[6] Grassroots elections were held as early as 1951, with Taiwanese members of the KMT winning virtually every seat. National elections were more problematic, however, since the nationally elected bodies -- the National Assembly, Legislative Yuan, and Control Yuan -- were intended to represent all of China, not merely Taiwan which was considered only a province of the Republic of China.[7] To provide legitimacy to the ROC claim of being the legal government of China, those elected on the mainland in 1947-1948 were allowed to hold office on Taiwan without having to run for reelection. Many of these senior parliamentarians remained in office until forced to retire at the end of 1991 by order of the Council of Grand Justices of the Judicial Yuan.[8]

Over time, the advanced age of many of the mainland-elected officials prevented them from fulfilling even minimal legislative duties. This institutional weakness, coupled with martial law, tended to concentrate political power in the hands of a few senior KMT officials, especially those who were members of the party's central standing committee.

Mindful that the *San Min Chu-i* intended China to become a democratic country and that Taiwan was increasingly important to the ROC cause, the Nationalist government in 1969 began to hold regularly scheduled "supplementary" elections to add new members to the legislative bodies. About 80 percent of the newly elected legislators were Taiwanese members of the KMT. Most of the others were independents. The formation of new political parties remained forbidden under martial law.

Beginning in 1977, political opposition to the KMT became more organized in the form of candidates who ran as *tangwai* (literally, non-party). The *tangwai*, who typically won 20-30 percent of the vote, were characterized by their Taiwanese ethnicity and their more or less open advocacy of Taiwan becoming a nation separate from mainland China. At the time, support for Taiwan independence was considered treason since it ran counter to the ROC principle of "one China," a united China including both the mainland and Taiwan. As the *tangwai* became more vocal in their opposition to KMT domination of the political system, clashes with ROC authorities were inevitable. The most serious of these occurred in December 1979 in the southern port city of Kaohsiung, when a riot resulting in police injuries led to the arrest and the imprisonment of several key opposition leaders, including Shih Ming-teh, an outspoken proponent of Taiwan independence.

In the 1980 national elections the *tangwai*, still banned from forming a new political party, organized an "association" with a common platform. The platform included demands for more locally elected seats in the National Assembly, Legislative Yuan, and Control Yuan; popular elections for the governor of Taiwan and the mayors of Taipei and Kaohsiung; more Taiwanese to be appointed to government positions; permission for new political parties to be formed; more freedom of the press, speech, and assembly; abolishment of martial law provisions; and the release of political prisoners. In the 1980 elections the KMT won about 80 percent of the seats, but individual *tangwai* won the highest number of votes for single candidates.

In the 1983 and 1986 elections, the KMT permitted political competition from the *tangwai* to become more open. In 1983, however, the *tangwai* were badly split due to policy differences over whether Taiwan independence should be demanded immediately or approached gradually. The KMT won about 85 percent of the seats. By 1986 the *tangwai* were organized sufficiently to mount a more serious challenge to the KMT. In September of that year, *tangwai* leaders founded the Democratic Progressive Party (DPP). Although the action was illegal under martial law, President Chiang Ching-kuo decided not to intervene. The next month President Chiang announced to American newspaper publishers that the ROC would shortly lift martial law and allow new political parties to be formed.[9]

The DPP's political platform in 1986 included demands that the government allow Taiwan's residents to determine the island's future, conduct relations with the PRC on the basis of equal status between the two governments, actively seek to rejoin the United Nations, reduce Taiwan's armed forces, and close all nuclear power plants. The KMT won about 70 percent of the vote in the elections and the DPP received just over 20 percent.

Passing the Torch to Lee Teng-hui

In January 1988 President Chiang Ching-kuo died. In passing, he expressed the wish that no member of his family should assume his offices, thereby ending the Chiang family dynasty which dominated ROC politics for six decades. Vice President Lee Teng-hui, a native Taiwanese with a Ph.D. in agricultural economics from Cornell University, became the new president. Lee was also elected chairman of the Kuomintang, over the objections of some mainlander KMT, during the party's thirteenth congress in July.

Although President Lee Teng-hui pledged to continue the policies of his predecessor, an important milestone in Taiwan politics had been passed. Henceforth, both the ROC government and the KMT began to reflect the interests of Taiwanese more than those of mainlanders. Within the KMT a majority "mainstream" faction, comprised mostly of Taiwanese with some liberal mainlanders, supported Lee. Most mainlanders were grouped in the minority "non-mainstream" faction of the KMT.[10] With the passing of Chiang Ching-kuo, the unity of the ruling party (and hence its control) began to unravel.

The 1989 elections saw the introduction of more equal competition between the KMT and the DPP, by then a legal political party. In the campaign the KMT stressed the importance of continuing the successful "Taiwan Experience" as a way to improve Taiwan's lifestyle and to achieve the eventual reunification of China under terms favorable to

Taiwan. The DPP, on the other hand, stressed the right of Taiwanese self-determination, the need to expand Taiwan's international presence, and the need to overhaul the island's political system.

In what was viewed as a setback for the Nationalists, the KMT won 60 percent of the vote while the DPP won over 30 percent. Most importantly, the DPP won six of the sixteen county magistrate seats up for election, including Taipei County, home of President Lee Teng-hui. As a result of the election, the DPP controlled the local government of half of the territory of Taiwan and about 35 percent of its population.

In June 1990 the ROC Council of Grand Justices ruled that the senior parliamentarians frozen in office to represent mainland constituencies would have to retire by December 31, 1991. This affected 76 percent of the members of Taiwan's legislative bodies, including 612 members of the National Assembly, 138 members of the Legislative Yuan, and eighteen members of the Control Yuan. The decision necessitated that new legislative bodies be elected. Subsequently, the government decided that members of a new (or Second) National Assembly would be elected in December 1991, while a Second Legislative Yuan would be elected in December 1992. In both elections, members were to be elected solely from Taiwan with some seats reserved for Overseas Chinese.

In the December 1991 National Assembly elections the DPP strongly pushed for Taiwan independence. The KMT, on the other hand, stressed caution in dealing with the mainland and the need to avoid radical changes in ROC policy. In results which surprised the DPP, the KMT won about 70 percent of the vote and the DPP won less than 25 percent. The open advocacy of Taiwan independence and factional differences within the opposition party contributed to the poor DPP showing.

In the December 1992 Legislative Yuan elections the KMT was plagued by factionalism but not the DPP. The Nationalists were deeply divided over ROC policy toward mainland China. A strong minority of mainlander KMT members believed that the mainstream KMT faction, led by President Lee Teng-hui and to which most Taiwanese belonged, was pursuing policies designed to delay the unification of China or even to abort the process entirely. A large number of Taiwanese KMT, on the other hand, felt the conservative mainlander KMT should turn over the reins of power to the Taiwanese people, whose interests would not be served by early unification. There was also disagreement over the party's candidate selection process, with non-mainstream members saying the selections were heavily biased in favor of Lee Teng-hui's faction.

These and other disagreements coalesced around a power struggle between President Lee Teng-hui and Premier Hau Pei-tsun, a mainlander who was former defense minister and chief of the general staff. A further complication was the fact that the 1947 Constitution did not define whether the ROC had a presidential system, in which case the president would have the most power, or a cabinet system, under which the premier would have the most power.[11] The clearly drawn factions supporting the two men severely weakened KMT party unity in 1992.

Reflecting the deep divisions within the ruling party, several popular KMT members (mostly non-mainstream mainlanders) who had not been selected as candidates for the 1992 elections decided to run over party objections. Since Taiwan's electoral system is single-vote, multimember district, the popularity of these rogue candidates drew heavily away from officially sponsored KMT candidates (mostly pro-Lee mainstream) and may have adversely affected the election outcome for the ruling party as a whole.[12]

In the 1992 elections the DPP campaigned vigorously against KMT "money politics" and stressed the need for change after nearly five decades of KMT rule. Learning its lesson from the 1991 National Assembly elections, the DPP did not emphasize Taiwan independence. For its part, the KMT argued for China's eventual unification under democratic rule and for continuity with successful policies of the past. Throughout the campaign, divisions within the KMT damaged the party's image and limited the ability of party officials to channel votes to designated candidates.

The election results were seen as a defeat for the KMT, with the ruling party receiving an all-time low of 53 percent of the vote, while the DPP won 31 percent. In terms of seats, the new 161-member Legislative Yuan had 103 KMT members (both officially sponsored candidates and those running without the party's approval), fifty DPP members, seven independents, and one member of a minor party. The KMT retained a nearly two-third's majority in the legislature, but the DPP doubled its size from the previous legislature and was in a much stronger position to challenge KMT policies. Moreover, within the legislature the DPP was more united than the KMT on many issues.

The 1992 elections shifted considerable political power from the executive to the legislative branch of government. Taiwan now had a fairly effective check-and-balance system in place, a division of power among branches of the national government, and a functional two-party system. The KMT no longer dominated the political process. Taiwan's political system could accurately be described as democratic and non-authoritarian.

A New Era of Taiwan Politics

Politics on Taiwan after the December 1992 elections became even more lively and confrontational. President Lee Teng-hui replaced Hau Pei-tsun as premier with Lee's ally and former Taiwan Governor Lien Chan in February 1993. Other government and party appointments further strengthened the mainstream KMT faction of the president. Armed with a popular mandate, the newly elected members of the Legislative Yuan often exercised their power in direct challenge to Executive Yuan and KMT-sponsored policies. Even sacrosanct projects such as the purchase of F-16 and Mirage fighters were threatened by the legislature's reluctance to provide funding, a fate which also greeted Taiwan's high-speed railroad project designed to ease the island's notorious transportation gridlock.

With the introduction of democracy in Taiwan politics, centralized KMT leadership in the government became impossible to maintain. Dissension was common even inside the ruling party. Factional competition for power moved to the level of fundamental policy differences, often exasperated by Taiwanese-mainlander rivalries and contrasting views of the future of Taiwan and China. In August 1993 several popular KMT politicians (mostly mainlanders) decided to abandon the KMT altogether and form a rival political organization, the Chinese New Party (later called simply the "New Party").

The new political party, most of whose members were originally part of the New KMT Alliance (a non-mainstream KMT faction within the Legislative Yuan), pledged to become a balance between the KMT and the DPP. The Chinese New Party (NP) criticized the KMT for being too involved in "money politics" and criticized the DPP for irresponsibly calling for Taiwan independence. In its charter the NP said it would cooperate with the KMT and DPP to keep Taiwan from being betrayed in contacts with the PRC; support the ROC's entry into the world community, direct transportation between Taiwan and mainland China, and promotion of a "Greater China" economic community; and work to establish a direct presidential election supervised by the legislature.[13]

The KMT held its Fourteenth National Party Congress in August 1993. President Lee secured a majority of his supporters in both the 210-

member central committee and the policy-making central standing committee. However, many of his non-mainstream opponents were elected to these committees as well, forcing the president to make several key appointments to powerful mainland rivals.

The party's 1993 congress made several historic changes to the KMT party charter. These included dropping the long-standing KMT goal of "recovering the Chinese mainland" and redefining the party from Sun Yat-sen's "revolutionary party" to a "democratic political party with a revolutionary spirit."[14] Charter amendments pledged the KMT would seek international recognition for the ROC on Taiwan as a sovereign state and that it would follow the government's national unification guidelines in relations with the mainland, details of which will be discussed below.[15]

Thus, in 1992-1993 the KMT faced a crisis of identity. The historic mission of the Nationalists was to unify China under a democratic government. But as the KMT itself became democratic, it faced the dilemma of deciding who were "the people" the party represented: the people of Taiwan, many of whom did not want to unify with mainland China; or the people of China (with Taiwan being considered only a small province), most of whom presumably did not want Taiwan to become an independent country. This uncertainty was expressed by senior KMT official John Kuan, who asked rhetorically: "Are we trying to reunite the country and lead towards a peaceful, democratic China? Or are we simply consolidating on this island and becoming a new republic and an independent Taiwan?" Expressing the view of many KMT mainlanders on Taiwan, Kuan said President Lee had blurred that distinction by seeking ideological accommodation with the pro-independence DPP.[16]

Important local elections were held on Taiwan in late 1993 and early 1994. The November 1993 elections for mayors and county magistrates were crucial because of the political power of the twenty-three offices and the fact that the elections were the first in which three major political parties -- the KMT, DPP, and NP -- competed for votes. At the time of the election, the KMT held thirteen of the twenty-three seats, while the DPP held seven.

Despite predictions that the KMT would do poorly, the ruling party won fifteen of the contested offices while the DPP won six. Independents won the other two seats; the Chinese New Party won no seats. The actual vote was much closer, however. For the first time the KMT won less than 50 percent of the vote, receiving 47.5 percent, while the DPP won a record 41 percent. Although the Chinese New Party won only 3 percent of the vote island-wide, it won nearly 17 percent of the vote in the six constituencies where it supported a candidate.[17]

Because the opposition party won far less than the eleven seats he had predicted, DPP chairman Hsu Hsin-liang of the moderate Formosa faction resigned to take responsibility for the disappointing performance. Shih Ming-teh, one of Taiwan's strongest advocates for independence, took over the DPP's leadership. Shih had spent twenty-five years in prison for his political views and represented the DPP's radical New Tide faction.

Under Shih Ming-teh, the DPP was more successful in the local elections of January 1994. The KMT won 214 of the 309 contested seats for mayor or town chiefs, a loss of forty-nine seats from the 1990 elections. The DPP won twenty-one seats, up from six seats in the earlier elections. The remaining seats went to independents. The local elections were marred by several incidents of violence and widespread accusations of vote-buying. By May 1994 more than 380 people had been charged with election fraud, including seventeen speakers and fourteen deputy speakers of city and county councils.[18]

In May 1994 the DPP held an election for a new chairman. Shih Ming-teh was elected over more moderate candidates. Upon being elected, Shih said: "I will continue to follow party policies, including the goal to make Taiwan an independent country. The party, however, will not seek to reach this goal with violence or any illegal means." He warned, however, of two circumstances under which the DPP would resort to violence: if the KMT "sells out" Taiwan to the PRC, or if the DPP wins an election but is not allowed to take office. If either of these two things occurred, Shih said, "the DPP would have to use force to defend democracy."[19]

Another sign of the democratization of Taiwan was the decision to hold direct elections for the governor of Taiwan Province and the mayors of Taipei and Kaohsiung at the end of 1994. Previously, these offices had been appointed by the central government. The KMT Central Committee decided in April 1994 to hold direct presidential elections in 1996. At the same meeting it concluded that the premier's constitutional right to countersign the appointment and dismissal of personnel by the president would be removed. Both KMT decisions required amendments to the Constitution by the National Assembly, a process completed in July 1994. The amendments dramatically increased the president's powers and moved the ROC decisively toward a strong presidential system. Non-mainstream KMT opposed increasing the president's power, preferring the existing system which enabled the premier to serve as a check on the president. The immediate effect of these constitutional changes was to further strengthen Lee Teng-hui and his mainstream KMT faction.

In December 1994 important elections were held in which the issue of Taiwan's identity played a key role.[20] The results of the elections were inconclusive on that issue, however. In the race for Taiwan's governor the incumbent KMT candidate James Soong, a mainlander and strong supporter of Lee Teng-hui, received 56.2 percent of the vote, while the DPP candidate Chen Ding-nan received 38.7 percent. The Chinese New Party (NP) candidate won 4.3 percent of the vote, and two independent candidates received 0.75 percent. In this election the DPP candidate emphasized Taiwan independence under the slogan of "Taiwanese for Taiwanese." James Soong stressed the need for stability and pointed to his record of service to the people. He also received effective campaign support from President Lee.

In the election for Taipei's mayor the DPP candidate Chen Shui-bian won 43.7 percent of the vote, New Party candidate Jaw Shau-kong won 30.2 percent, and the KMT incumbent Huang Ta-chou won 25.9 percent. Unlike other DPP candidates, Chen Shui-bian played down the independence issue and campaigned under a slogan of "Happiness and Hope." Chen publicly supported the government's policy of defending the offshore islands of Kinmen and Matsu, whose abandonment had been proposed by DPP chairman Shih Ming-teh. For his part, Jaw Shau-kong attacked the pro-independence elements of the DPP, saying, "All you anti-independence people out there, please vote for me."

In the Kaohsiung mayor's race the incumbent KMT candidate won 54.5 percent of the vote, the DPP 39.3 percent, the NP 3.45 percent, and independents 2.8 percent.

In the seventy-nine member Taiwan provincial assembly the KMT won forty-eight seats, the DPP won twenty-three seats, the NP won two seats, and independents won six seats. In the Taipei city council election the KMT won twenty of the fifty-two seats, the DPP won eighteen, the NP won eleven, and independents won three seats. In the Kaohsiung city council election the KMT won twenty-three of the forty-four seats, the DPP won eleven, the NP won two, and independents won eight.

In the December 1994 elections the KMT won the strategically important office of governor and the mayorship of Taiwan's second largest city; but it lost the mayorship of Taipei, six provincial assembly seats, sixteen Taipei city council seats, and six Kaohsiung city council seats. The DPP captured the mayorship of Taiwan's largest city and a large percentage of Taipei city council seats (a DPP magistrate already was seated in Taipei County). The opposition party was greatly disappointed, however, over not winning the governorship of Taiwan. The outcome of that crucial election prompted members of the DPP's moderate Formosa faction to demand that the party's call for a plebiscite on Taiwan's independence be scrapped. In response, DPP chairman Shih Ming-teh and other leaders from the New Tide faction threatened to resign and even to leave the DPP if the party's charter was amended.

The election results also indicated fairly strong support for the pro-unification New Party, at least in the Taipei area where the NP exercised a "swing-vote" which could spell the difference between KMT victory or defeat. The elections further highlighted the importance of personalities in voters' preference, and a desire on the part of most Taiwan residents to avoid confrontation with the mainland by openly endorsing the goal of Taiwan independence.

Thus, by 1995 most political power in Taiwan had shifted to the liberal Taiwanese faction of the ruling party. In the minds of many, there was not a great distinction between this wing of the KMT and more moderate elements of the DPP. The decision-making power of the conservative mainlander faction of the KMT, the strongest traditional advocate for a reunited China, had been greatly reduced; although many of its ideals had been resurrected by the New Party and the emergence of dynamic second-generation mainlander politicians. For its part, the DPP had proven its ability to win key elections, but it was deeply divided between those advocating immediate and go-slow approaches on independence. The party's leadership was controlled by the strongly pro-independence New Tide faction.

With such a fundamental shift in political power taking place since 1988, many mainlanders on Taiwan feared that the Taiwanese-dominated KMT and moderate DPP might form a coalition to gradually move Taiwan in the direction of greater independence or, at minimum, a "two Chinas" policy. Concerns about the shift in Taiwan's power structure were shared by Beijing, which saw in the rise of Lee Teng-hui and the DPP signs that Taiwan might move more decisively in the direction of independence. These concerns were also held by some Americans who viewed with apprehension the potential negative impact of Taiwan's political developments on the "one China" policy of the United States and Sino-American relations in general. But, overall, the most common U.S.

reaction to political evolution on Taiwan was wholehearted approval of Taiwan's successful transition to a democracy from authoritarian rule.

Foreign Policy

As defined by the Nationalist government, the ultimate purpose of ROC diplomacy is to help create international conditions making possible the reunification of China under a democratic system. As the smaller portion of a divided country, the ROC faces great challenge in its foreign policy. This include not only the normal duty of the state to protect its national interests in the community of nations, but also the more frustrating task of gaining political recognition from other members of that community. From the mid-1980s through 1994 the ROC adopted a pragmatic (sometimes called flexible) style of diplomacy to achieve its international objectives. Pragmatic diplomacy was in sharp contrast to the inflexible anticommunism which distinguished much of ROC foreign policy until the 1980s.

White Paper on Foreign Policy

In January 1993 the ROC Ministry of Foreign Affairs released a "white paper" describing Taipei's foreign policy in the post-Cold War era.[21] The document divided ROC foreign policy into four stages. In the first stage of "consolidation" between 1946 and 1971, the Nationalist government was mostly concerned about land reform and agricultural development, as well as maintaining its seat on the U.N. Security Council. Steadfast anticommunism was a characteristic of this stage. The second stage of "evolution" occurred in the 1970s, as the United States entered into detente with the PRC and the ROC suffered serious diplomatic setbacks in the international community. The third stage of "adjustment" occurred during the 1980s, as ROC economic development increased and unofficial ties with other countries began to expand. The current fourth stage of "expansion" has occurred under President Lee Teng-hui in the 1990s, as Taiwan moved in several simultaneous directions to increase its international presence. These directions included developing official ties where possible, upgrading existing non-diplomatic relations, and actively participating in international organizations.

The white paper noted, "Obstruction from the Chinese Communists is perhaps the greatest challenge to the ROC in foreign relations....The Chinese Communist regime aims to destroy the ROC's relations with other countries, politically, economically and militarily. Peking uses every means at its disposal to prevent the ROC from joining any international organizations or participating in international activities." "Fortunately," the report continued, "the ROC is now in an advantageous position, as the focus of international relations has gradually moved away from an emphasis on political settlements to fostering economic cooperation. Taiwan's economic success has given the ROC government more diplomatic bargaining chips."

The new international situation provided Taiwan with an opportunity to present "a new look in foreign relations." However, fundamental ROC national policies remained "unaltered." These included the "principles of `one China' and `peaceful unification.'" According to the report, the ROC, "applying its new-found political and economic resources and pragmatic diplomacy, [is now] holding the line against Chinese Communist suppression, winning praise and gaining higher status in the international community."

The white paper pointed to three pillars in current ROC foreign policy:

1. "solidify and improve relations with countries that maintain diplomatic ties with the ROC"
2. "upgrade non-official relations with countries that do not recognize the ROC"
3. "actively participate in international organizations."

At the end of 1993, the ROC maintained diplomatic relations with twenty-nine countries.[22] The number of ROC representative offices in countries with no official ties increased from sixty-six in forty-three countries in 1989 to eighty-nine in fifty-eight countries in 1992. Of these, seventeen bore the name of "Republic of China" and fifty-three used "Taipei." In addition to embassies, forty-four "offices" were set up in thirty-eight countries. Taiwan's participation in international organizations also increased, with APEC being joined in 1991 and GATT observer status being granted in September 1992. At the end of 1992 Taiwan was a member of ten government-to-government international organizations such as the Asian Development Bank. It held membership in over 780 international non-governmental organizations. According to the white paper, "returning to the United Nations remains the ROC's foremost goal."

As part of its international outreach, Taiwan maintained a fairly large foreign assistance program centered on technical aid, humanitarian relief and loans, investment loans, and technological cooperation. Much of this was directed to developing nations in Latin America. Taiwan's efforts were rewarded in August 1993 when seven Central American countries wrote to U.N. Secretary General Boutros Boutros-Ghali asking that the issue of ROC representation be placed on the agenda for the September 1993 General Assembly meeting.[23] The issue never made the agenda, but the fact that several Third World countries were willing to sponsor the ROC's return to the United Nations generated considerable interest abroad -- and some anxiety in Beijing.

One of Taipei's most successful strategies to ensure that it remained recognized as an international political entity was the use of strong economic assets to attract other countries into complex sets of relationships. Most of these links were based on mutual economic benefit, but they had the important foreign policy result of integrating Taiwan into the global international system in ways generally denied it on the diplomatic level.

Relations with the United States remained central to ROC foreign policy. According to the white paper, during the 1993-1994 stage in ROC-U.S. relations, "the feasible goal is to enhance substantive relations between the two sides." In this, "there are several directions for developing ROC-U.S. relations: urging Washington to increase arms sales to Taiwan; strengthening economic ties between the two sides; and promoting mutual visits of high-level officials."

Concerning arms sales, the document stated: "The ROC has to maintain a steady supply of arms, military materials, military technologies and spare parts necessary to preserve its security. This is one of the major concerns of the ROC's diplomatic efforts in America." The report noted that the 1979 Taiwan Relations Act,

> together with concerns over a shifting balance of military power across the Taiwan Straits, led former President George Bush to announce on Sept. 2, 1992, that the United States would sell 150 F-16 A/B fighter planes to the ROC. These planes will cost Taiwan about US$6 billion when they are all built and delivered.
>
> Later in the same month, Washington went on to approve the sale of 12 SH-2F Light Airborne Multipurpose System helicopters and spare engines to Taiwan despite strong protests from the Chinese Communists.

The ROC's resolve to purchase U.S. arms has been encouraged by President Bill Clinton, who expressed his support for the F-16 sale while he was still running for president.

The report noted the "very close" trade relations between the ROC and the United States, including efforts by Taiwan to reduce its large trade surplus with the United States. The white paper said, "to expand pragmatic diplomacy, the ROC is seeking more channels for contacts between higher-level officials of the two countries," noting the visit of U.S. Trade Representative Carla Hills in November 1992.

Success and Disappointment

In late December 1992 Minister of Foreign Affairs Fredrick Chien reported on the successes and failures of ROC diplomacy during that year. He cited as examples of success: progress was made in the application to enter GATT; diplomatic relations were established with Niger; major arms purchases were negotiated, including modern fighters from the United States and France; and there were visits by many high-level government officials from countries with which the ROC did not maintain diplomatic relations, including visits by ninety-six minister-level officials. Chien said the "biggest setback and disappointment of the year" was the severing of formal ties with South Korea in August 1992. As to the future, Chien said, "the biggest challenge for us...would be re-entry to the United Nations."[24]

ROC diplomatic achievements in 1993 included the establishment of trade offices in Tatarstan, Israel, Columbia, Morocco, Russia, and the Czech Republic; the establishment of direct air links with Germany and France; the signing of investment agreements with Malaysia and Vietnam; the visits of several former heads of state to Taiwan, including President George Bush, Philippine President Corazon Aquino, and Outer Mongolian Prime Minister Byambasuren Dashyn; and the visit of African National Congress leader Nelson Mandela. In another sign of Taiwan's gradually improving international status, France began to issue tourist visas to ROC citizens in Taipei for the first time in forty years.

In November 1993 the ROC was able to participate in the Asia-Pacific Economic Cooperation (APEC) forum in Seattle on an equal basis with other participants, despite PRC efforts to minimize Taipei's role. Taiwan was represented by Economics Minister Chiang Pin-kung in the

APEC meetings and by Vincent Siew, Chairman of the Council for Economic Planning and Development and personal representative of President Lee Teng-hui, at the APEC leaders' conference with President Clinton.

Perhaps the most bold initiative taken by the ROC in the international sphere in 1993 was the priority placed on gaining readmittance into the United Nations. A ROC-financed advertisement in the *Washington Post* and other major U.S. newspapers in September 1993 argued: "This is the time to convince the PRC that the ROC should not be barred from the United Nations. This is the time for the United Nations to honor its principle of universal membership. This is the time for the United Nations to respect and protect the basic human rights and dignity of the 21 million people of the Republic of China on Taiwan. This is also the time for nations around the world to separate fiction from fact, rhetoric from reality."[25] As of early 1995, there was little positive response from the international community for the ROC's readmission into the United Nations. The hurdle of overcoming the threatened veto of the PRC on the Security Council was simply too high.

ROC foreign policy in 1994 also saw incremental advance. Most notable: successful trips to Southeast Asia by President Lee Teng-hui and Premier Lien Chan to initiate a "southern strategy" designed to strengthen economic ties with the region; trips by the two statesmen to Latin America (marred by a U.S. refusal to allow Lee to stay overnight on American soil); several visits to Taipei by heads-of-state of countries maintaining diplomatic relations with the ROC; many visits by cabinet-level officials to discuss commercial and other non-diplomatic ties; and some improvement in relations with Japan. The upgrading of U.S. unofficial relations with Taiwan in September 1994 will be discussed in Chapter Five.

Taiwan's constricted international presence in 1994 was brought home by treatment accorded President Lee Teng-hui. In addition to the snub administered by the Clinton administration in denying Lee permission to sleep in the United States on his way to Latin America, the ROC president was at first invited, and then disinvited, to participate in the Asian Games in Hiroshima, Japan, in October and in the APEC summit meeting in Bogor, Indonesia, in November. PRC pressure on the host countries grew so intense that Lee was compelled to tactfully agree not to attend. In the case of the Asian Games, Lee's invitation was actually withdrawn under humiliating circumstances.

Taipei's determination to participate in the international community, which has led to some foreign policy accomplishments, presents a new challenge to U.S. policy. Washington must decide to what extent the United States should support Taiwan's expanded role in international affairs. An ad hoc approach of deciding the U.S. response on a case-by-case basis will be difficult to maintain indefinitely, particularly in view of growing congressional demands for stronger U.S. support of Taiwan. How to define new guidelines that are both congruous with developments on Taiwan and yet not overly offensive to the PRC is a policy issue of great complexity for the Clinton administration.

Taiwan's Economy

ROC diplomacy has experienced difficulty from the inception of Nationalist rule on Taiwan, but Taiwan's economic growth has been phenomenal during the same period. Taiwan today has one of the world's strongest economies. Ranking twentieth in gross national product in 1993, Taiwan was the world's thirteen largest trading nation, its twelfth largest exporter and fifteenth largest importer, the world's ninth largest foreign investor, and the world's largest holder of foreign exchange reserves.

Known as one of Asia's four "little dragons" or "four tigers" (the others being South Korea, Hong Kong, and Singapore), Taiwan's twenty-one million inhabitants enjoyed a per capita GDP in 1993 of nearly $10,400.[26] Economic growth was 6.2 percent, lower than the official goal of 7 percent but still very strong when compared to the rest of the world.

In 1993 Taiwan's nominal GDP was $216.3 billion; nominal GNP was $220.2 billion. Unemployment was a low 1.5 percent; the consumer price index rose only 2.9 percent. Industrial production increased 3.4 percent over 1992. Taiwan's foreign debt was only $500 million, making the ROC one of the world's most creditworthy nations. Taiwan's total worldwide trade was $162.2 billion, with a trade surplus of $7.9 billion. Taiwan accounted for 2.6 percent of the world's $7.5 trillion in trade during 1993 (exports accounting for 2.3 percent and imports 2 percent of the world's total). Foreign exchange reserves at the end of 1993 stood at $83.6 billion, the world's largest. Long a favorite site in Asia for foreign investment, the cumulative foreign investment in Taiwan at the end of 1993 was $16.5 billion, of which nearly $4.5 billion came from American-owned corporations. Total foreign direct investment in 1993 was about $920 million. Domestic private investment totalled $26.2 billion in 1993, and Taiwan's investment overseas totalled $2.4 billion.

Taiwan's economic strength compensates to some extent for the ROC's diplomatic isolation. This is especially important in the post-Cold War period, when economic power has become a key determinant of national prestige in the international community. Taiwan's economic accomplishments have been achieved through a market economy and reasonably fair trading practices, a significant achievement from the point of view of U.S. interests in promoting market democracies.

Economic Development

At current prices Taiwan's per capita GNP in 1951 was $145. In 1993 it stood at $10,400 -- an amazing economic accomplishment when compared to most other countries. The ROC economy grew an average of 8.9 percent annually between 1952 and 1989, far above the average 3.5 percent growth rate among industrialized countries and considerably higher than the 5 percent growth among developing nations.

Taiwan went through several stages of economic development. During the 1945-1952 period, emphasis was placed on recovery from the devastation of World War II. Considerable emphasis was placed on land reform, whereby agricultural holdings were redistributed to tenant farmers with the large landowners being compensated by bonds and stocks in government-owned industries. From 1953 through 1960, Taiwan increased agricultural and industrial production. U.S. economic assistance, totalling nearly $2 billion through 1965, played an important role during this period, as did its advice and not-infrequent pressure for reform. A third stage of development occurred between 1961 and 1972, when industrial exports expanded dramatically. Between 1973 and 1991, Taiwan's economy became heavily dependent upon expanding exports. During times of international recession, the government introduced major infrastructural projects that pumped billions of dollars into an otherwise stagnant economy.

Since 1992 the ROC has been restructuring its economy to one built more on domestic demand than exports. In 1993 private consumption accounted for 56 percent of GDP and two-thirds of the economy's real growth. Other aspects of Taiwan's current economic restructuring include upgrading exports into high value added products and high-tech goods and services and, despite cultural preferences to the contrary, attempting to consolidate Taiwan's many small and medium-sized businesses into larger, more efficient exporters.

Such restructuring is necessary because of several problems in Taiwan's economy. These include a shortage of low-skilled labor, especially in the construction and other labor-intensive industries; rapidly rising wages which make many of Taiwan's labor-intensive products noncompetitive in international markets; the appreciation of the New Taiwan Dollar against the U.S. Dollar (a trend that may have been reversed beginning in 1993); growing public demands for environmental protection, often at the expense of needed public construction projects; a sluggish world economy, particularly in the key American and Japanese markets; and the hesitation of many local businessmen to invest in Taiwan, preferring instead to place their capital in the United States, Southeast Asia, or mainland China.

ROC economic priorities in 1993-1994 period included: (1) the restructuring of Taiwan's trade policies to maintain ROC competitiveness in the international market, including the renewal of guidelines with key trading partners in North America, Japan, and Europe; (2) the adjustment of Taiwan's trade and economic laws to bring them into alignment with GATT guidelines and to facilitate Taiwan becoming a regional commercial hub; (3) the finalization of government policies for the development of industry and specific sectors over the next ten years to restore the confidence of Taiwan's investors; (4) the institutionalization of Taiwan's trade relationship with mainland China through a series of regulations aimed at managing and integrating cross-straits trade.[27]

National Development Plan

A six-year infrastructure development plan was introduced in 1990 to achieve the ROC goals of becoming a regional financial center, a regional transportation hub, and a major technological leader in the Western Pacific. The national development plan was designed to bring Taiwan into the ranks of developed nations by the year 2000. Under the plan, Taiwan's economy was projected to grow at an average of 7 percent between 1991 and 1996, with per capita GNP rising from $8,000 in 1990 to $14,000 in 1996. The plan sought to raise the national income, provide sufficient resources for continuous industrial growth, balance regional development within Taiwan, improve the overall quality of life on the island, stimulate domestic demand, increase infrastructural investment, improve macroeconomic balance, strengthen production potential, and promote higher environmental quality. Nearly 800 projects were outlined in the plan, with expenditures from both the public and private sectors projected to reach just over $300 billion.

Firms from the United States and other nations scrambled to Taiwan to gain a piece of the action. International competition to win construction and other contracts on Taiwan contributed greatly to ROC diplomatic advances in the early 1990s. Eager for business, corporations lobbied their governments to upgrade ties with Taipei to improve their chances of winning lucrative contracts. The plan thus became an important tool for the ROC in its efforts to expand Taiwan's role in international affairs.

One weakness of the national development plan was its enormous cost, necessitating substantial increases in public sector spending and public borrowing. Taiwan's bonded debt increased from $5.9 billion in FY1990 (3.5 percent of GNP) to an estimated $42.6 billion in FY1994 (17.4 percent of GNP).[28] Because of the financial burden, parts of the plan became politically untenable. In 1993 the government froze public expenditures and trimmed the six-year plan. The number of projects was cut from the original 772 to 632, expenditures were cut by 26 percent to around $220 billion, and the completion of many projects were delayed for a number of years. Since public expenditures for the plan had become one of the most important engines for Taiwan's economic growth (export growth being minimal due to the sluggish world economy), reductions in the plan resulted in a lowering of estimates for Taiwan's economic growth from 7 percent to just over 6 percent through 1996. Despite the slowdown, Taiwan's economic strength remains its most powerful asset in seeking to expand its international presence.

International Economic Relations

The expansion of exports was the lifeblood of Taiwan's economy from the 1960s until very recently. In the last few years, especially since 1987, the share of GNP attributable to exports has declined sharply. In 1993 Taiwan's exports (FOB) totalled $84.9 billion, while imports (CIF) totalled $77 billion. This gave Taiwan a trade surplus of $7.9 billion, down from $9.5 billion in 1992 and $13.3 billion in 1991. Taiwan's trade surplus in 1993 was the lowest in ten years, mostly due to economic weakness in the U.S., Japanese, and European markets. Nonetheless, in

1992 and 1993 Taiwan had the only trade surplus among Asia's four tigers.

Taiwan's principal trading partners are the United States, Japan, Hong Kong, and mainland China. The combined share of Taiwan's exports to the United States and Japan was 37.5 percent in 1993, a percentage which has been dropping in recent years. Japan and the United States together supplied over 50 percent of Taiwan's imports, a more consistent pattern.[29] Taiwan's rapidly growing trade with the PRC is usually transshipped through Hong Kong and will be discussed momentarily.

The United States is Taiwan's most important trading partner, and Taiwan is the sixth largest trading partner of the United States. In 1993 the United States imported (FOB) $23.5 billion from Taiwan and exported (CIF) $16.7 billion, with Taipei enjoying a $6.8 billion trade surplus.

In the late 1980s the United States was concerned over its large trade deficit with Taiwan, which hit a record $16 billion in 1987.[30] Other U.S. trade complaints included the counterfeiting of American products, the dumping of Taiwan-made goods at below-market prices in the United States, and the maintenance of an artificially low value of the New Taiwan Dollar relative to the U.S. Dollar. Significant tariff and non-tariff barriers also existed. In May 1989 the Bush administration included Taiwan on a "priority watch list" for possible violations of intellectual property rights (IPR) under the "Super 301" provisions of the 1988 Omnibus Trade and Competitiveness Act.

As U.S. pressure mounted in the late 1980s, Taiwan made significant alterations in its conduct of trade. Export markets were diversified to reduce dependency on the U.S. market, the New Taiwan Dollar was appreciated over 60 percent,[31] major purchases were made of American "big ticket" items like airplanes, several "Buy America" missions were sent to the United States to purchase billions of dollars of U.S. goods, most tariff and non-tariff barriers were removed, various IPR agreements were negotiated with Washington, and a trade action plan was adopted in 1988 with a goal of reducing the ROC trade surplus with the United States by 10 percent a year. Much of the trade surplus problem was resolved by shifting Taiwan-owned manufacturing to mainland China, which now has the burden of a large surplus with the United States.

In December 1992 the ROC reviewed its 1988 Action Guideline for ROC-U.S. Trade, concluding that the goal to reduce Taiwan's huge trade surplus with the United States had been reached. (By Taipei's calculations, in 1991 Taiwan's trade surplus with the United States was

$8.3 billion; in 1992 it was $7.8 billion; in 1993 it stood at $6.8 billion.) Taipei decided that the 1993 trade guidelines would be refocused because of the probable enactment of the North American Free Trade Agreement (NAFTA). In anticipation of the passage of the agreement Taiwan began to plan for several contingencies, including the possibility of Taiwan becoming a contracting party to NAFTA or signing a bilateral free trade agreement with the United States.[32]

Thus, through a combination of U.S. pressure and ROC accommodation, most of the U.S.-Taiwan trade difficulties arising in the late 1980s have been managed. Those issues continuing under the Clinton administration will be addressed in the next chapter.

Trade with China

By 1993 mainland China became the most important growth market for Taiwan's exports. According to the ROC Board of Foreign Trade, Taiwan's trade with the PRC reached $13.8 billion in 1993, or 8.4 percent of Taiwan's total foreign trade. Of this amount, $12.7 billion were exports to the mainland, or 14.9 percent of Taiwan's total global shipments.[33] According to the March 1994 American Institute in Taiwan (AIT) economic report, since 1988 Taiwan has increased its exports to the PRC at an annual rate of about 30 percent, compared to 0.4 percent to the United States and 5.9 percent to Japan. AIT estimated that Taiwan's exports to the mainland represented 21.7 percent of total ROC exports in 1993, up from 7.7 percent in 1987. In a reverse trend, the combined share of Taiwan's exports to the United States and Japan in 1993 was 37.5 percent, down from 57.2 percent in 1988.[34]

According to ROC statistics, Taiwan had a $16.7 billion trade surplus with Hong Kong in 1993, the largest surplus ever with any trading partner. ROC exports to Hong Kong, most of which make their way to the PRC, rose to a 21.7 percent share of Taiwan's total exports, second only to the 27.6 percent absorbed by the United States. These figures reflected a shift in focus in ROC trade from the U.S. market to that of mainland China. By 1994 Taipei viewed its polarized trade -- a huge deficit with Japan and a huge surplus with China -- as a serious problem and one proving to be intractable.[35]

In the early 1990s most of Taiwan's imports from China were raw materials, agricultural products, and Chinese medicines. The ROC government carefully regulated these imports, but the categories of approved items were expanded several times each year. Taiwan's exports to the mainland were mainly consumer goods such as textiles and dyestuffs, tobacco, motorcycles, shoes and other leather goods, television sets, machines and machine tools, electrical goods, and paper and plastic products.

A great deal of the mainland's increased demand for Taiwan products was generated from Taiwan-owned production facilities built in China. These facilities imported machinery and materials, components, and semi-finished goods to be assembled and then exported to the United States and other countries under the country-of-origin label, "Made in China."

Since 1987 investment in China has become an important trend among Taiwanese businessmen. Nearly 40 percent of Taiwan's direct foreign investment in 1993 consisted of registered investment in the mainland. Much more investment was unregistered. Official cumulative Taiwan investment on mainland China was about $6 billion at the end of 1993, but unofficial estimates placed it far in excess of $10 billion. Investment approval statistics from Beijing placed the figure at $20 billion at the end of 1993, second only to Hong Kong and ahead of investments from the United States and Japan. Even by official ROC figures, mainland China was second only to the United States as the most popular destination for Taiwan's offshore investment.

Taipei has tried to limit economic interaction with the PRC on the grounds that too much trade would make Taiwan businessmen vulnerable to Beijing's manipulation. The ROC government also argues that too much investment on the mainland will "hollow out" Taiwan's industrial base, build too great an economic competitor on the mainland, transfer technology that will harm ROC security interests, and divert needed investment capital from Taiwan itself. The problem that the government faces is that a huge number of Taiwan businessmen find it in their vital interest to deal with China. Hence, despite ROC government efforts "to go slow" in cross-strait exchanges, there is constant and growing pressure from the business community to expand and make more efficient these contacts.

In September 1992 the first ROC Government Coordination Conference on Mainland Affairs was held. One decision was to divide products and technologies into three categories for approval on mainland investment: those that are banned, those that are permitted, and those that must be reviewed on a case-by-case basis. At the end of 1992, some 4,250 products were permitted for investment. Those products denied for investment included items on the COCOM (Coordinating Committee on

Export Controls) list, those related to national defense, those developed through government assistance, those belonging to newly developed industries, and certain other key parts and components identified by the government.[36]

Also in late 1992, Taipei scrapped its policy restricting exports to China to less than 10 percent of Taiwan's total exports. The policy was intended to ensure that Taiwan would not become overly dependent on the mainland and susceptible to PRC political pressure. Taiwan businessmen, however, bitterly complained of losing opportunities at a time when economic slowdowns in the United States and Japan were forcing ROC exporters to look elsewhere for markets. The vast mainland market was simply too important to ignore. Public pressure forced the ROC government to bring policy into closer alignment with economic reality.

The prospects for increased trade and investment between Taiwan, Hong Kong, and mainland China are excellent. The three Chinese societies seem to be merging into a highly competitive export-oriented economic zone, now often referred to as "Greater China." This new international entity is already having an enormous impact on the region's economy. As the production and trade zone becomes more integrated, the U.S. deficit with mainland China will probably grow larger while its trade deficit with Taiwan will stabilize or even decrease.[37] In part this change in trade patterns has occurred because a great many of Taiwan's production facilities (especially labor-intensive industries such as footwear, apparel, umbrellas, toys, and sporting goods) have already moved to the mainland to take advantage of lower labor costs and other financial incentives. On American shelves these goods are now labelled "Made in China" rather than "Made in Taiwan."

ROC Dollar Diplomacy

The economic strength of Taiwan has very important influence on ROC international relations. Diplomatically isolated from much of the world, the ROC has found that it can use "dollar diplomacy" to gain political support from countries needing financial and technological assistance to modernize. Taiwan is the largest or second largest foreign investor in most Southeast Asian countries. In a pattern similar to that found on mainland China, most Taiwan investments in Southeast Asia have set up multistage production operations which export to the United

States or, increasingly, to other Asian countries, using the host's "country-of-origin" labels on the assembled products. One result of this economic activity is the willingness of most Southeast Asian governments to receive quasi-official visits from ROC dignitaries, as seen by the friendly reception given to President Lee Teng-hui and Premier Lien Chan during their "vacation diplomacy" trips to the region in 1994.

Dollar diplomacy plays a key role in ROC relations with the United States and the European Community. In recent years both have increased the level of their political contact with Taiwan to ensure that their businessmen have equal or favorable access to the rapidly expanding Taiwan market. Taiwan also uses its economic resources to establish quasi-political relations with many former Soviet republics and Eastern European countries. This serves the dual purpose of gaining new markets and pressuring Beijing to moderate its policies toward Taiwan. Two of the best examples of dollar diplomacy are Taiwan's economic ties with Russia and Vietnam.[38]

Dollar diplomacy is used to enhance Taiwan's participation in international economic organizations -- a crucial step in breaking out of diplomatic isolation. One of the most important initiatives in this regard was a 1990 effort to join the General Agreement on Tariffs and Trade (GATT) as the "Customs Territory of Taiwan, Penghu, Kinmen, and Matsu."[39] In 1992 Taiwan assumed observer status within the trade organization, and GATT established a working party to consider Taiwan's application for membership. Also in 1992 Taiwan became a non-regional full member of the Central American Bank for Economic Integration. Taiwan joined APEC as a full member in 1991, attaining equal status with both mainland China and Hong Kong. In recent years Taiwan has made substantial financial contributions to the European Bank for Reconstruction and Development and the Inter-American Development Bank in bids to gain membership or influence. In January 1993 Taiwan formed a task force to join the Organization of Economic Cooperation and Development and the International Monetary Fund. Also in 1993 the Bank for International Settlement (BIS) recognized the Central Bank of [the Republic of] China as a non-stockholder member. The ROC Central Bank is BIS's largest correspondence bank. These multilateral efforts pay off bilaterally as well. In 1992 Taiwan added fourteen new trade offices in foreign countries, bringing its total to fifty-eight.

One tool of ROC dollar diplomacy is international financial assistance. A total of forty-four technical assistance missions from Taiwan help developing countries improve their economies, mostly in the area of agriculture. Taipei recently added a disaster relief program which has helped sixty countries with grants and loans totalling about $100 million. Nearly a billion dollars in low-interest ROC loans have been given to developing nations since 1988 to finance development projects.

These humanitarian and development assistance programs cultivate friends for Taiwan in the international community. The United States, for instance, has benefitted from Taipei's financial assistance to strategically important countries in the Persian Gulf, Latin America, and Southeast Asia. This assistance has served U.S. interests but without cost to the American taxpayer. For example, Taipei contributed $30 million to countries friendly to the United States adversely affected by the Persian Gulf War.

Political Relations with Mainland China

One of the most important political developments in East Asia since 1987 has been the increased contact between Taiwan and mainland China.[10] The two sides are becoming ever more closely intertwined, with the PRC being one of the most important export markets for Taiwan and the mainland relying heavily on Taiwanese investments for its modernization. Between 1987 and 1992, residents of Taiwan made more than 4.2 million trips to the PRC; about 40,000 visits were made by mainlanders to Taiwan. In 1992 more than 18 million pieces of mail were exchanged and nearly 27 million phone calls were placed.

To manage the growing interaction across the Taiwan Strait, Taipei and Beijing established institutions with quasi-official status to represent their interests. In February 1991 the ROC created the Foundation for Exchanges Across the Taiwan Strait (or Straits Exchange Foundation) with the following major responsibilities:

- accepting, ratifying, and forwarding on entry and exit documents from the two Chinese sides
- verifying and delivering documents issued on the mainland
- deporting fugitives on both sides of the Taiwan Strait
- arbitrating trade disputes
- promoting cultural and academic exchanges
- providing consultation on general affairs
- helping to protect the legal rights of ROC citizens during their visits to the mainland.

In December 1991 Beijing created its counterpart to the Straits Exchange Foundation: the Association for Relations Across the Taiwan Straits. The Association is closely tied to the Taiwan Affairs Office of the PRC State Council. Both the ROC and PRC representative offices have direct links with their respective governments and act in accordance with their governments' instructions.

Koo-Wang Talks

In an historic breakthrough in relations, Taiwan and mainland China held their first high-level meeting in more than forty years in Singapore in April 1993, when the chairmen of Beijing's Association for Relations Across the Taiwan Straits and Taipei's Straits Exchange Foundation (Wang Daohan and Koo Chen-fu, respectively) met to discuss a variety of non-political bilateral issues.[41] The meeting produced four documents. Three dealt with the delivery of registered letters, document verification, and the schedule of future contacts between the two quasi-official organizations. The other accord set forth the areas in which both sides wanted greater cooperation: fishing disputes, repatriation from Taiwan of illegal immigrants from the mainland, joint efforts to fight crime, protection of intellectual property rights, and efforts to reconcile differences in the two sides' legal systems. The joint exploitation of natural resources was also discussed, along with cooperation in science, culture, and education.

The two sides were unable to agree on the protection of Taiwan investments on the mainland, partly because Taipei wanted Beijing to sign a bilateral investment accord giving Taiwan a claim to be an equal political entity in relations with the mainland. The PRC side refused to do this, proposing instead that it provide investment guarantees directly with individual investors.

Subsequent meetings over the next few months between the Straits Exchange Foundation and the Association for Relations Across the Taiwan Straits were not as productive as the Koo-Wang talks. Differences over definitions of sovereignty effectively blocked agreements on trade and cultural links throughout the remainder of 1993. Practical problems such as airline hijacking (ten PRC airlines were hijacked to Taiwan in 1993 alone), fishing disputes, immigration, and extradition could not be resolved due to their political implications. In essence, the PRC side refused to give Taipei any semblance of political equality, while the ROC side refused to compromise on key issues as long as Beijing placed obstacles in the way of Taipei's participation in international affairs and did not rule out the use of force in resolving the Taiwan issue. Despite the stalemate, both sides wanted to continue the talks.[42]

In early 1994 the two sides decided to continue their discussions at a slightly higher level and with a less formal agenda. In a key meeting in Taipei in August 1994 the two organizations were able to reach agreement in principle on three issues: each side will handle its own citizens who hijack planes, procedures for handling illegal entrants, and procedures for settling fishing disputes. Little progress was made on the protection of Taiwan business interests on the mainland, travel safety, press freedom, or the return of previous hijackers.

The slow progress of the talks reflected the caution with which the ROC approached political contact with the PRC. Beijing, on the other hand, sought to expand contact with Taiwan to the official level as soon as possible. This coincided with the apparent interests of the two Chinese governments: the ROC wanted to postpone reunification until such time as the Chinese Communist Party could no longer dominate the mainland's political system; the PRC wanted to expedite reunification while its position was stronger than that of Taipei.

Democracy and Unification

The reunification of China has become vastly more complicated since the emergence of democracy on Taiwan. This is reflected most clearly in the rise to political prominence of the Democratic Progressive Party (DPP). The DPP, which by 1994 received 30-40 percent of the vote in various elections, openly advocates Taiwan independence. Its supporters see few advantages for Taiwan to be united with the mainland under any circumstances. The democratization of the KMT has led to sharp differences within the ruling party itself over the merits of reunification. As a democratically elected government, the ROC can no longer be seen as a political instrument of the mainlander Nationalist Chinese. The ROC government must represent the interests of all Taiwan citizens, including the strong minority who oppose reunification. The divisiveness of the reunification issue on Taiwan necessitates a slow -- if not obstructionist -- policy toward increased ROC political contact with the PRC.

Taiwan's security is closely linked to the reunification issue, since the most likely reason for the PRC to use force against Taiwan would be to prevent the island from becoming an independent country separate from China. This is the "one China, one Taiwan" option adamantly opposed by both Beijing and pro-unification forces on Taiwan. Both prefer a "one China" option whereby the mainland and Taiwan are united eventually under a single political entity called "China." A middle ground formally rejected by the two sides is the "two Chinas" option, whereby both the PRC and ROC adhere to the goal of "one China" but accept each other as equal governments in control of separate Chinese territories temporarily divided over ideological differences.[43]

The official positions of the two Chinese governments on the reunification issue were contained in the "Guidelines for National Unification" adopted by the ROC in March 1991 and the August 1993 PRC white paper on "The Taiwan Question and the Reunification of China."

ROC Guidelines for National Unification

The ROC position on reunification was enunciated by the National Unification Council in a 1991 document called "Guidelines for National Unification."[44] The National Unification Council was established in October 1990 as a non-partisan body under the Office of the President to provide policy guidance and determine consensus for ROC policy toward the mainland. It represents a wide spectrum of Chinese interests at home and abroad. The guidelines, which were formally accepted by the ROC cabinet in March 1991, set forth as fundamental principles:

1. Both mainland and Taiwan areas are parts of Chinese territory. Helping to bring about national unification should be the common responsibility of all Chinese people.
2. The unification of China should be for the welfare of all of its people and not be subject to partisan conflict.
3. China's unification should aim at promoting Chinese culture, safeguarding human dignity, guaranteeing fundamental human rights, and practicing democracy and the rule of law.
4. The timing and manner of China's unification should first respect the rights and interests of the people in the Taiwan area, and protect their security and welfare. It should be achieved in gradual phases under the principles of reason, peace, equity, and reciprocity.

The guidelines proposed a three-stage process of unification. The immediate first stage was one of building "exchanges and reciprocity." During this period, exchanges across the Taiwan Strait would increase, while at the same time "not endangering each other's safety and stability...and not denying the other's existence as a political entity." Mainland China would begin to implement democratic reform, and Taiwan would accelerate its constitutional reform. This stage was meant to end the PRC threat to use force against Taiwan, to allow Taipei to play a meaningful role in international affairs without interference from Beijing, and to phase out communism on the mainland. All exchanges between the two sides would be through intermediary organizations such as the Straits Exchange Foundation and its PRC counterpart, the Association for Relations Across the Taiwan Straits.

The mid-term phase of the unification guideline focused on building "mutual trust and cooperation." During this stage, "Direct postal, transport and commerce links should be allowed." Also, Taipei and Beijing would cooperate economically to develop the coastal areas to narrow the gap between the two sides' standards of living. "Official communication channels on equal footing" would be established, both sides would assist each other "in international organizations and activities," and "high-ranking officials on both sides" would exchange visits.

The final stage would be one of "consultation and unification." During this phase,

> A consultative organization for unification should be established through which both sides, in accordance with the will of the people in both the mainland and Taiwan areas, and while adhering to the goals of democracy, economic freedom, social justice and nationalization of the armed forces, jointly discuss the grand task of unification and map out a constitutional system to establish a democratic, free, and equitably prosperous China.

Several policies resulting from these guidelines were spelled out by Ma Ying-jeou, then vice chairman of the Mainland Affairs Council, in February 1992.[45] The Mainland Affairs Council was established in August 1988 under the Executive Yuan to coordinate the various government agencies in charge of implementing mainland policy and to control the pace of exchanges across the Taiwan Strait. The Straits Exchange Foundation is overseen by this government body. The Council became a permanent government agency in October 1990 with the responsibility of policy planning and coordination. The policies noted by Ma Ying-jeou included:

- The ROC will not use force in the process of national unification.
- "Under the one-China principle, Taipei practices `pragmatic diplomacy,' that is, creating opportunities to resume suspended diplomatic ties or to establish new ones, and to join or rejoin global or regional intergovernmental organizations."
- "Taipei regards itself as the central government of China while Peking is a `political entity' that controls the mainland area. Taipei proposes a `one country, two areas, two political entities' scheme, a pragmatic characterization of political reality across the Taiwan Strait, allowing sufficient `creative ambiguity' for each side to live with."
- Taipei opposes any political negotiations with Beijing until the second stage of the guidelines' process. At that time the ROC government, not the KMT party, will conduct the negotiations because only the government can represent all of the Taiwan people.
- Direct trade, postal, and transportation links will only occur "when Peking is ready not to deny Taipei's existence as a political entity, not to use force to settle bilateral disputes, and not to interfere with Taipei's conduct of external relations under the one-China principle." Until then, those links will be indirect, as will investment in the mainland. Direct two-way exchanges, however, have rapidly expanded and will continue to do so.
- The ROC intends to "build, with Taiwan's security and the welfare of its 20 million people in mind, a national consensus on orderly exchanges with the mainland to foster mutual understanding."

In August 1992 an important clarification of Taiwan's policy toward mainland China was made when the National Unification Council defined what was meant by Taipei's "one China principle." The term meant "one China, two regions and two political entities." "One China" referred to the Republic of China established in 1912 with sovereignty extending to mainland China, although only Taiwan, Penghu (Pescadores Islands), Kinmen, and Matsu were now under ROC rule. The term also signified that China was temporarily split into two political entities as a result of a civil war fought over ideological differences. The National Unification Guidelines were "intended to promote the development of China as a whole and the welfare of all the Chinese people to bring about eventual peaceful unification." The guidelines were also intended "to encourage mainland China to take concrete steps and a pragmatic attitude in handling cross-strait relations and working with Taiwan to build a free, democratic and better China."[46] As summarized in a later document, the "one China" policy of the ROC "acknowledges division, promotes exchanges and seeks unification."[47]

PRC White Paper on Taiwan

The PRC position on the unification of China was set forth in an August 1993 document called "The Taiwan Question and the Reunification of China."[48] As its fundamental premise, the white paper noted that the Taiwan issue is a remnant of China's dismemberment in the past, a period of history that cannot be brought to a close until Taiwan and the mainland are reunited. Most of the blame for the continued division of China is placed on the United States. The white paper said, "Against the backdrop of East-West confrontation, in the wake of the Second World War and guided by its conceived global strategy and national interest considerations, the U.S. government gave full support to the Kuomintang." After normalization of Sino-American relations in 1979, the document stated, the United States continued its interference in China's internal affairs by passing the Taiwan Relations Act. "Invoking this legislation, the U.S. Government has continued its arms sales to Taiwan, interference in China's internal affairs, and obstruction to Taiwan's reunification with the mainland."

To resolve the issue of arms sales to Taiwan, the PRC and the United States negotiated the August 17, 1982, joint communique in which the United States promised to end its arms sales. However, the white paper said, "in the past dozen or more years the U.S. Government has not only failed to implement the communique in earnest, but has repeatedly contravened it. In September 1992 the U.S. Government even decided to sell 150 F-16 high-performance fighter aircraft to Taiwan. This action of the U.S. Government has added a new stumbling block in the way of the development of Sino-U.S. relations and settlement of the Taiwan question."

The PRC document continued:

> It is clear from the foregoing that the U.S. Government is responsible for holding up the settlement of the Taiwan question. Since the 1970s many Americans of vision and goodwill in or outside the administration have contributed much by way of helping to resolve the differences between China and the U.S. on the Taiwan question. [The] three joint communiques testify to their effort and contribution of which the Chinese Government and

people are highly appreciative. On the other hand, one cannot fail to note that there are people in the U.S. who still do not want to see a reunified China. They have cooked up various pretexts and exerted influence to obstruct the settlement of the Taiwan question.

The Chinese Government is convinced that the American and the Chinese peoples are friendly to each other and that the normal development of the relations between the two countries accords with the long-term interests and common aspiration of both peoples. Both countries should cherish the three hard-won joint communiques guiding the development of bilateral relations. As long as both sides abide by the principles enshrined in those communiques, respect each other and set store by their overall common interests, it will not be difficult to settle the Taiwan question that has been left over from history and Sino-U.S. relations will surely see steady improvement and development ahead.

The white paper noted, it "is a sacrosanct mission of the entire Chinese people [to] settle the Taiwan question and achieve national reunification." The PRC's "basic position on this question is: peaceful reunification; one country, two systems." As outlined by the white paper, the main contents of this proposal were:

1. *Only one China.* There is only one China in the world, Taiwan is an inalienable part of China and the seat of China's central government is in Beijing. This is a universally recognized fact as well as the premise for a peaceful settlement of the Taiwan question.

   The Chinese Government is firmly against any words or deeds designed to split China's sovereignty and territorial integrity. It opposes `two Chinas,' `one China, one Taiwan,' `one country, two governments' or any attempt or act that could lead to `independence of Taiwan'. The Chinese people on both sides of the Straits all believe that there is only one China and espouse national reunification. Taiwan's status as an inalienable part of China has been determined and cannot be changed. `Self-determination' for Taiwan is out of the question.

2. *Coexistence of two systems.* On the premise of one China, socialism on the mainland and capitalism on Taiwan can coexist and develop side by side for a long time without one swallowing up the other. This concept has largely taken account of the actual situation in Taiwan and practical interests of our compatriots there. It will be a unique feature and important innovation in the state system of a reunified China.

   After reunification, Taiwan's current socio-economic system, its way of life as well as economic and cultural ties with foreign countries can remain unchanged. Private property, including houses and land, as well as business ownership, legal inheritance and overseas Chinese and foreign investments on the island will all be protected by law.

3. *A high degree of autonomy.* After reunification, Taiwan will become a special administrative region. It will be distinguished from the other provinces or regions of China by its high degree of autonomy. It will have its own administrative and legislative powers, an independent judiciary and the right of adjudication on the island. It will run its own party, political, military, economic and financial affairs. It may conclude commercial and cultural agreements with foreign countries and enjoy certain rights in foreign affairs. It may keep its military forces and the mainland will not dispatch troops or administrative personnel to the island. On the other hand, representatives of the government of the special administrative region and those from different circles of Taiwan may be appointed to senior posts in the central government and participate in the running of national affairs.

4. *Peace negotiations.* It is the common aspiration of the entire Chinese people to achieve reunification of the country by peaceful means through contacts and negotiations. People on both sides of the Straits are all Chinese. It would be a great tragedy for all if China's territorial integrity and sovereignty were to be split and its people were to be drawn into a fratricide. Peaceful reunification will greatly enhance the cohesion of the Chinese nation. It will facilitate Taiwan's socio-economic stability and development and promote the resurgence and prosperity of China as a whole.

    In order to put an end to hostility and achieve peaceful reunification, the two sides should enter into contacts and negotiations at the earliest possible date. On the premise of one China, both sides can discuss any subject, including the modality of negotiations, the question of what parties, groups and personalities may participate as well as any other matters of concern to the Taiwan side. So long as the two sides sit down and talk, they will always be able to find a mutually acceptable solution.

    Taking into account the prevailing situation on both sides of the Straits, the Chinese Government has proposed that pending reunification the two sides should, according to the principle of mutual respect, complementarity and mutual benefit, actively promote economic cooperation and other exchanges. Direct trade, postal, air and shipping services and two-way visits should be started in order to pave the way for the peaceful reunification of the country.

Sounding a warning that the use of force cannot be ruled out to achieve unification, the white paper said: "Peaceful reunification is a set policy of the Chinese Government. However, any sovereign state is entitled to use any means it deems necessary, including military ones, to uphold its sovereignty and territorial integrity. The Chinese Government is under no obligation to undertake any commitment to any foreign power or people intending to split China as to what means it might use to handle its own domestic affairs."

The report emphasized that the Taiwan issue "bears no analogy to the cases of Germany and Korea which were brought about as a result of international accords at the end of the Second World War....The Chinese Government has always opposed applying the German or Korean formulas to Taiwan. The Taiwan question should and entirely can be resolved judiciously through bilateral consultations and within the framework of one China."

The white paper noted that the PRC and Taiwan authorities had taken positive steps in recent years to improve cross-straits relations. "Thus, an atmosphere of relaxation prevails in the Taiwan Straits for the first time in the past four decades. This is auspicious to peaceful reunification."

Despite these signs of progress, the white paper pointed to several obstacles to reunification that were of grave concern to the PRC. The document said, "It should be pointed out that notwithstanding a certain measure of easing up by the Taiwan authorities, their current policy vis-a-vis the mainland still seriously impedes the development of relations across the Straits as well as the reunification of the country. They talk about the necessity of a reunified China, but their deeds are always a far cry from the principle of one China. They try to prolong Taiwan's separation from the mainland and refuse to hold talks on peaceful reunification. They have even set up barriers to curb the further development of the interchanges across the Strait."

Even more disturbing, the PRC observed, were calls for Taiwan independence:

> In recent years the clamors for `Taiwan independence' on the island have become shriller, casting a shadow over the course of relations across the Straits and the prospect of peaceful reunification of the country. The `Taiwan independence' fallacy has a complex socio-historical root and international background. But the Taiwan authorities have, in effect, abetted this fallacy by its own policy of rejecting peace negotiations, restricting interchanges across the Straits and lobbying for `dual recognition' or `two Chinas' in the international arena. It should be reaffirmed that the desire of Taiwan compatriots to run the affairs of the island as masters of their own house is reasonable and justified. This should by no means be construed as advocating `Taiwan independence'. They are radically distinct from those

handful of `Taiwan independence' protagonists who trumpet `independence' but vilely rely on foreign patronage in a vain attempt to detach Taiwan from China, which runs against the fundamental interests of the entire Chinese people including Taiwan compatriots. The Chinese Government is closely following the course of events and will never condone any maneuver for `Taiwan independence'.

Certain foreign forces who do not want to see a reunified China have gone out of their way to meddle in China's internal affairs. They support the anti-Communist stance of the Taiwan authorities of rejecting peace talks and abet the secessionists on the island, thereby erecting barriers to China's peaceful reunification and seriously wounding the national feelings of the Chinese people.

The white paper went on to clarify the PRC's position on Taiwan's role in international affairs: "As part of China, Taiwan has no right to represent China in the international community, nor can it establish diplomatic ties or enter into relations of an official nature with foreign countries." However, "the Chinese Government has not objected to non-governmental economic or cultural exchanges between Taiwan and foreign countries." The report emphasized, "In recent years the Taiwan authorities have vigorously launched a campaign of `pragmatic diplomacy' to cultivate official ties with countries having diplomatic relations with China in an attempt to push `dual recognition' and achieve the objective of creating a situation of `two Chinas' or `one China, one Taiwan'. The Chinese Government is firmly against this scheme."

In terms of Taiwan's participation in international organizations, the white paper said:

> The Government of the People's Republic of China, as the sole legal government of China, has the right and obligation to exercise state sovereignty and represent the whole of China in international organizations. The Taiwan authorities' lobbying for a formula of `one country, two seats' in international organizations whose membership is confined to sovereign states is a maneuver to create `two Chinas'. The Chinese Government is firmly opposed to such an attempt....Only on the premise of adhering to the principle of one China and in the light of the nature and statutes of the international organizations concerned as well as the specific circumstances, can the Chinese Government consider the question of Taiwan's participation in the activities of such organizations and in a manner agreeable and acceptable to the Chinese Government.

Special mention was made of the United Nations, where Taipei had been attempting with increasing vigor to gain reentry:

> All the specialized agencies and organizations of the United Nations system are inter-governmental organizations composed of sovereign states. After the restoration of the lawful rights of the People's Republic of China in the United Nations...the issue of China's representation in the U.N. system has been resolved once and for all and Taiwan's re-entry is out of the question. However, it should be pointed out that recently some elements of the Taiwan authorities have been clamoring for `returning to the United Nations'. Apparently, this is an attempt to split state sovereignty, which is devoid of any legal or practical basis. The Chinese Government is convinced that all governments and organizations of the U.N. system will be alert to this scheme and refrain from doing anything prejudicial to China's sovereignty.

The report then discussed various models of Taiwan's participation in international organizations:

> As to regional economic organizations such as the Asian Development Bank (ADB) and the Asia-Pacific Economic Cooperation (APEC), Taiwan's participation is subject to the terms of agreement or understanding reached between the Chinese Government and the parties concerned which explicitly prescribe that the People's Republic of China is a full member as a sovereign state whereas Taiwan may participate in the activities of those organizations only as a region of China under the designation of Taipei, China (in ADB) or Chinese Taipei (in APEC). This is only an ad hoc arrangement and cannot constitute a `model' applicable to other inter-governmental organizations or international gatherings.
>
> As regards participation in non-governmental international organizations, the relevant bodies of the People's Republic of China may reach an agreement or understanding with the parties concerned so that China's national organizations would use the designation of China, while Taiwan's organizations may participate under the designation of Taipei, China or Taiwan, China.[49]

The document paid special attention to foreign arms sales to Taiwan, thought by the PRC to firm up the will of Taipei to resist unification:

> The Chinese Government has always firmly opposed any country selling any type of arms or transferring production technology of the same to Taiwan. All countries maintaining diplomatic relations with China should abide by the principles of mutual respect for sovereignty and territorial

integrity and non-interference in each other's internal affairs, and refrain from providing arms to Taiwan in any form or under any pretext. Failure to do so would be a breach of the norms of international relations and an interference in China's internal affairs.

All countries, and especially big powers shouldering major responsibilities for world peace, are obligated to strictly abide by the guidelines laid down by the five permanent members of the U.N. Security Council to restrict the proliferation of conventional weapons so as to contribute to maintaining and promoting regional peace and stability. However, at a time when relations across the Taiwan Straits are easing up, certain powers have seen fit to renege on their undertakings under international agreements and to flout the Chinese Government's repeated strong representations by making arms sales to Taiwan, thereby whipping up tension between the two sides of the Straits. This not only constitutes a serious threat to China's security and an obstacle to China's peaceful reunification, but also undermines peace and stability in Asia and the world at large. It stands to reason that the Chinese people should voice strong resentment against this conduct.

ROC Response to PRC White Paper

On September 16, 1993, the ROC Mainland Affairs Council responded to the PRC white paper on Taiwan in a document titled "There Is No `Taiwan Question'; There Is Only a `China Question'."[50] Some of the major points in the ROC document were:

1. There is no Taiwan question, only a question of the future of China and how to make the country democratic and free.
2. The Chinese Communists regime cannot be equated with China. "The term `China' connotes multifaceted geographical, political, historical and cultural meanings. We have always asserted that both the mainland and Taiwan are Chinese territories....It is an undeniable fact that the two have been divided and ruled separately since 1949. Although the Chinese Communists have enjoyed jurisdiction over the mainland area, they cannot be equated with China. They can in no way represent China as a whole, much less serve as the `sole legal government of all Chinese people.'"
3. The ROC is a member of the international community, and the PRC cannot represent the people of Taiwan. "The Chinese Communists have never extended their governing power to the Taiwan area, so they are not entitled to represent Taiwan in the international community, nor

have they advocated the rights or fulfilled the obligations of the people in the Taiwan area in any international organizations."

4. The PRC's one country, two systems proposal "is the main obstacle to China's unification....It is clear that the `one country, two systems' premise is nothing but a demand for the Taiwan area to surrender to the Chinese Communists. Thus, objectively, `one country, two systems' is infeasible, and, subjectively, it is unacceptable to the people in the ROC."

5. "The ROC government pursues China's unification not only to unify the territories of China through peaceful and reasonable means. The loftier goal is to allow the 1.2 billion people on the Chinese mainland to enjoy the same democratic, free and equitably prosperous lifestyle and the basic human rights and freedom that the people in the Taiwan area do."

6. "The two sides of the Taiwan Straits should resolve the unification question peacefully....we believe that so long as the Chinese Communists do not implement democracy and the rule of law, and do not renounce the use of force to resolve problems, the threat they pose to the stability and prosperity of Asia, and even the world, will continue."

The ROC document concluded:

We believe that the value of national unification lies not in a single jurisdiction over China's territories but in enabling the people on the Chinese mainland to enjoy the same democratic, free and equitably prosperous lifestyle as is enjoyed by the people in the Taiwan area....We sincerely call upon the Chinese Communist authorities to quickly relinquish the anachronistic communist system; commit themselves to political, economic and social reforms on the Chinese mainland; and place the fundamental rights and welfare of the 1.2 billion Chinese people above the narrow interests of the Chinese Communist Party. Only so can the reunification of China be meaningful.

We would also like to once again urge the Chinese Communist authorities to recognize the reality that the two sides of the Taiwan Straits are divided and ruled separately, and to renounce the use of force in the Taiwan Straits.

In comparing the positions of the two sides on reunification, it is clear that principles of sovereignty and political power are at the heart of the issue. Under existing conditions, Beijing has little incentive to change its position other than to deflect the possibility of Taiwan independence -- a possibility that appears to be growing. PRC strategy is to present Taipei with a choice of either global isolation or capitulation under fairly generous terms. In addition to the economic benefits received by the PRC, trade and other contact across the Taiwan Strait are seen as ways to bind Taiwan ever closer to the mainland's embrace. Held in the background is the iron fist of the PLA to deter outside interference and Taiwan independence and to serve as a final option to achieve reunification.

The ROC maintains a defensive position, but it claims the moral high ground by arguing that reunification can only occur after the communists allow the Chinese people on the mainland to enjoy the democracy and prosperity found on Taiwan. In addition to providing a large market for Taiwan businessmen, contact across the Taiwan Strait is viewed as an effective means to undermine the authority of the CCP. To counter the PRC strategy of isolation, Taipei uses its growing economic power to expand its international presence. One goal of pragmatic diplomacy is to widen international recognition of Taipei as a government representing the interests of Taiwan. Later, if that effort is successful, Taipei may seek to be acknowledged once again as a legitimate government representing the interests of the people of China. At present, the ROC strategy is one of survival, patiently waiting for a shift in circumstances to make possible the resolution of the reunification issue on terms favorable to its own interests.

The strategies of both the PRC and ROC have been upset recently by the emergence of greater public support for Taiwan independence. The surfacing of pro-independence sentiment among Taiwanese in the KMT is a development that may prove more ominous to mainland-Taiwan relations than obstacles posed by the DPP. Certainly, such a development has posed additional challenges to U.S. policy toward Taiwan and Sino-American relations in general.

Conclusion

Political, economic, social, and other changes since 1986 have altered fundamentally the character of the Republic of China on Taiwan. Especially important in terms of this study have been the democratization of Taiwan and ROC policy changes toward mainland China and the international community. Developments on Taiwan have created a new political entity in East Asia, one that is not widely recognized as an independent nation-state but one that can no longer be described with absolute certainty as being part of China.

Although Taiwan has made remarkable political and economic progress in recent years, there is great danger to a polity that is unsure of its national identity. Most mainlanders on Taiwan consider themselves Chinese and seem to be in favor of a united China. Many Taiwanese within the ruling party share with the DPP the conviction that Taiwan should never unify politically with the mainland. A great many of these individuals view themselves as being Overseas Chinese, that is, Chinese in the sense of race and culture but not Chinese in the sense of national identity. Since Taiwanese have largely taken control of the ruling party's direction, the "one China" policy of the ROC can no longer be taken for granted. Nor can it be assumed that reunification is the true goal of top KMT decision-makers. At minimum, these policies -- once thought unassailable principles of the Republic of China -- are beginning to metamorphose under the pressure and heat of Taiwan politics.

At present, the ROC government has two fundamental interests: avoiding a military confrontation with the PRC, and maintaining the political support of the majority of the Taiwanese people. This requires the ROC to pursue a China policy with two separate objectives: a commitment to the historical goal of unification (albeit under a democratic form of government), and a continuation of Taiwan's autonomy from the communist mainland. The status quo in the Taiwan Strait serves these dual interests and objectives, but neither the PRC nor domestic critics of Taipei's "one China" policy seem willing to tolerate the status quo indefinitely. Both perceive time as being against their interests: the PRC is concerned that Taiwan is drifting toward independence, while critics of the ROC's "one China" policy view increased contact across the Taiwan Strait as undermining Taiwan's autonomy. Perhaps more than any other factor, this creates the dynamic that is driving the Taiwan issue toward a resolution as yet unknown but profoundly consequential for all concerned.

The challenge for the ROC government is to devise a China policy that is tolerable to both Beijing and the majority Taiwanese. Pressure from both sides is forcing the government to be creative and exploratory. Efforts to seek readmittance into the United Nations is a clear example of ROC willingness to accept a "two Chinas" solution. And in February 1994 Premier Lien Chan told the Legislative Yuan that unifying the mainland and Taiwan under a federal or confederal system would be a feasible way to end the sovereignty dispute between the two Chinese sides.[51]

Thus, while Beijing continues to adhere rigidly to its "one country, two systems" formula for reunification, Taipei is becoming quite flexible in its China policy and in its foreign policy in general, a flexibility enhanced to a degree by fear and desperation in a perceived "life-threatening" international and domestic environment. How the Clinton administration has responded to the "new" Taiwan will be the subject of the next chapter.

Notes

1. For a description of the "new" Taiwan and its policy implications for the United States, see Martin L. Lasater, *U.S. Interests in the New Taiwan* (Boulder, CO: Westview Press, 1993).

2. The legal revisions necessary to remove all vestiges of martial law (first declared on Taiwan in May 1949) were complex. The major steps in this direction were as follows: June 1987, Taiwan's Legislative Yuan (parliament) passed a National Security Law to replace the Period of National Mobilization for Suppression of the Communist Rebellion; July 1987, the state of emergency degree in the Taiwan area was lifted; April 1991, the National Assembly passed articles amending the ROC constitution and approved abolishment of the Temporary Provisions Effective During the Period of National Mobilization; May 1991, President Lee Teng-hui terminated the Period of National Mobilization and abolished the Temporary Provisions. For details, see Hungdah Chiu, *Constitutional Development and Reform in the Republic of China on Taiwan* (Baltimore, MD: University of Maryland School of Law, 1993).

3. The population of Taiwan is almost entirely Han Chinese, with a few thousand aborigines. "Taiwanese" are those Chinese whose relatives moved to Taiwan before and during the Japanese occupation of the island from 1895 to 1945. Most Taiwanese have ancestral roots among the Fukien (from Fujian province) and the Hakka (from Guangdong province). "Mainlanders" are Chinese who came to Taiwan from mainland China after 1945, the vast majority of whom accompanied General Chiang Kai-shek to the island following his defeat by the communists on the mainland. The ancestral homes of mainlanders are from throughout China. Taiwanese comprise about 85 percent of the population, while mainlanders comprise about 15 percent. The two groups are heavily intermarried.

4. Because of the PRC threat against Taiwan, martial law was declared on May 20, 1949. According to some scholars, the form of "martial law" on Taiwan was actually similar to a "state of siege." Martial law involves the suspension of normal rules of law, whereas state of siege maintains existing civil law except where there exists a threat to public safety and order. This distinction

is explained in the case of Taiwan in Chiu, *Constitutional Development and Reform in the Republic of China*, pp. 14-19.

5. The *San Min Chu-i* were formulated by Dr. Sun Yat-sen, the founder of the KMT and the "father" of the Republic of China. The three principles are sometimes translated as national independence, political democracy, and social well-being. Dr. Sun theorized that the ROC would go through three stages in the implementation of his philosophy. The first would be a military administration to unite the country. The second would be political tutelage under the KMT to educate the Chinese people in the ways of democracy. The third and final stage would be constitutional democracy. The KMT holds that the ROC is now in this final stage.

6. For detailed analysis of Taiwan's political liberalization, see Hung-mao Tien, *The Great Transition: Political and Social Change in the Republic of China* (Stanford, CA: Hoover Institution Press, 1989). See also John F. Copper with George P. Chen, *Taiwan's Elections: Political Development and Democratization in the Republic of China* (Baltimore, MD: University of Maryland School of Law, 1984); John F. Copper, *Taiwan's Recent Elections: Fulfilling the Democratic Promise* (Baltimore, MD: University of Maryland School of Law, 1990); and John F. Copper, *Taiwan's 1991 and 1992 Non-Supplemental Elections: Reaching a Higher State of Democracy* (Lanham, MD: University Press of America, 1994).

7. According to the 1947 ROC Constitution, the national government has five branches, or yuan. Three -- the Executive, Legislative, and Judicial -- parallel Western institutions. Two, the Control Yuan (to enforce standards of behavior among government officials) and the Examination Yuan (to select members of the civil service), are traditional Chinese political institutions. The National Assembly elects the President and Vice President and amends the Constitution. Elections for the National Assembly, Legislative Yuan, and Control Yuan were held in 1947-1948 in those parts of China under the control of the Nationalists. Many of these officials moved to Taiwan in 1949 with other remnants of the ROC government. The 1947 Constitution is now being extensively amended on Taiwan.

8. The Council has the constitutional authority to interpret the ROC Constitution. On June 21, 1990, the Council rendered Interpretation No. 261, stating that all life-tenured parliamentarians had to resign by December 31, 1991.

9. Individual Americans, including several Members of Congress, had advised the ROC government for years to liberalize its political system to reflect the progress made in economic development. President Chiang made his announcement about the lifting of martial law to *Washington Post* chairperson Mrs. Katharine Graham.

10. Although not precise, these factional differences within the KMT can be seen in liberal-conservative terms. The mainstream faction is liberal and includes some mainlanders. The non-mainstream faction is conservative and contains

some Taiwanese. Liberals are more inclined to support the one China, one Taiwan position and no unification in the foreseeable future. The conservatives support one China and reunification. Both sides more or less support the status quo in the Taiwan Strait for the immediate future, but they have different timetables and objectives in expanding contacts with the PRC. The liberals prefer a more gradual approach to expanding contacts, whereas the conservatives want to integrate the two Chinese societies more rapidly. Neither faction wants to see Taiwan controlled by the Chinese communists. KMT liberals have pushed for a more rapid democratization and Taiwanization of Taiwan's politics than have the conservatives. The key issue has been the amount of change Taiwan's society can bear given its domestic and international situation. The conservatives favor the use of government regulatory powers to manage the society; the liberals favor less government regulation. In addition to the mainstream and non-mainstream, there are many other factions within the KMT, some of which are based on generational differences, family ties, and professional interests such as the military or big business. With the exception of a few fundamental issues (e.g., Taiwan-mainland relations and the pace of democratization), factional identification often means very little in terms of what an individual KMT member supports or opposes. But the nature of these fundamental issues -- having to do with the nation's identity and the future direction of the KMT -- are far more divisive than most liberal-conservative issues in U.S. politics.

11. Article 35 of the ROC Constitution stated, "The President shall be the head of state," whereas Article 53 said, "The Executive Yuan shall be the highest administrative organ of the state." Article 37 provided that laws must be signed by both the president and the premier.

12. In this type of electoral system, legislative districts have one or more representatives, depending upon the district's population. Voters have one vote. Those candidates with the largest number of votes win the available seats. To win the maximum number of seats in a given district, party discipline and financial resources are key, since the party must convince voters to spread their votes among several candidates. In the 1992 elections, KMT party discipline disintegrated and popular KMT members running as independents received huge numbers of votes from increasingly independent voters. The DPP, on the other hand, exercised greater discipline and was able to better proportion votes among its candidates. Under this electoral system, an organized minority is almost assured of a seat. In the 1992 elections, non-mainstream candidates did much better on average than mainstream candidates, partly because mainlander members of the KMT voted in blocks for second-generation mainlander candidates.

13. The formal launching of the Chinese New Party in a press conference on August 10, 1993, was reported in *Free China Journal*, August 13, 1993, p. 2.

14. In the 1920s the KMT was organized along Leninist lines with the help of Soviet Comintern agent Mikhail Borodin to be a revolutionary party. The

question of whether the KMT should continue to be a revolutionary party or a democratic party split the KMT in recent years. In the late 1980s party leaders said the KMT could be both a revolutionary party and a democratic party, but that proved difficult to accomplish in the context of Taiwan politics.

15. For a summary of the KMT Congress, see *Far Eastern Economic Review*, September 2, 1993, p. 15.

16. *Far Eastern Economic Review*, August 19, 1993, pp. 10-11.

17. For election results, see *Free China Journal*, December 3, 1993.

18. The unprecedented prosecution of election fraud by the ROC government signalled an end to the KMT's reliance on local party bosses to turn out the vote. Under President Lee Teng-hui, the KMT shifted the foundations of the party's power from the elite ruling class to the general populace. See *Far Eastern Economic Review*, April 28, 1994, p. 18; May 12, 1994, p. 13.

19. *Free China Journal*, May 6, 1994, p. 2; *Far Eastern Economic Review*, June 23, 1994, pp. 22-23.

20. Results and analysis of the December 3, 1994, election can be found in *Free China Journal*, December 9, 1994, and December 15, 1994.

21. *Foreign Affairs Report: Foreign Relations and Diplomatic Administration* (Taipei, Taiwan: ROC Ministry of Foreign Affairs, 1993). An English summary of the white paper can be found in issues of *Free China Journal* between March 26 and May 11, 1993.

22. These countries were Bahamas, Belize, Central African Republic, Costa Rica, Commonwealth of Dominica, Dominican Republic, El Salvador, Grenada, Guatemala, Guinea-Bissau, Haiti, the Holy See, Honduras, Lesotho, Liberia, Malawi, Nauru, Nicaragua, Niger, Panama, Paraguay, Saint Christopher and Nevis, Saint Lucia, St. Vincent and the Grenadines, Solomon Islands, South Africa, Swaziland, Tonga (South Pacific), and Tuvalu. In 1994 the ROC severed diplomatic ties with Lesotho but resumed official relations with Burkina Faso.

23. The seven countries were El Salvador, Guatemala, Nicaragua, Costa Rica, Honduras, Panama, and Belize. In July 1994 twelve nations sent a joint proposal to the U.N. asking that it set up an ad hoc committee to consider ROC representation. The proposal was later dropped.

24. *China News*, December 30, 1992, p. 3.

25. *Washington Post*, September 21, 1993, p. A16. The DPP supports Taiwan's entrance into the United Nations, but as "Taiwan" not the "Republic of China." As one Taiwanese professor at the New York Law School wrote: "Taiwan is Taiwan and China is China. They are two separate, sovereign states, diverging fundamentally in their political, economic and social systems. Taiwan is *not* an internal affair of China....It is time for Taiwan to be made a member of the United Nations and of other international governmental organizations...*as Taiwan, not as a truncated China*." Lung-chu Chen, "The Nation of Taiwan," *Washington Post*, December 24, 1993, p. A15. Emphasis in original.

26. Most of the statistics in this section were taken from "Foreign Economic Trends and Their Implications for the United States: Taiwan" (Taipei, Taiwan: American Institute in Taiwan, July 1993 and March 1994). (Hereafter cited as FET: Taiwan.) The AIT report is largely based on statistics from the ROC Directorate General of Budget, Accounting and Statistics. Due to different accounting procedures, some figures, especially those dealing with trade, differ from U.S. statistics.

27. See remarks of Economics Minister Vincent Siew in *China News*, January 1, 1993, p. 8.

28. In New Taiwan Dollar (NT$), outstanding bonds in FY1990 (ending June 30, 1990) totalled NT$147 billion. The debt in FY1994 was estimated to be NT$1,064 billion.

29. Japan is Taiwan's second largest trading partner and its most important source of imports. In 1993 12 percent of Taiwan's global trade was with Japan. Taiwan's persistent trade deficit with Japan, which rose to $14.2 billion in 1993, is a source of constant irritation to Taipei.

30. By U.S. calculations, the trade deficit with Taiwan was $8.9 billion in 1993, the third largest after Japan and China. The U.S. trade deficit with Taiwan was $10.1 billion in 1984, $12.1 billion in 1985, $15.7 billion in 1986, $19 billion in 1987, $13 billion in 1988, $12 billion in 1989, $11.2 billion in 1990, $10 billion in 1991, and $9.4 billion in 1992.

31. The New Taiwan Dollar (NT$) appreciated another 10 percent against the U.S. Dollar in 1992. In 1993 the NT$ depreciated 6 percent against the dollar.

32. *China News*, December 17, 1992, p. 3.; *China Post*, December 18, 1992, p. 9.

33. *Free China Journal*, March 25, 1994, p. 3.

34. FET: Taiwan (March 1994).

35. *Free China Journal*, January 14, 1994, p. 3.

36. *China News*, January 1, 1993, p. 8. COCOM was established in 1949 to control the export of strategic products and technical data to proscribed destinations such as the communist bloc.

37. In 1993 PRC exports to the United States totalled $31.5 billion, while Taiwan exports were $23.5 billion. The PRC had a 5.5 percent share of the U.S. market, while Taiwan had a 4.3 percent share.

38. In October 1992 Russian President Boris Yeltsin approved an agreement ending more than four decades of broken relations between Moscow and the ROC. The agreement set up private organizations with the authority to issue visas. On Taiwan's side, the Taipei-Moscow Economic and Cultural Commission will have offices in Moscow, St. Petersburg, and Vladivostok. See *Far Eastern Economic Review*, September 24, 1992, p. 17; *China News*, October 7, 1992, p. 3. Former Soviet President Mikhail Gorbachev visited Taiwan in March 1994. See *Free China Journal*, March 25, 1994, p. 1. As of September 1993, Taiwan

had invested $1.4 billion in Vietnam, the largest single foreign investor in that country. See *Wall Street Journal*, August 5, 1993, p. A4.

39. See "The Accession of the Customs Territory of Taiwan, Penghu, Kinmen and Matsu: GATT" (Taipei, Taiwan: ROC Ministry of Economic Affairs, January 1990).

40. For details of this interaction through 1991, see Ralph N. Clough, *Reaching Across the Taiwan Strait: People-to-People Diplomacy* (Boulder, CO: Westview Press, 1993).

41. See Hungdah Chiu, *Koo-Wang Talks and the Prospect of Building Constructive and Stable Relations Across the Taiwan Strait* (Baltimore, MD: University of Maryland School of Law, 1993).

42. For a detailed report on the December 1993 meeting in Taipei between representatives of the Straits Exchange Foundation and the Association for Relations Across the Taiwan Straits, see *Free China Journal*, December 24, 1993; *Wall Street Journal*, December 23, 1993, p. A8, and January 31, 1994, p. A5A.

43. Despite official renunciation of the idea by the ROC and PRC, "two Chinas" accurately describes the status quo in the Taiwan Strait. Admission of this reality is politically difficult, for different reasons, for both Beijing and Taipei. Of the two sides, however, Taipei would be much more willing to adopt this option if it became acceptable to the international community. Now widely recognized as the sole legal government of China, the PRC would have more to lose if "two Chinas" gained international support.

44. "Guidelines for National Unification" (Taipei, Taiwan: National Unification Council, 1991).

45. Ying-jeou Ma, "The Republic of China's Policy Toward the Chinese Mainland," *Issues and Studies*, Vol. 28, No. 2 (February 1992), pp. 1-10.

46. *China News*, August 2, 1992, p. 10.

47. *Free China Journal*, December 24, 1993, p. 7.

48. "The Taiwan Question and the Reunification of China" (Beijing, China: Taiwan Affairs Office and Information Office, State Council, August 1993). An English version of the document can be found in *Beijing Review*, September 6-12, 1993, pp. I-VIII.

49. The PRC document even defined policy in regards to international airline service to Taiwan: "the opening of aviation services with Taiwan by any airlines, including privately-operated ones, of countries having diplomatic relations with China is a political issue affecting China's sovereignty and cannot be regarded as a non-political transaction. State-run airlines of countries having diplomatic relations with China certainly must not operate air services to Taiwan. Privately-operated airlines must seek China's consent through consultations between their government and the Chinese Government before they can start reciprocal air services with privately-operated airlines of Taiwan."

50. An abridged version of the ROC response can be found in *Free China Journal*, September 24, 1993, p. 7.

51. *Free China Journal*, March 4, 1994, p. 1.

5

Clinton's Taiwan Policy

The Republic of China did not expect great change in U.S.-Taiwan relations under President Clinton. In December 1992 ROC Foreign Minister Fredrick Chien said that bilateral relations would continue to be sensitive to both countries. Taipei would not make high-profile efforts to establish good relations with Bill Clinton, Chien said, but rather would allow the relationship to evolve naturally. In a statement characteristic of pragmatic diplomacy, the Foreign Minister said mutual benefit (not shared ideology) should be the goal of all future ROC relations with the United States. The best way to improve bilateral relations, he explained, was to have a clear understanding of the possible difficulties the United States might have in dealing with Taiwan on a diplomatic level.

Chien downplayed the implications of the F-16 sale as a breakthrough in relations with the United States, noting that Taipei had sought to purchase an advanced fighter since the late 1960s. These efforts were not successful, he pointed out, until the U.S. domestic situation had changed and the military balance between the ROC and mainland China had been disrupted by PRC purchases of advanced aircraft from the Soviet Union.[1]

Taipei did hope for some improvement in relations with the United States, however. In mid-December 1992 Foreign Minister Chien noted that Clinton had visited Taiwan four times in the past, had firsthand knowledge about Taiwan, and was quite friendly to the Taiwan people. Chien said the ROC wanted the Clinton administration to take two important steps to improve their bilateral relationship:

1. Clinton should lift the administrative directive established by the Carter administration forbidding U.S. government officials above the assistant secretary level to visit Taiwan and prohibiting other forms of official contact, such as denying the right of Taiwan diplomats to visit the State Department.

2. Clinton should agree to the renaming of the two representative offices (Coordination Council for North American Affairs and the American Institute in Taiwan) "so that newcomers will not be confused."[2]

The appointment of Warren Christopher as Clinton's secretary of state raised some concern in Taiwan because of his unpleasant experiences there during the Jimmy Carter administration. Christopher was sent to Taipei in December 1978 to explain the U.S. decision to break diplomatic relations with the ROC and to establish ties with the PRC. When he arrived, crowds gathered around his car to hurl eggs, tomatoes, and other abuse. His car was nearly overturned before police moved in to protect the U.S. diplomat. Despite this negative encounter, Christopher's professionalism was highly respected in the ROC government. Vice Foreign Minister C.J. Chen said, "There indeed were some unpleasant experiences for him fourteen years ago, but he is a rational and calm person. Bilateral relations would not change much with him in office."[3]

Continued Friendly Ties

The ROC reaction to the election of Clinton was cautiously optimistic, since the new president had signalled on several occasions his recognition of the importance of Taiwan to U.S. interests. During the campaign, Clinton approved of President Bush's decision to sell F-16s to Taiwan and promised to implement the decision if elected. Clinton also voiced support for the U.S. commitment to help Taiwan defend itself under the TRA. Clinton's campaign promises to take strong action against the PRC for its human rights abuses and missile proliferation contributed to the perception in Taiwan that ties with the United States might improve somewhat under the new president.

The most important reason the ROC expected continuity in U.S. policy was a continuation of U.S. interests in maintaining a balanced relationship with both Taipei and Beijing. Nothing had changed in the international or domestic environment to alter that fundamental U.S. policy, which had been in place since the early 1970s. This was affirmed by Ambassador Winston Lord in his confirmation hearing as assistant secretary of state for East Asia and the Pacific. In his overview of U.S. policy toward China, Lord said the Clinton administration:

- "will continue to be guided by the three Sino-American communiques that have provided a flexible framework for our relations."
- "It is up to China and Taiwan to work out their future relationship; we insist only that the process be peaceful."
- "Consistent with our undertakings not to challenge the principle of `one China,' we will continue to build upon our unofficial relations with Taiwan based on the Taiwan Relations Act."[4]

These principles were identical to those of the Reagan and Bush administrations from late 1982 through 1992 under which Washington-Taipei relations quietly prospered. They reflected U.S. recognition that there were good reasons to improve relations with Taiwan but that the United States had extremely important interests in China. This necessitated a balanced policy toward both Taipei and Beijing. The Clinton administration sought to maintain this balance, but developments in Taiwan, China, and the United States made it more difficult for Washington to sustain such a policy.

Public Statements

President Clinton spoke favorably of Taiwan on several occasions during the first year of his administration. In his Waseda University speech in Tokyo in July 1993, for example, Clinton referred to Taiwan as an example of the forces of market democracy at work in Asia: "The experience of the Philippines, Taiwan, Korea, and others prove that the move toward more open economies also feeds people's hunger for democracy and freedom and more open political systems." During the same speech Clinton said that Taipei, along with Seoul, Bangkok, and Shanghai, were "providing consumer goods and services to people who could not have even dreamed of them just a generation ago." He spoke favorably of Taiwan's trade practices, which he contrasted with those of Japan, noting that Taiwan "moved closer to trade balance with the U.S. as [it became] more prosperous."[5]

These positive themes were reiterated by Ambassador Natale H. Bellocchi, chairman of the American Institute in Taiwan (AIT), in several of his speeches under the new administration. In Boston in June 1993, Bellocchi described how the United States saw the profound changes taking place on Taiwan.[6] Suggesting that Clinton might broaden U.S. support for Taiwan's participation in international organizations, Bellocchi said:

> As the world's 14th largest trader, Taiwan has become an important element in the international economic community. It is a major producer of both hi-tech and consumer goods; and an important source of capital. In some form, it is in everyone's interest that Taiwan should not only follow but also where appropriate, participate in establishing trade and other standards. Taiwan is a member of APEC and the GATT accession process has begun, both of which are positive developments. It is still barred from most international economic and scientific organizations and agreements. International organizations in finance, in trade, in environment, in transnational issues such as narcotics, police, terrorism, etc., in humanitarian efforts, and in regulatory bodies, all could benefit from Taiwan's involvement.

But Bellocchi also signalled the new administration's sensitivity to the Taiwan issue in Sino-American relations: "in dealing with international organizations the form of [Taiwan's] involvement becomes a multilateral matter, not a bilateral one and thus it becomes much more complex."

Bellocchi cited several areas in which "the U.S.-Taiwan relationship has significantly expanded" while Taiwan has strengthened its economy and democratized its political system:

- AIT and the Coordination Council for North American Affairs (CCNAA) sign some twenty agreements each year.
- In representing U.S. interests in Taiwan, AIT must deal with almost every department in the U.S. government.
- AIT Taipei has the world's third largest workload on non-immigration visas.
- Some 35,000 students from Taiwan are studying in the United States, one of the largest foreign student populations in the world.
- A very large number of political leaders, leading businessmen, and academics on Taiwan have advanced degrees from the United States.
- Some forty science and technology agreements have been signed with Taiwan.
- A number of Taiwan firms are making direct investments in U.S. firms, and there is a rapidly growing number of high-tech joint ventures in locations such as Silicon Valley in California.
- In 1992 U.S. companies won over one billion dollars in major contracts in Taiwan.

- Taiwan continues to be one of the world's largest buyers of U.S. Treasury Certificates.

Because of these and other close ties, Bellocchi said, "The U.S. relationship remains Taiwan's most important while increasing its importance to us."

The AIT chairman also discussed recent changes in Taiwan and noted their impact on U.S.-Taiwan relations in a speech before the U.S.-ROC Economic Council in September 1993.[7] Bellocchi again emphasized the constructive role Taiwan could play in the international economic system and the positive example Taiwan provided to other developing market democracies. Once again suggesting that the United States might support a larger international economic role for Taiwan, he said, "The U.S. will increasingly expect Taiwan to assume its share of the responsibilities in supporting resolution of transnational problems that advanced economies around the world are [facing]." Noting that Taiwan's political model furthers several U.S. global and regional interests, Bellocchi observed:

> Taiwan's progress in reforming political institutions and creating an atmosphere in which democracy can prosper, can be a factor in the spread of democracy. Fundamental in Taiwan's concept of development, and one which is fundamental to any aspiring democracy, has been the ability to bring about change while maintaining stability. While each country has its own unique set of conditions, culture, and history, Taiwan can show that democracy is flexible enough to fashion a system that is both free and productive regardless of the circumstances.
>
> Accordingly, in our mutual interest, American will encourage continued policies [on Taiwan] that lower tension in the area, and that demonstrate the benefits of the open economic and political systems to other countries in the area.

Trade and Arms Sales

In addition to positive statements from the Clinton administration, trade and arms sales were measurable indicators of continued close U.S. ties with Taiwan.

In 1993 Taiwan was the sixth largest trading partner of the United States. U.S. imports from Taiwan totalled $23.5 billion and exports to the ROC were $16.7 billion. Taiwan's trade surplus of $6.8 billion ($8.85 billion by U.S. calculations) was the lowest in a decade, reflecting the efforts of both Washington and Taipei to lower the U.S. trade deficit to more acceptable levels. In 1993 the U.S. share of Taiwan's total exports was 28 percent, while the U.S. share of Taiwan's total imports was around 22 percent. The principal U.S. exports to Taiwan were transportation equipment, electronic parts, chemicals, machinery, corn, soybeans, and basic metals. Taiwan's principal exports to the United States included electronic parts, machinery, information/communications equipment, garments, transportation equipment, toys/sporting goods, and footwear.

The potential for expansion of U.S. trade and investment with Taiwan is large. In 1992, for example, one-third of the increase in global exports to the Pacific Rim were to Taiwan. It represented the largest market in the world for infrastructure work and equipment. As AIT explained in its March 1994 report on Taiwan's economy, one of the most important future U.S. interests in Asia is commercial ties with Taiwan:

> Taiwan is fast emerging as a high consumption economy. With per capita income in excess of $10,000 there is disposal income available for the purchase of consumer goods and services unimagined a decade ago. This is a new market, in which brand loyalties for the most part are not yet strongly established.
>
> Accordingly, U.S. firms may have a good opportunity to increase their presence, before competitors become entrenched, since in many cases mass market imported consumer goods have only just arrived and have allure their Taiwan based competitors do not.
>
> Apart from consumer goods, Taiwan's very rapid transition from a producer of simple, labor-intensive goods to a producer of more sophisticated capital- and technology-intensive goods has created a market for industrial equipment and industrial and business technology. There may also be a better opportunity to explore joint ventures with Taiwan businesses to tap the rich East Asian market, especially in mainland China.

The 1994 AIT report listed the following areas as providing excellent commercial opportunities for American businessmen: food and beverages; integrated circuits; electronic laboratory instruments; customer premise equipment, such as cellular phones; public ACE services, such as infrastructure engineering assistance; skin care and makeup; refrigeration equipment; insurance services; pollution control equipment; aircraft and parts; automobiles and light trucks/vans; computers and peripherals; travel and tourism services; education and training; computer software; electronics industry production/test equipment; building products; chemical production machinery; electric power systems; and industrial process control systems.

Since economic expansion in the Asian Pacific was viewed by the Clinton administration as vital to future U.S. economic growth, Taiwan's potential as a trading and investment partner was a powerful inducement for continued friendly U.S. relations with Taiwan.

Another measurable indicator of Clinton's intention to maintain friendly relations with Taiwan was the level of arms sold to Taipei during the first year of the new administration. In addition to promising to implement President Bush's decision to sell F-16s to Taiwan, Clinton authorized several new arms transfers.

In March 1993, for example, it was announced that Taiwan and Raytheon Company, manufacturer of the Patriot missile system, were negotiating the coproduction of the hardware and software for a Patriot derivative known as the Modified Air Defense Systems (MADS). MADS would replace Taiwan's existing air defense system, based on the Nike, now considered incapable of protecting the island against air attacks from China.[8] In April 1994 the ROC Army announced that it would purchase 200 of the Patriot missiles at a cost of about $377 million.[9]

In September 1993 the United States agreed to sell Taiwan forty-one Harpoon antiship missiles for $68 million. The Harpoon had been sought by Taiwan for almost as long as the F-16. The agreement included training and was considered the most significant U.S. arms sale since the F-16 transaction announced in September 1992.[10]

In October 1993 it was reported that the United States would sell Taiwan the Stinger ground-to-air missile, used so effectively in countering Soviet aircraft in Afghanistan. At U.S. insistence, the Stingers would be installed on military vehicles and not carried by individual soldiers to keep the missiles out of the hands of terrorists.[11]

Bill Clinton's promises to adhere to the Taiwan Relations Act, his praise of Taiwan's democratization and trade liberalization policies, the level of trade and investment between the two countries, and the continued sale of modern weapons to Taiwan reflected the new administration's determination to maintain friendly U.S. relations with Taiwan. There were, however, some problem areas in the U.S.-Taiwan relationship which should also be noted.

Problem Areas

Trade Sanctions

The most serious issue centered on trade, especially Taiwan's violations of U.S. copyrights. AIT Chairman Bellocchi said in March 1993 that the Clinton administration would include Taiwan on a list subject to Section 301 U.S. Omnibus Trade Act sanctions if Taipei did not take concrete action in resolving its copyright violations. Bellocchi also said the United States would continue to support Taiwan's entrance into GATT, but that Washington would focus on four areas of needed improvement in regards to that membership: intellectual property rights (IPR), agricultural subsidies, transparency of government procurement, and regulation of telecommunications.[12]

Little progress was made in negotiations over the next few months, so in May 1993 the Clinton administration placed Taiwan, along with Hungary, on a "priority watch list" for IPR violations. U.S. Trade Representative Mickey Kantor said, "We have given Taiwan and Hungary very special action plans, and expect them to meet the plans by the end of July....Taiwan needs to enact legislation to legitimize cable TV systems, control copyright piracy by cable TV stations in Taiwan and eliminate piracy of videogames." Kantor added, "We have presented Taiwan with an immediate action plan to address problems in the level of protection for IPR and market access for U.S. audio-visual products." At the same time, Kantor praised Taiwan for clamping down on IPR violators, approving a strict bilateral copyright agreement, and banning unauthorized parallel imports of copyrighted works.[13] Taiwan responded to the increased pressure, and by August 1993 the United States declared its satisfaction with Taipei's efforts to end industrial piracy.[14]

In December 1993 the Clinton administration presented the ROC with a list of 2,800 import items on which Washington wanted Taipei to reduce tariffs or make duty-free in order to advance Taiwan's GATT application process in Geneva. During the same period, the ROC legislature approved amendments to Taiwan's Trademark Law strengthening IPR protection for U.S. products as a means of avoiding possible future trade sanctions under Section 301 and to move Taiwan's regulations closer into alignment with GATT requirements. Another area of trade contention in 1993-1994 was U.S. sanctions placed on Taiwan for trade in endangered species such as tigers and rhinoceroses.[15]

Challenge to "One China" Principle

In addition to trade controversies, some in Washington were concerned that Taiwan's democratization might eventually pose a problem for U.S. policy. Taiwan was no longer a Nationalist Chinese bastion for the recovery of the mainland (a goal sometimes ridiculed in the United States but one which fit perfectly with the U.S. "one China" policy). Since the late 1980s, the political fate of Taiwan rested ever more firmly in the hands of the Taiwanese people. Since virtually no one on Taiwan wanted to unify with the mainland as long as it was controlled by the communists and a large portion of Taiwanese apparently wanted national independence instead of any form of unification with China, a fundamental contradiction arose in U.S. China policy. For decades the United States had supported democracy for the Chinese people (including those on Taiwan), while acknowledging since the early 1970s the Chinese position on both sides of the Taiwan Strait that there was only one China with Taiwan being considered part of China. By 1994, however, there existed the possibility of a democratically elected government on Taiwan abandoning the ROC's traditional "one China" policy and pursuing either "two Chinas" or Taiwan independence.

There was, in other words, growing evidence that maintaining the deliberate ambiguity in U.S. policy over Taiwan's sovereignty and international legal status might not be possible for much longer. This would require hard policy choices which no administration wanted to face, particularly the Clinton administration with its emphasis on human rights and democracy, on the one hand, but clear desire for cooperative relations with the PRC, on the other. Setting aside Beijing's human rights record to preserve Sino-American trade benefits through MFN was one thing; to ignore PRC pressure on the people of Taiwan as they pursued national self-determination would be quite a different policy problem.

The emerging U.S. difficulty in maintaining a balanced China-Taiwan policy was summarized in a *New York Times* guest editorial in November 1993:

> Americans who still think of Taiwan as "Nationalist China" are in for a shock. The most conspicuous nationalism to be encountered on the island these days is not Chinese but Taiwanese....
>
> There's a real chance...that a pro-independence government could take power in Taipei this decade. If saner heads prevail on both sides, this needn't necessarily lead to crisis. But because Beijing openly threatens to

greet any move toward Taiwan independence with military force, the issue could bring on a large-scale regional confrontation....

The sensible course is to begin diplomatic efforts now to preempt any future military confrontation. That involves working out broadly acceptable formulas to reinforce Taiwan's present political and economic autonomy and to include Taiwan in the regional economic and security organizations now taking shape.

For Washington, it always seems to be the wrong moment to raise new contentions into an already troubled relationship with Beijing. But waiting for the right moment poses even more serious risks.[16]

From a more immediate, pragmatic perspective, AIT Chairman Bellocchi noted in his June 1993 Boston speech that many of the changes underway on Taiwan presented new challenges to the United States. He cited as examples:

- The growing diversification of Taiwan's markets means a much more competitive atmosphere for American businessmen.
- Taiwan's eventual entry into the GATT means that the barriers to Japanese imports into Taiwan will be removed, presenting greater competition to American products.
- Large numbers of European businessmen are being attracted to the Six-Year National Development Plan, making competition for U.S. contractors very intense.
- More openness in society and democratization means that contracts and other business dealings involving Americans are coming under closer scrutiny and becoming more complex.
- Democratization on Taiwan has resulted in a far more complex U.S.-Taiwan relationship, since the United States must deal with a much more diversified political entity.
- Interest groups are proliferating on Taiwan, power is being redistributed to the national legislature and local governments, information is more readily available -- all this makes the task of representing American interests in Taiwan more challenging and difficult.
- Taiwan's government policies and decisions, including those involving the United States, are more often challenged and open to public scrutiny.[17]

Thus, despite U.S. approval and even encouragement of most developments on Taiwan, many aspects of the "new" Taiwan brought to the surface difficult questions for the Clinton administration. For instance,

1. Should the United States do more to assist in the peaceful reunification of China?
2. How would the United States respond to a plebiscite on Taiwan calling for the island's independence?
3. To what extent should the United States assist Taiwan to broaden its participation in international affairs?
4. How would the United States respond if the PRC acted with force to prevent Taiwan's independence?

What occurred in the 1992-1993 period was greater recognition that the United States faced a major policy dilemma in regards to Taiwan. Developments on Taiwan necessitated some adjustment in U.S. policy in the direction of greater support of Taipei, but such adjustments would likely come at a cost in damaged relations with the PRC, in which the United States also had very important interests. How to maintain that cost-benefit balance, and thereby to serve U.S. interests in both Chinas, was a growing problem for the Clinton administration.

Sensitivity of Taiwan Issue

Despite changes on Taiwan which made some adjustment in U.S. policy necessary, the Clinton administration made it clear that it did not intend to allow improved U.S. relations with Taiwan to undermine U.S. relations with the PRC. There were several indications of this.

For example, the Clinton administration would not allow President Lee Teng-hui to attend a meeting of Asian-Pacific heads of state in November 1993. President Clinton had proposed a one-day summit meeting of APEC leaders following the November 17-19 APEC foreign ministers meeting in Seattle. Despite the fact that Taiwan was admitted as a full and equal member to APEC in 1991 under the designation "Chinese Taipei," the PRC insisted that Taiwan's president or prime minister could not be invited because they represented only a local government, not a country. After intense negotiation between Washington, Beijing, and Taipei, it was agreed that President Lee Teng-hui would decline President Clinton's invitation to attend the summit and instead send as his personal representative Vincent Siew, head of the ROC Council for Economic Planning and Development.[18]

The U.S. decision was proof that the Clinton administration would not upgrade the officiality of its relations with Taiwan beyond very limited levels, despite U.S. support for Taipei's participation in APEC and despite strained relations with the PRC. The United States would continue to apply a careful calculus weighing the effects of its policies toward Taiwan on U.S. relations with China. The care exercised by Clinton on this issue could be seen in his press remarks following his meeting in Seattle with PRC President Jiang Zemin on November 19, 1993. Clinton emphasized, "In our meeting I reaffirmed the United States support for the three joint communiques as the bedrock of our one China policy." In responding to a question as to whether the Taiwan issue was raised in his talks with Jiang, Clinton said:

> I have been there [Taiwan] many times. I've been there five times, actually. And I have been very impressed with the remarkable transformation of the country as it has gotten more prosperous and more democratic, and impressed also by the amount of investment from Taiwan into China. So it seems that the two countries are getting along on a commercial basis, even as the rest of us are confronted with political dilemmas from time to time.
> We did not really discuss [the Taiwan issue] today in any detail whatever. The policy of the United States on one China is the right policy for the United States. It does not preclude us from following the Taiwan Relations Act, nor does it preclude us from the strong economic relationship we enjoy with Taiwan. There's a representative [from Taiwan] here at this meeting. So I feel good about where we are on that. But I don't think that will be a major stumbling block in our relationship with China. I think we can work through these other things that the practical ingenuity of the Chinese people themselves seems to be at least on a course to resolve...in some form or fashion in the years ahead.[19]

U.S. sensitivity on the issue of "one China" was also apparent in the State Department's refusal in May 1994 to allow President Lee Teng-hui to stay overnight in Los Angeles en route to a state visit to Latin America. Instead, Lee was allowed a ninety-minute refueling stop in Honolulu where he was greeted on board his plane by AIT Chairman Bellocchi. The treatment of President Lee prompted several Members of Congress to criticize Secretary of State Christopher and to invite the ROC president to visit their own states.[20] The U.S. action was in sharp contrast to the willingness of several Southeast Asian leaders to meet socially with Lee during his "vacation" to the Philippines, Indonesia, and Thailand in February 1994. The Southeast Asian nations shrugged off PRC protests in the interests of promoting closer economic ties with Taiwan.[21] ROC Premier Lien Chan received a similar warm welcome in Malaysia and Singapore in December 1993-January 1994.[22]

The administration's efforts to walk a fine line between improving ties with Taiwan yet not undermining Sino-American relations was also reflected in its maneuvering to stop congressional legislation amending the Taiwan Relations Act in ways favorable to Taiwan.

Murkowski Amendment to TRA

On July 15, 1993, the Senate Foreign Relations Committee adopted by a vote of 20-0 the following amendment to the 1979 Taiwan Relations Act (TRA) introduced by Senator Frank H. Murkowski of Alaska:

Section 3 of the Taiwan Relations Act (22 U.S.C. 3301) is amended by adding at the end the following:
"(d) The provisions of Subsection (a) and (b) of this section shall supersede any provision of the August 17, 1982, Joint United States-China Communique related to these matters; and regulations, directives, and policies based thereon."[23]

The subsections of the TRA referred to in the Murkowski amendment were as follows:

SEC.3.(a)...the United States will make available to Taiwan such defense articles and defense services in such quantity as may be necessary to enable Taiwan to maintain a sufficient self-defense capability.
(b) The President and the Congress shall determine the nature and quantity of such defense articles and services based solely upon their judgment of the needs of Taiwan....

In an apparent contradiction to the Taiwan Relations Act, the Reagan administration signed a joint communique with the PRC on August 17, 1982, which stated in paragraph six:

[The] United States Government states that it does not seek to carry out a long-term policy of arms sales to Taiwan, that its arms sales to Taiwan will not exceed, either in qualitative or in quantitative terms, the level of those supplied in recent years since the establishment of diplomatic relations between the United States and China, and that it intends to reduce gradually its sales of arms to Taiwan, leading over a period of time to a final resolution....

In explaining the August 17 communique to Congress, officials in the Reagan administration emphasized that the U.S. promise to reduce arms sales to Taiwan was conditioned on a continuation of Beijing's policy of striving for a peaceful solution to the Taiwan issue.[24] The administration also said the TRA took legal precedence over the communique. A State Department legal advisor told Congress:

> [The communique] is not an international agreement and thus imposes no obligations on either party under international law. Its status under domestic law is that of a statement by the President of a policy which he intends to pursue....The Taiwan Relations Act is and will remain the law of the land unless amended by Congress. Nothing in the joint communique obligates the President to act in a manner contrary to the Act or, conversely, disables him from fulfilling his responsibilities under it.[25]

Despite administration assurances that Taiwan's security would not be adversely affected by the August 17 communique, the implementation of U.S. arms sales policy under the communique may have had that unintended effect. The quantitative and qualitative restrictions contained in the communique resulted in the creation of a "Taiwan bucket" for U.S. arms sales, which were reduced about $20 million a year from a 1982 high of $820 million to a level of about $580 million in 1993.

Although ways were found to circumvent much of the communique's restrictions -- such as the sale of U.S. defense technology to enable Taiwan to manufacture its own advanced weapons -- by the late 1980s the "Taiwan bucket" had begun to shrink to dangerously low levels. Also, Taiwan simply could not manufacture some of the equipment needed for its defense, such as modern air defense fighters. The problem became more apparent after the collapse of the Soviet Union, when Moscow began to offer advanced Soviet weapons systems to the PRC.

The Murkowski amendment was intended to do away with the "Taiwan bucket" altogether by explicitly stating the legal precedence of the TRA over the August 17 communique. The TRA specified that U.S. sales of defense equipment would be governed by Taiwan's security requirements, whereas the communique mandated a gradual reduction of arms sales to Taiwan, regardless of the PRC's military capabilities to use force against the ROC.

The Senate concurred with its Foreign Relations Committee and included Murkowski's amendment in its version of the FY 1994-1995 State Department Authorization Bill. No such provision was contained in the House version of the bill, however. When the Senate and House met in conference in April 1994 to work out differences in their respective versions, a non-binding sense of Congress substitute for the Murkowski amendment was adopted, which stated:

SEC. 531. TAIWAN

In view of the self-defense needs of Taiwan, the Congress makes the following declarations:

(1) Sections 2 and 3 of the Taiwan Relations Act are reaffirmed.

(2) Section 3 of the Taiwan Relations Act take primacy over statements of United States policy, including communiques, regulations, directives, and policies based thereon.

(3) In assessing the extent to which the People's Republic of China is pursuing its "fundamental policy" to strive peacefully to resolve the Taiwan issue, the United States should take into account both the capabilities and intentions of the People's Republic of China.

(4) The President should on a regular basis assess changes in the capabilities and intentions of the People's Republic of China and consider whether it is appropriate to adjust arms sales to Taiwan accordingly.

In the conference report on the revised bill (such reports are widely used by Congress to convey its intention in writing legislation), the conferees stated:

With this provision [Sec. 531], the committee of conference expresses its continued concern for the security of Taiwan. It reaffirms the commitments made in the Taiwan Relations Act (TRA) to enable Taiwan to maintain a sufficient self-defense capability. Among the policy statements over which Sections 3(b) of the TRA takes precedence is the communique concluded between the United States and the People's Republic of China on August 17, 1982.

The congressional statement reflects concern on the part of the committee of conference over the effect of stability in the Asia-Pacific region of China's military modernization, its increased military spending, and its territorial claims. If the President, in consultation with the Congress as provided in Section 3(b) of the TRA, finds that PRC capabilities and intentions have increased the threat to Taiwan, then a compensating adjustment in the transfer of defense articles and services to Taiwan should be seriously considered. Pursuant to the TRA, U.S. policy on arms sales to Taiwan should be based on Taiwan's defense needs and be formulated jointly by the Congress and the President.

The Taiwan Relations Act is explicit that the nature and quantity of defensive articles and defensive services to be transferred to Taiwan shall be based solely upon the judgment of the President and Congress of the needs of Taiwan, in accordance with procedures established by law. Consequently, the transfer of particular defense articles and services -- such as advanced ballistic missile defense systems and conventionally powered coastal patrol submarines -- should be based on Taiwan's needs and not on arbitrary principles, such as prohibiting the incorporation of U.S. equipment on defensive platforms produced by other nations or the exclusion of entire classes of defensive weapons. The committee of conference calls on the Executive Branch to streamline and rationalize the procedures for implementation of U.S. policy concerning arms sales to Taiwan.

The conference bill, H.R. 2333, was passed by both Houses of Congress in late April 1994 and signed into law by President Clinton on April 30, 1994. In addition to the arms sales provision, the new law (P.L. 103-236) contained language urging high-level U.S. official visits to Taiwan and U.S. support for Taiwan in multilateral organizations.

As might be expected, Taiwan's reaction to passage of the bill was positive. The ROC Foreign Ministry said the president's signing of the bill "lay a good foundation for further substantive relations" between the two countries. The ministry said the law not only conformed to the principles of the Taiwan Relations Act but also reflected U.S. concern for the interests of the two countries.[26]

The reaction of the administration to the Murkowski amendment was illustrative of U.S. policy toward Taiwan under Clinton. From the outset the White House, but particularly the State Department, tried to block the amendment. State Department officials warned the Senate Foreign Relations Committee that the amendment would set U.S.-China relations back twenty years. One official said the August 17 communique was a "cover [for arms sales to Taiwan], so as not to provoke China's wrath....We're afraid to change this."[27]

The administration did not want to change the ground rules for handling the Taiwan issue in Sino-American relations. It feared jeopardizing the delicate balance between the three communiques governing U.S. diplomatic relations with China and the Taiwan Relations Act governing unofficial ties with Taiwan. The State Department preferred flexibility and ambiguity in U.S. policy rather than clear precedence of the TRA being established over the communiques.

The State Department's opposition to the Murkowski amendment centered around the use of the word "supersede," which the department chose to interpret as meaning that the Sino-American communiques would become null and void, thus destroying the foundation of U.S.-PRC relations. Acting Secretary of State Strobe Talbott wrote a March 8,

1994, letter to Senator Claiborne Pell, Chairman of the Senate Foreign Relations Committee, urging that the Congress delete the amendment during the Senate-House conference on H.R. 2333. Described as an issue of concern on which change was "essential to the Administration's ability to support the final bill," Talbott wrote: "In particular, section 706 of the Senate bill [the Murkowski amendment], regarding the Taiwan Relations Act, would seriously undermine the foundation of the peace and stability we have helped create in the Taiwan Strait over the last fourteen years. It is critical to the Administration that the conference committee adopt a conference report that does not include this section."

After considerable negotiation to find an appropriate compromise, the Senate and the White House National Security Council agreed on new wording that would assert the "primacy" of the TRA over the communiques. At first, the State Department resisted even this non-binding language, arguing that it needed flexibility in its China diplomacy, that U.S. China policy had worked to date and should not be changed, and that Taiwan had been treated quite well even with the communiques in place. Under intense pressure from Congress, the State Department finally agreed to the revised amendment and promised to send a private letter to Congress clarifying the U.S. position on the TRA and the communiques.

When the final version of the amendment was passed and signed into law by President Clinton, the administration said the non-binding language in the conference report would not change U.S. policy toward Taiwan or China.[28] Nonetheless, to assuage congressional concerns over Taiwan's security, Secretary of State Warren Christopher reaffirmed the TRA's legal precedence over the August 17 communique in a private letter to Senator Murkowski. His letter also promised to streamline the process of approving arms sales to Taiwan.[29] The fact that Clinton signed the bill into law demonstrated his commitment to Taiwan's security. At the same time, administration statements that the law would not change U.S. policy suggested the president's determination to adhere to a "one China" policy and to seek cooperative relations with the PRC on a priority basis.

One immediate effect of Clinton's signing of the bill was the sale of advanced U.S. naval electronic equipment to Taiwan for six new LaFayette frigates purchased from France. The equipment included radar, electronic countermeasures, and an entire electronic combat suite. Thus, as has often been the case in U.S.-Taiwan relations, actions by the Congress strengthened the relationship over the objections of the administration. The passage of H.R. 2333 may open wider the door for future U.S. arms sales to Taiwan.

Congressional Hearing on Taiwan and the U.N.

On July 15, 1994, two subcommittees of the U.S. House of Representatives held a joint hearing to consider Taiwan's participation in the United Nations.[30] The Subcommittee on International Security, International Organizations and Human Rights and the Subcommittee on Asia and the Pacific of the House Foreign Affairs Committee heard testimony generally in favor of Taiwan joining the U.N., although few thought the veto power of the PRC could be overcome in the near future. Testimony focused on the legitimate right of the Republic of China to be a member of the international community rather than an assessment of the probability of it being accepted.

Significantly, ten members of the two subcommittees spoke in favor of Taiwan's increased role in international affairs and membership in the U.N. Representative Tom Lantos (D-Calif.), chairman of the subcommittee on international security and organizations, said: "Taiwan's exclusion [from the U.N.] cannot be justified in terms of international law as Taiwan more than meets the traditional criteria of statehood. Nor would granting Taiwan U.N. representation in any way prejudice the resolution of Taiwan's ultimate status....The two Germanys reunited, although both had seats in the U.N., and so could mainland China and Taiwan at some future date, if that were the wish of both nations."

Representative Gary L. Ackerman (D-N.Y.), chairman of the subcommittee on Asia and the Pacific, said Taiwan's future was inextricably linked to U.S. interests in Asia and that Taiwan could play an important role in the U.N. He commented, "we must face reality. And that reality is that Taiwan is an economic goliath and the interrelationship and interdependency between the community of nations and Taiwan will only grow more important as time goes on."

The subcommittees were considering two House resolutions on the issue. One, offered by Representative Gerald Solomon (R-N.Y.), called for a seat in the United Nations for the Republic of China on Taiwan, while the other, offered by Representative Robert Torricelli (D-N.J.), called for Taiwan's representation at the U.N. but not specifically for a seat in the international organization. At the time of the hearing, Torricelli's resolution had sixty-five cosponsors in the House. The bills were indicative of a trend in the Congress toward more vocal and active support for Taiwan. This trend, while resisted by the administration, could not be ignored. Congressional pressure and other growing support for Taiwan in the media and among the general public eventually found its way into Clinton's Taiwan policy.

Taiwan Policy Review

In July 1994 the Clinton administration concluded a year-long interagency review of U.S. policy toward Taiwan. The review was one of several initiated by the president to examine various aspects of American foreign policy. When the Taiwan policy review was first undertaken, it was seen as low priority and a pro forma exercise. State Department officials expected the review to conclude that no change was necessary. It became apparent by mid-1994, however, that some adjustment in U.S. policy was necessary due to several unanticipated factors: growing congressional pressure for better treatment of Taiwan, strong public approval of Taiwan's democratization, business demands to make it easier to deal with Taiwan, and widespread concern that Clinton was leaning too much in Beijing's favor -- despite continued human rights violations, missile sales, and the PLA's modernization -- while ignoring Taiwan's rapid progress toward becoming a market democracy.

The *Los Angeles Times* reported in July 1994 that the review was being considered by President Clinton. The draft review recommended that the United States not alter its "one China" policy and not change its views on Taiwan's sovereignty.[31] Nonetheless, certain adjustments in the conduct of U.S. relations with Taiwan could be made to enable the United States to deal more effectively with Taipei. The proposed changes included:

1. Some American cabinet-level officials would be permitted to visit Taiwan, and some ROC cabinet-level officials would be permitted to visit the United States.
2. Taiwan officials would be permitted to meet with their American counterparts in U.S. government buildings.
3. Taiwan would be allowed to call its offices in the United States something like "Taipei Representative Office" instead of the nondescript "Coordination Council for North American Affairs."[32]

The final results of the policy review were announced in a background briefing to reporters by a senior State Department official on September 7, 1994.[33] The official said President Clinton had authorized certain "refinements" to better serve America's increasingly extensive and complicated interests in Taiwan while preserving the U.S. "one China" policy and unofficial relations with Taiwan. "There is only one China," he reiterated, "and Taiwan is a part of China." He said U.S. policy toward China and Taiwan was a delicate balancing act, designed to help maintain stability in Asia.

To allow more effective meetings between U.S. and Taiwan officials, "We...are willing to establish under the AIT auspices, a sub-cabinet economic dialogue with Taiwan. We will permit high-level U.S. government officials of economic and technical agencies to visit Taiwan....All such meetings and visits will be focused sharply on solving practical problems and doing business. They carry with them no implication that we consider the relationship to be official and should not be interpreted by anyone as being so." He explained that top-level U.S. officials having no economic, commercial, or technical portfolio will not be allowed to visit Taiwan. Similarly, Taiwan's top leadership -- including the president and vice president -- will not be issued permits to visit the United States. They will be allowed, however, "to transit the United States when necessary." Exchange visits by cabinet-level officials with economic, commercial, or technical portfolios will be considered on a case-by-case basis. "We don't rule anything out," he said.

The U.S. official explained further that senior Taiwan officials will be able to meet with undersecretary-level U.S. officials in the State and Defense departments in unofficial settings, while high-level economic and trade officials from Taiwan will be able to meet with the leadership of U.S. economic, commercial, and technical agencies in official settings.

He said the U.S. government acknowledges that Taiwan has a legitimate role to play in international organizations such as APEC and GATT and that it was in the general interests of the world community that Taiwan's voice be heard in some additional international organizations. However, he emphasized, the United States does not support Taiwan's entry into the United Nations.

The U.S. official said Taiwan could change the name of its representative office in the United States from "Coordination Council for North American Affairs" to the "Taipei Economic and Cultural Representative Office in the United States." He said the United States would continue to provide material and training for Taiwan's self-defense as mandated by the Taiwan Relations Act, while adhering to the August 17, 1982, Sino-American communique.

Congressional reaction to Clinton's new Taiwan policy was critical because of the policy's cosmetic nature. Senator Paul Simon called the policy adjustments "slight improvements" and "official pettiness," saying, "We continue to give Taiwan the cold shoulder....Taiwan has a multiparty system, free elections, and a free press -- the things we profess to champion -- while we continue to cuddle up to the mainland government, whose dictatorship permits none of these." Senator Hank Brown said the administration's policy treats "one of our closest democratic allies in the Pacific worse that we treat North Korea, Cuba, or Libya....The policy does not even recognize Taiwan as a political entity....It is a tragic mistake to treat corrupt dictators better than democratic allies. The administration's so-called `policy change' is a slap in the face to Taiwan. This sends a terrible message to emerging democracies around the world." Representative Robert Torricelli said the new policy was "an attempt to have things both ways. We ignore the significant movement toward democracy in Taiwan, while we seek its trade and, having retreated from the idea of using trade preferences to influence China's behavior, we now shrink from the possibility that better treatment of Taiwan could exert pressure for better behavior from China." Senator Frank Murkowski welcomed the change as "a good first step" but said, "the administration should have taken bolder and more substantive steps to recognize the more mature relationships between the U.S. and Taiwan. The people and the government of Taiwan should be rewarded for their tremendous strides toward building a free and prosperous country."[34]

Taipei's reaction to the shift in U.S. policy was ambivalent. ROC Foreign Minister Fredrick Chien said, "There's some progress, but basically speaking we are disappointed." Indirectly setting new markers for ROC-U.S. relations, Chien said his government wanted some sign from Washington that the United States regarded Taiwan as a political entity equal to other nations. Also, Taiwan was disappointed the Clinton administration would not allow the ROC president, vice president, premier, or vice premier to visit the United States. Further, Taipei was disappointed because the United States would not support Taiwan's bid to reenter the United Nations alongside China. Chien said, "I think it is unfair that Washington's representative can come to my ministry, but that our representatives cannot enter the State Department." He added, "We are dissatisfied that the changes could not add `Republic of China' to the name [of Taiwan's representative office in the United States.]" Foreign

Minister Chien was briefed in his office by AIT director in Taiwan Lynn Pascoe. Pascoe also called on Premier Lien Chan in the Executive Yuan and briefed President Lee Teng-hui. Pascoe's visits to these ROC government offices were the first for an AIT official and were meant to symbolize the new American policy.[35]

Beijing's reaction was bitter. The PRC Foreign Ministry said the measures "have seriously violated the three joint communiques signed between China and the United States....This act of the United States brazenly interferes with the internal affairs of China and is something we are firmly opposed to....This will seriously, adversely affect the future development of bilateral relations."[36]

The official New China News Agency (Xinhua) reported that Deputy Foreign Minister Liu Huaqiu handed an official protest to U.S. Ambassador to China J. Stapleton Roy. Calling Taiwan an "explosive issue," Liu told Roy that Washington should "correct its erroneous action on the question of Taiwan to spare our relationship from severe damage." Liu said the U.S. move was "a political move...to deliberately create `two Chinas' or `one China, one Taiwan'." The Chinese official repeated the threat that the PRC would not sit idle if Taiwan moved toward independence "with support from foreign forces" and turmoil broke out on the island as a result. Liu warned the U.S. ambassador: "If not handled properly, the question of Taiwan will become an explosive issue for China and the United States....In that case, the growth of our bilateral relations will not only be stalled, but also retrogress....We demand that the U.S. government approach the question of Taiwan with every seriousness and caution."[37]

At the same time that China issued these protests and warnings, Beijing re-extended its invitation to President Clinton to visit China at a time of his convenience. This signalled that Sino-American relations had not suffered irreparable damage due to the U.S. policy change toward Taiwan.

Beijing no doubt was concerned that the U.S. policy adjustment might be followed by similar adjustments in the relations of other countries with Taiwan. Two days after the new policy's announcement, Japan's Foreign Ministry said it would relax its ban on trips to Taiwan by cabinet ministers.[38] Tokyo's announcement was significant because the Japanese government had been under intense pressure from Beijing not to allow ROC President Lee Teng-hui to visit Japan during the Asian Games in October 1994, else risk serious political consequences. After Lee's invitation was withdrawn by the Olympic Council of Asia, Japan invited

Taiwan's Vice Premier Hsu Li-teh.   Beijing again reacted strongly, warning Japan,

> We again solemnly request the Japanese government...to reconsider the proposed visit of Hsu Li-teh to Japan to prevent the impairment of the normal development of Sino-Japanese relations and the disruption of the Asian Games....The Chinese government cannot accept the Japanese government deciding to allow Hsu Li-teh and other important political figures from Taiwan to visit Japan....It does not matter what name Hsu Li-teh uses to visit Japan.   Such a visit has clear political motives and is an attempt and a political incident deliberately created by the Taiwanese authorities.   The Taiwan issue is a major issue in Sino-Japanese relations. The position of the Chinese government on that is clear and unshakable.[39]

Thus, the adjustments in U.S. policy toward Taiwan under President Clinton were minor in substance but symbolically important.   Most importantly, they were not intended to upset the balanced nature of U.S. relations with both China and Taiwan.   Rather, they were pragmatic acknowledgments of the significant political and economic progress Taiwan had made in recent years and, subsequently, of the increased importance of Taiwan to U.S. interests.   Having somewhat altered U.S. policy toward Taiwan for the first time in fifteen years, it remained to be seen whether future U.S. policy alternations would benefit or harm the Republic of China.

Disturbing Precedents

Despite the slight nod in Taiwan's favor from the policy review, other adjustments in Taiwan policy might have placed the Clinton administration on a "slippery slope" that could have long-term negative impact on Taiwan. These adjustments included a possible willingness to discuss the F-16 sale with Beijing, possible U.S. support for a "unified" China, and possible acceptance (as opposed to acknowledgment) of Taiwan being part of China.

In January 1994 it was announced that the PRC would discuss with the United States a new understanding on China's adherence to the Missile Technology Control Regime (MTCR). Beijing's cooperation on this issue was an important strategic goal of the United States to further its global nonproliferation interests. In return for Beijing's willingness to discuss the MTCR guidelines, it was reported that the Clinton administration agreed to discuss the sale of F-16s to Taiwan, a sale approved by President Bush in 1992 and which Clinton promised to implement.[40]

Although U.S. officials said the talks would not give Beijing a veto over arms sales to Taiwan, such discussions could establish a dangerous precedent of consulting the PRC before deciding which weapons systems would be sold to Taiwan in the future. Such consultations had been a PRC objective since at least 1982. In January of that year the Reagan administration decided not to sell a new fighter to Taiwan, approving instead the extension of the existing F-5E coproduction program on Taiwan. Assistant Secretary of State John Holdridge was sent to the PRC to explain this decision, with the anticipation that the Chinese would be pleased and allow strategic cooperation with Washington against Moscow to proceed. Instead, the Chinese strongly criticized the U.S. decision to continue the production of F-5Es. In January 1982 the PRC Foreign Ministry lodged a strong protest against the extension, saying, "The Chinese Government will never accept any unilateral decision made by the U.S. Government" on arms sales to Taiwan. The PRC was insisting that it be notified in advance of future arms sales to Taiwan.[41]

Given Beijing's opposition to virtually all major U.S. weapons sales to Taiwan, for Washington to include the PRC in discussions over arms sales would further complicate the already labyrinthine process of deciding which U.S. arms and defense technologies to sell to Taipei. Over time, such consultation with the PRC could result in the degrading of Taiwan's defense capabilities.

Another dangerous precedent involved possible Clinton support for China's unification. According to press reports, as part of his efforts to "re-engage" China in September 1993, President Clinton sent a personal letter to President Jiang Zemin, along with a document clarifying U.S. intentions in Sino-American relations. The documents were said to mention a U.S. "commitment to a `unified' China."[42] Such a commitment would be a significant change in U.S. policy, which since 1987 had supported the *process* of peacefully resolving the Taiwan issue without backing a specific *outcome* of that process.[43] The difference between U.S. support for the process and outcome of Taiwan-mainland talks is important for the future of Taiwan because:

1. A consensus on Taiwan's future does not yet exist among the people of Taiwan themselves. Such a consensus may, or may not, support unification with the mainland.

2. Taipei has many motives in increasing contact with the mainland, not all of which are designed to achieve unification. The United States should not assume unification in the near future is the preferred choice of the Taiwan government.

3. For the United States to support reunification would weaken Taiwan's negotiating position with the mainland and thus may harm the interests of the Taiwanese people.

4. Beijing has not yet worked out the mechanisms for a successful integration of a capitalist economy with the mainland's socialist economy. The fate of Hong Kong after 1997 should first be observed before considering whether to encourage Taiwan to unify with the mainland.

5. The continuation of China's reform program and open policies after the death of Deng Xiaoping is not assured. The leadership succession in the PRC should first be observed before changes in U.S. policy toward reunification are considered.

6. Adequate studies have not been made on the impact of China's reunification on U.S. interests. Such analysis is especially important in the post-Cold War period as the PRC modernizes its armed forces and acquires power projection forces.

7. The status quo in the Taiwan Strait continues to serve U.S. interests admirably well. A change in U.S. China-Taiwan policy should be undertaken only with great caution.

Yet another disturbing precedent was the Clinton administration's possible *acceptance*, as opposed to *acknowledgment*, that Taiwan is part of China. The day after the results of the Taiwan policy review were announced on September 7, 1994, State Department spokesman Michael McCurry was asked whether the United States actually considers Taiwan part of China. He said: "Absolutely. That's been a consistent feature of our one-China policy, consistent with the three China communiques and the Taiwan Relations Act."[44]

Assuming that McCurry did not err, this is an admission of an important evolution of U.S. policy. In the past the United States merely "acknowledged" the Chinese position on both sides of the Taiwan Strait that there is only one China and Taiwan is part of China. In recent years, however, a larger portion of Taiwan's population and even some in the ROC government have questioned whether Taiwan is indeed part of China or some separate political entity.

The McCurry statement would seem to place the United States firmly on the side of Beijing (Taiwan is part of China) and against democratic trends on Taiwan supporting the concept of Taiwan being separate from

China. The previous U.S. position of "acknowledging" Taiwan as being part of China straddled this issue nicely, preserving U.S. flexibility as both Chinese sides evolved their relationship. There is no reason to abandon this time-honored formulation in favor of one so obviously supporting the PRC claim of sovereignty over Taiwan. By accepting Beijing's view that Taiwan is part of China, the Clinton administration moves very close to accepting Beijing's view that the Taiwan issue is strictly China's internal affair.

In sum, during the first two years of his administration, the policies of President Clinton toward Taiwan were very similar to those of Presidents Reagan and Bush. There were, however, changes underway in the United States, China, Taiwan, and the international system that were compelling a reexamination of those policies. These changes were reflected in the largely cosmetic "refinement" of U.S. policy toward Taiwan announced by the Clinton administration in September 1994. Whether U.S. policy will change significantly in the future and what the impact of those changes might be on Taiwan's security remain open to speculation at this point. But it is clear that the Taiwan issue is reemerging with a new urgency in ways that cannot be ignored by Washington policymakers.

Conclusion

Most ROC policy changes since 1986 have been in directions favorable to U.S. goals and interests in East Asia. Accordingly, the Clinton administration during its first two years in office worked to improve unofficial ties with Taiwan. This was demonstrated by favorable presidential comments about Taiwan, high level public commitments to honor the Taiwan Relations Act, cordial trade relations, expanding cultural and educational ties, support for Taiwan's policies toward mainland China, greater support for Taipei's participation in some international organizations, advanced arms sales, and a slight upgrading of relations as a result of the year-long Taiwan policy review. But there were clearly defined limits beyond which the new administration would not go in improving relations with Taiwan. These limits were, in essence, contained in the three joint Sino-American communiques of 1972, 1979, and 1982 which recognized the PRC government as the sole legal government of China and acknowledged the Chinese position on both sides of the Taiwan Strait that there is but one China and Taiwan is part of China.

Fundamentally, there was little difference between Clinton's policies toward Taiwan and those of his immediate predecessors. Clinton, Bush, Reagan, and Carter sought to optimize U.S. interests through a dual-track China policy of maintaining official relations with the PRC and unofficial relations with Taiwan. While Clinton and Bush felt it necessary to improve the quality of U.S.-Taiwan relations in the post-Cold War period, both presidents moved in that direction with great deliberation because of highly important U.S. interests in sustaining cooperative relations with Beijing. During Clinton's first term in office, these areas of cooperation included the need to stop proliferation of weapons of mass destruction and their advanced delivery systems, the containment of the North Korean nuclear weapons program, the avoidance of war on the Korean peninsula, and the proper management of rapidly expanding U.S.-PRC trade.

U.S. relations with Taiwan were important in their own right in the areas of the expansion of market democracies, protection of human rights, trade and investment, and symbols of the continued American commitment in Asia. Additionally, Clinton's friendly policies toward Taiwan served at least three long-range (but unstated) U.S. strategic goals in regards to China:

- to influence changes in the PRC in directions favorable to U.S. interests
- to support positive change in Taiwan both for its own merit and as a moderating influence on PRC behavior in East Asia
- to ensure that the PRC, if it did become hostile to the United States in the future, would not be a greater threat to U.S. interests in Asia.

To date, nothing in the domestic or international environment has changed sufficiently to justify a fundamental shift in the balanced, dual-track U.S. policy toward China and Taiwan. Despite the continuity, Washington, Beijing, and Taipei face increased pressure to adjust their policies in ways that could have an important impact on Taiwan's security in the 1990s. Congressional pressure in 1993-1994 to increase U.S. arms sales to Taiwan and to support the ROC's participation in the United Nations are but two examples. Other forces of change in Taiwan's security environment will be discussed in the next two chapters.

Notes

1. *China News*, December 2, 1992, p. 3.
2. *China News*, December 19, 1992, p. 3.
3. *China News*, December 24, 1992, p. 2.
4. Winston Lord, "A New Pacific Community: Ten Goals for American Policy," opening statement at confirmation hearings for Assistant Secretary of State, Bureau of East Asian and Pacific Affairs, Senate Foreign Relations Committee, March 31, 1993, ms.
5. "Remarks by the President to Students and Faculty of Waseda University" (Tokyo, Japan: The White House, Office of the Press Secretary, July 7, 1993).
6. Natale H. Bellocchi, "Speech to New England-Taiwan Business Council," Boston, Massachusetts, June 22, 1993, ms. See also his "Speech to the Dallas Chinese Community," Dallas, Texas, April 10, 1993, ms.
7. Natale H. Bellocchi, "Taiwan and the U.S. Relationship," speech before the U.S.-ROC Economic Council, Hilton Head, North Carolina, September 23, 1993, ms.
8. *Free China Journal*, March 12, 1993, p. 1.
9. *Free China Journal*, April 22, 1994, p. 1.
10. *Far Eastern Economic Review*, September 16, 1993, p. 11; *Free China Journal*, September 10, 1993, p. 1.
11. *Far Eastern Economic Review*, November 4, 1993, p. 15.
12. *China Post*, March 25, 1993, p. 1.
13. *China Post*, May 2, 1993, p. 1.
14. See *Wall Street Journal*, May 3, 1993, p. A13; August 4, 1993, p. A5.
15. *Free China Journal*, December 3, 1993, p. 3. Many of these endangered species were used in traditional Chinese medicines.
16. David C. Unger, "Nationalist China or Nationalist Taiwan?" *New York Times*, November 9, 1993, p. A16.
17. Natale H. Bellocchi, "Speech to New England-Taiwan Business Council," June 22, 1993, ms.
18. *Far Eastern Economic Review*, October 7, 1993, p. 20.
19. "Remarks by the President After Meeting with President Jiang of China" (Seattle, Washington: The White House, Office of the Press Secretary, November 19, 1993).
20. *Far Eastern Economic Review*, June 9, 1994, p. 18.
21. For a report on Lee Teng-hui's "vacation diplomacy," see *Far Eastern Economic Review*, February 24, 1994, pp. 18-19.
22. Premier Lien Chan's "vacation diplomacy" to Southeast Asia was reported in *Free China Journal*, January 7, 1994, p. 1.
23. Related legislation was introduced by other Members of Congress. H.R. 763 was introduced by Congressman Crane in February 1993, calling for the establishment of free trade areas with Pacific Rim countries, including Taiwan.

S. 1467 was introduced by Senator Pell in September 1993, calling for high-level official exchanges between the United States and Taiwan. S.Con.Res. 20 was introduced by Senator Lieberman in March 1993 expressing the sense of Congress that Taiwan should be represented in the United Nations and other international organizations. Similar resolutions were introduced by Congressman Solomon (H.Con.Res. 148), Senator D'Amato (S.Con.Res. 45), and Senator Simon (S.Res. 148). For a discussion of the role of Congress in the Taiwan issue in 1993-1994, see Robert G. Sutter, "Taiwan: Recent Developments and U.S. Policy Choices," Library of Congress, Congressional Research Service *Issue Brief*, No. IB94006 (updated May 26, 1994).

24. See the August 18, 1982, testimony of Assistant Secretary of State John Holdridge in U.S. Congress, House of Representatives, Committee on Foreign Affairs, *China-Taiwan: United States Policy* (Washington, D.C.: Government Printing Office, 1982), pp. 2-29.

25. Prepared statement of Davis R. Robinson, Legal Advisor, Department of State, given before U.S. Congress, Senate, Committee on the Judiciary, Subcommittee on Separation of Powers, September 27, 1982, pp. 1-2, ms.

26. *Free China Journal*, May 6, 1994, p. 2. At first, Taiwan was not necessarily in favor of the amendment, since it would open the TRA to future amendments which might be more damaging to ROC interests.

27. *Far Eastern Economic Review*, August 5, 1993, p. 15.

28. On May 16, 1994, the State Department reiterated that the various Taiwan provisions in P.L. 103-236 would not alter U.S. policy and practice toward Taiwan. Sutter, "Taiwan: Recent Developments and U.S. Policy Choices," p. 12.

29. Statement of Senator Murkowski before the U.S. Senate on May 3, 1994, from *Congressional Record* reprint provided by the Senator's office.

30. The proceedings of the congressional hearing were summarized in a CNA (China News Agency) report filed by N.K. Han from Washington, D.C., July 15, 1994.

31. Jim Mann, "U.S. May Ease Limits on Ties with Taiwan," *Los Angeles Times*, July 6, 1994, p. 1.

32. It will be recalled that these were the specific adjustments in U.S. policy requested by Taipei in December 1992, shortly after Clinton's election as president.

33. The official's remarks are taken from a CNA report from Washington, D.C., September 7, 1994. For a much briefer formal explanation of the policy adjustments, see "Statement of Assistant Secretary Winston Lord, Senate Foreign Relations Committee, Hearing on Taiwan Policy," September 27, 1994, ms.

34. *New York Times*, September 8, 1994, p. A5; *Washington Post*, September 8, 1994, p. A10; CNA report from Washington, D.C., September 8, 1994.

35. *Wall Street Journal*, September 9, 1994, p. A7A; CNA report from Taipei, Taiwan, September 8, 1994; UPI report from Taipei, September 8, 1994; Reuters report from Taipei, September 8, 1994.

36. *New York Times*, September 9, 1994, p. A13.

37. *Washington Post*, September 11, 1994, p. A26; Reuters report from Beijing, China, September 10, 1994.

38. CNA report from Tokyo, Japan, September 9, 1994.

39. *Wall Street Journal*, September 9, 1994, p. A7A; Reuters report from Beijing, China, September 15, 1994.

40. See *Washington Post*, January 7, 1994, p. A8. Compare with a *Washington Post* wire dated September 8, 1994, reporting that China repeatedly told the United States it would discuss its sale of M-11 missiles to Pakistan only if the Clinton administration agreed to discuss the sale of F-16s to Taiwan. To date, the wire story said, Washington had refused this condition.

41. For details, see Martin L. Lasater, *The Taiwan Issue in Sino-American Strategic Relations* (Boulder, CO: Westview Press, 1984), pp. 182-191.

42. Don Oberdorfer, "Replaying the China Card: How Washington and Beijing Avoided Diplomatic Disaster," *Washington Post*, November 7, 1993, p. C3. Also, Julian Baum, "On the Sidelines: Taipei Anxious about US-China Warming," *Far Eastern Economic Review*, November 25, 1993, p. 20.

43. For a discussion of this and other nuanced changes in U.S. policy on the reunification issue, see Martin L. Lasater, *Policy in Evolution: The U.S. Role in China's Reunification* (Boulder, CO: Westview Press, 1989), especially pp. 170-173, 179-187.

44. CNA report from Washington, D.C., September 9, 1994.

6

Taiwan's Security Environment

Many factors influence Taiwan's security: geography, international trends and the attitude of the international community toward the Taiwan issue, ROC political and economic conditions, relations across the Taiwan Strait, U.S.-PRC-ROC relations, the intentions of PRC leaders, the military capabilities of the PLA, and the capabilities and intentions of the United States to intervene on Taiwan's behalf. Together, these form Taiwan's security environment, the circumstances within which Taipei must formulate its strategy for deterring and, if need be, for winning a war in the Taiwan Strait.

This chapter provides an overview of Taiwan's security environment by examining briefly each of the above factors. Chapter 7 will consider ROC military capabilities, Taiwan's deterrence strategy, and several scenarios for a possible PRC-ROC military confrontation in the 1990s.

Geography

Geography plays an important role in ROC security. Taiwan is an island approximately one hundred miles off the coast of China. It is close enough to be considered Chinese territory (Chinese military expeditions were sent to Taiwan as early as the third century AD), yet far enough away to prevent easy colonization or investment.

Taiwan has few natural resources, but it is one of the most densely populated lands in the world. Trade is essential to the island's survival. Taiwan is a very large island with several ports around its coastline.

Thus, while Taiwan is vulnerable to blockade, it would be difficult to enforce a blockade effectively without large naval deployments and air cover. These blockading forces would be exposed to Taiwan's small, but modern, air and naval forces. To isolate Taiwan the PRC would have to establish both air and sea control over much of the island and its surrounding waters, including the Taiwan Strait. Because of Taiwan's distance from the mainland, however, most PRC aircraft (which lack air refueling capability) cannot fly combat air patrol over Taiwan for long before they have to return to their bases.

Due to the mountainous terrain of Taiwan, the island's population is concentrated on the western plains where cities are vulnerable to bomb and missile attack. But Taiwan's large population and rough terrain also mean that any invasion and occupation of the island could be costly. Thousands of fortified positions dot the island at strategic locations; opportunities for sustained guerrilla operations are endless. The fact that Taiwan is defended by 360,000 active duty troops and over 1.6 million in the reserves increases the size of the amphibious force necessary to invade Taiwan to very high levels. It was estimated in World War II, for example, that 300,000 American troops would be required to defeat 32,000 Japanese soldiers then defending Taiwan.

The offshore islands of Kinmen (Quemoy) and Matsu have quite different geographical features. Small islands approximately a mile from the mainland, both are vulnerable to blockade, bombardment, and invasion. The islands are strongly defended, however, with 70,000 crack ROC troops armed with heavy weapons. Kinmen and Matsu are not necessary to the defense of Taiwan, but the offshore islands do have great symbolic value as a territorial link between the ROC government and the Chinese mainland.[1]

The Pescadores (Penghu) are small, windswept islands in the middle of the Taiwan Strait. Because of air and naval stations and proximity to Taiwan, Penghu is relevant to Taiwan's security. Penghu must be defended by the ROC; it must be captured or neutralized by the PRC. Whichever side controls the air and sea in the Taiwan Strait would control the fate of Penghu.

Taipei claims as ROC territory the Pratas Islands, Spratly Islands, Paracel Islands, and the Macclesfield Bank in the South China Sea. ROC naval and marine forces occupy a few of the major islands in these groups. They have little direct relevance to Taiwan's security, but their occupation is important to Chinese territorial claims. (The PRC also claims the islands as Chinese territory.) Since the islands are far removed from the mainland and Taiwan, their control is dependent upon the power projection capabilities of the two Chinese sides.

In sum, despite being an island, geographical factors tend to favor Taiwan's security. Because of its size and distance from the mainland, successfully blockading or invading Taiwan would be difficult for Beijing. On the other hand, Kinmen and Matsu are vulnerable to PRC attack, although if defended they could be captured only at great cost. Penghu's fate is tied to the much more problematic issue of air and sea control of the Taiwan Strait. The South China Sea islets occupied by the ROC are not essential to Taiwan's security, but they could provide setting for a contest between ROC and PRC naval and marine forces.

International Trends

Taiwan's security is also related to various international trends, especially the balance of power in East Asia, the growing importance of trade in international relations, and trends toward multilateralism including the expanding role of the United Nations.

The balance of power in East Asia has shifted considerably since the end of the Cold War. Overall, the relative power of the United States is perceived as diminishing, while the relative strength of the PRC and Japan is increasing. Russia, while still powerful in terms of armed forces assigned to the Far East, is considered far weaker than before the August 1991 collapse of the Soviet Union.

From the point of view of Taiwan's security, this shift in the regional balance of power is not favorable: its main ally (the United States) is seen as less predominant and its main adversary (the PRC) is growing stronger. Since Moscow poses no major threat to the PRC, Beijing has enormous military forces it can redeploy to concentrate on Taiwan if necessary. Japan, always considered a threat to Chinese interests on Taiwan, also has significant military potential.

The growing emphasis on trade in international relations, on the other hand, works strongly to Taiwan's security advantage. Taipei has trade relations with most of the countries of the world. Its largest trading partners are rich and powerful nations, including the United States, Japan, the European Community, and the ASEAN states. Taiwan is also deeply intertwined economically with the PRC.

Taiwan's trading strength works to its security advantage in several ways. First, since increased importance is given to economic matters by virtually all nations, Taiwan's standing in the world community has been enhanced. Second, since most nations are concentrating on economic development in the post-Cold War era, they take seriously any potential disruption of normal trade and investment patterns. Given Taiwan's status as a major trading partner and source of investment capital, Taiwan's security is thus of concern to many countries. Third, economic interdependency means that any harm done to Taiwan's economy would adversely affect the economies of other nations, including that of the PRC. Fourth, the probable negative reaction from the international community to a PRC use of force against Taiwan is a powerful incentive for Beijing to maintain peace in the Taiwan Strait. Fifth, strong trade and investment ties with the mainland give Taipei leverage to urge Beijing not to use force to resolve the reunification issue.

It should be noted, however, that just as Taiwan's international status has grown because of global trade, so China's importance has grown as well. The mainland, not Taiwan, is seen by many businessmen as the richest potential market in Asia and the major engine for economic growth in the region. China's importance as a U.S. trading partner has already been noted. The PRC uses its growing economic importance in much the same manner as it uses its superior diplomatic and strategic status to pressure Taiwan and limit ROC international activities.

Another factor in Taiwan's security environment is the trend toward multilateral approaches to security. Unilateral intervention by the United States, while held out as an ever-present option, has been increasingly rare as Washington has found it in its interests to solicit political, economic, and even military backing before committing U.S. forces to combat. This has special relevance to Taiwan, since countries in Asia would be most reticent in their support of U.S. intervention in case of conflict in the Taiwan Strait. This is not to say they would approve of a PRC use of force against Taiwan, but they would keep in mind that China has a long memory and that Taiwan is considered an especially sensitive issue in Beijing.

One example of the trend toward multilateralism in Asia is the meeting of Asian governments under ASEAN auspices to discuss regional security issues. The ASEAN Regional Forum (ARF) met for the first time in Bangkok in July 1994. Taiwan has not been invited to participate in these dialogues, primarily because other Asian governments want to ensure Chinese involvement in rather than isolation from the process. In the past the PRC has refused to participate in any international security discussion which included Taiwan as a participant or as an issue.[2]

The expanding role of the United Nations also is a factor in Taiwan's security. On the positive side, a more active United Nations adds considerable weight to incentives for Beijing not to use force against Taiwan. The issue of rejoining the United Nations provides Taipei with an important forum around which to publicize its case to the international community. Pursuing a U.N. seat also helps to defuse domestic criticism of ROC foreign policy, thus contributing to social stability at home.

On the negative side, as a permanent member of the U.N. Security Council the PRC is well positioned to defeat any effort by Taipei to join the U.N. or to use the international body to its advantage. Most U.N. members accept the principle of there being only one China, including Taiwan, and that the government of the People's Republic of China is the sole legal government of China. Given Beijing's influence in global and regional affairs, it will be difficult for Taipei to outmaneuver the PRC in the United Nations.

A closely related factor is the attitude of the international community toward Taiwan's security. Although most nations recognize the PRC as the legitimate government of China and acknowledge Taiwan as being part of China, Taiwan is accepted as a substantial international entity with global economic ties and many powerful friends. Most countries wish the ROC well and do not want to see Beijing establish control over the island, especially by force. A PRC use of force against Taiwan would be protested strongly by the international community. The condemnation of Beijing could have far-reaching negative consequences for PRC security relations with the United States, Western Europe, Russia, Japan, and other Asian countries. Most of these nations would view the PRC as a greater threat to their interests and perhaps allocate more resources to counter that threat. There would be significant political and economics costs to the PRC as well.

Actual intervention on Taiwan's behalf, however, would likely be circumspect. Many diplomatic entreaties would be made to convince Beijing to resolve its differences with Taipei through negotiations, but only the United States and possibly some Western European countries would assist Taiwan militarily. Of these, only the United States would likely go beyond the sale of arms.

In sum, Taiwan's stature as a trading partner and source of investment is its principal security advantage in the international community. Under conditions of regional peace, this advantage may be decisive in ensuring that force will not be used against Taiwan. However, as illustrated in the case of Bosnia, the international community can shun risks when violence is threatened. If Beijing is determined to press the issue of China's reunification at any cost, Taipei's trading strength might not be sufficient to draw effective international intervention on Taiwan's behalf. In terms of international support across the spectrum of political, economic, and military dimensions, only the United States can be considered a powerful (if somewhat unpredictable) ally of Taiwan.

Domestic Factors

Taiwan's political and economic conditions are very important factors in ROC security. Of these, one of the most critical is Taiwan's evolution toward democracy, which has both strengthened and weakened the island's security. Security has been strengthened in that the majority of people on Taiwan now have a greater personal stake in defending their country against a hostile PRC. Also, especially in the eyes of the American public, a democratic Taiwan is more worthy of military support than a non-democratic Taiwan.

Democracy has weakened Taiwan's security by giving vent to strong, persistent efforts among a segment of society to create an independent Taiwan state. The public's desire for national autonomy is growing on Taiwan. Since Beijing has warned repeatedly it would use force to stop Taiwan independence, democracy has increased the PRC threat to Taiwan.

Democracy weakens Taiwan's security in other ways. The KMT is no longer a strong centralized party; it is deeply split over fundamental policy issues and competing leadership. Many mainlander KMT question whether they want to remain part of Taiwan, now that it is, in their view, moving down a path of self-destruction. The redistribution of power between the executive and legislative branches presents another challenge to Taiwan's security. Some legislators doubt the seriousness of the PRC threat and prefer to focus budgetary resources on domestic programs rather than defense. Those warning of PRC intervention are frequently called "alarmists," "lackeys" of Beijing, or even "traitors" to Taiwan. Of course, if a major threat were to emerge, some -- but not all -- of these divisions would heal for the duration of the crisis.

The economic development of Taiwan is also an important factor in ROC security. Nowhere is this more apparent than in increased economic ties between Taiwan and mainland China. The mainland is Taiwan's most important market for export growth and one of the most important destinations for its capital and technological investments. But economic integration with the mainland has both positive and negative impact on Taiwan's security.

In a positive sense, increased economic ties lower Beijing's incentives to use force against Taiwan because the goal of reunification seems to be advancing. Also, a war with Taiwan would cause great economic hardship to the mainland, especially in the rapidly modernizing coastal provinces that are a principal engine of growth for the entire Chinese economy.

The main disadvantage to ROC security from economic integration with the mainland is Taiwan's susceptibility to economic pressure from Beijing. Taiwan's export growth is becoming dependent on the mainland market, a dependency that Beijing can manipulate by opening or closing market opportunities. The mainland has a much larger economy than that of Taiwan, a faster rate of economic growth, and is less dependent on trade. All these factors enable the PRC to withstand economic hardship better than Taiwan. To some extent, therefore, the greater the economic interaction of Taiwan and the mainland, the more economically vulnerable the ROC becomes. Unavoidably, this increases the risk to Taiwan's security, especially from a blockade.

Taiwan's economic development has other important implications for ROC security. These include:

- A strong economy expands Taiwan's international presence, involving more countries in Taiwan's future and thus contributing to ROC deterrence against the PRC. At the same time, more international activity by Taiwan sends warning signals to Beijing that Taipei is becoming politically stronger in the global community. This could prompt the PRC to consider whether force should be used to settle the reunification issue earlier, while Taiwan is still relatively weak, rather than later, when Taiwan is stronger.
- A strong ROC economy enables Taipei to purchase advanced weapons from foreign countries eager to sell more arms in the wake of post-Cold War military reductions. Many Western governments now allow these sales to go forward to provide jobs and business opportunities for their citizens. Taiwan also uses the lure of multimillion dollar contracts in its current national development plan to encourage Western governments to expand arms sales to Taiwan.

Thus, political and economic factors play both positive and negative roles in Taiwan's security. Greater democracy and a stronger economy have strengthened Taiwan's security and improved its international standing. At the same time, the rise of Taiwanese nationalism and economic dependency on the mainland have increased Beijing's wariness over political developments on Taiwan and made Taiwan more vulnerable to PRC economic pressure. Also, Taiwan's success in dollar diplomacy has caused the PRC to place additional obstacles in the path of Taipei's participation in most international organizations and activities.

ROC-PRC Relations

One of the most vital factors in Taiwan's security environment is the ROC relationship with the PRC. This relationship has become much more complex in recent years with the emergence of Taiwanese leadership in the KMT, the pro-independence DPP, and the establishment of the Chinese New Party as a breakaway party (mostly comprised of disgruntled mainlanders) from the mainstream-dominated KMT.

In this political environment, many within the non-mainstream faction of the KMT and the Chinese New Party favor China's unification in the not-too-distant future -- assuming continued political and economic evolution on the mainland. A majority of the KMT mainstream faction would seem to prefer to keep Taiwan's options open -- unification, a "two Chinas" policy, or independence -- depending upon future developments. Some Taiwanese members of the KMT openly support the goal of eventual independence. Most DPP members favor independence as soon as possible.

Despite these differences of opinion over Taiwan's future, there is broad consensus that Taipei's mainland policy should support the status quo of two separate, sovereign Chinese political entities in the short-term. But consensus on this issue is unraveling due to the tremendous internal and external pressures being placed on Taiwan. There is growing distrust between the various political factions, which -- in a democratic environment -- can stymie effective policy. Increasingly, many mainlanders on Taiwan doubt President Lee Teng-hui's sincerity in working toward China's reunification. Many Taiwanese treat mainlanders as second-class citizens. Mainlanders and Taiwanese are becoming less cooperative in certain instances. Some elements of the ROC armed forces might not even defend Taiwan if its political leaders pursue independence.[3]

The net result of increased distrust over the direction of China policy on Taiwan is that Taiwan's security is less secure. Increased tension between mainlanders and Taiwanese on Taiwan has also caused Beijing's anxiety to grow over Taipei's policy. There are many in the PRC who believe forceful action might eventually be necessary to prevent Taiwan from drifting toward independence.

A countervailing trend is that increased contact between Taiwan and the mainland, which is propelled more by private interests than by government policy, is rapidly merging the destiny of the two Chinese societies. It would be difficult for Taipei to halt exchanges across the Taiwan Strait, and it would be damaging to PRC interests for Beijing to do so. The cultural affiliation between the two sides and the potential for personal profit are powerful integrative forces that are seen as positive from the point of view of unification advocates and as negative from the standpoint of independence supporters. Since the PRC is firmly committed to unification, there seems to be little reason for Beijing to use force against Taiwan as long as reunification through cross-straits exchanges is moving forward.

But the emergence of "Greater China" is deeply troubling to supporters of Taiwan independence who think the high volume of cross-straits exchanges works against national autonomy. There is the possibility that a sense of racing against time might prompt desperate moves to further the cause of Taiwan independence. The DPP's increasingly bold efforts to push Taiwan's reentry into the United Nations and to expand Taiwan's international diplomatic presence are symptomatic of the time pressures being felt by the pro-independence party. If the DPP were to gain sufficient political power on Taiwan or if the KMT were to adopt more independence-leaning policies, a major crisis could be precipitated in the Taiwan Strait.

Given the steady integration of Taiwan and the mainland through cultural and economic links, it is unlikely Beijing would use force to speed up the reunification process or to prevent Taiwan from achieving greater international recognition under the "one China" principle (or perhaps even under the principle of "two Chinas" temporarily divided). The most important PRC goal is unification. Of the various reasons for a PRC use of force, the most likely would be a move on the part of Taipei to attain Taiwan independence.

In short, the nature of the Taiwan-mainland relationship is such that the PRC probably would not attack Taiwan unless it believed force was necessary to prevent Taiwan independence. A move toward independence cannot be ruled out, however, given political trends on Taiwan itself and some increase in international support for Taiwan's existence as a separate political entity.

U.S.-PRC-ROC Relations

The triangular relationship between the United States, the People's Republic of China, and the Republic of China is yet another important factor in Taiwan's security environment. The United States is deeply involved in Taiwan's security because of multifaceted U.S. roles:

- Washington is the principal external deterrent to a PRC use of force against Taiwan.
- The United States is the principal supplier of arms and defense technology to Taiwan.
- The 1979 Taiwan Relations Act is the most important international document relating to Taiwan's security.
- The United States is Taiwan's most important trading partner and a key source of investment and civilian technology.
- Washington is Taipei's most important political ally in the international community.
- For its own interests, the United States reinforces Beijing's policy of peaceful reunification.
- U.S. efforts to maintain a favorable balance of power in East Asia usually works to Taipei's advantage.

In general, when U.S.-PRC relations are strained, the United States is more supportive of Taiwan, but not to the point of completely undermining Sino-American relations. When U.S.-PRC relations are cooperative, Washington is more circumspect in its dealings with Taipei. Because of Taiwan's strong base of political support in the Congress and among the American public, however, it is very difficult for any administration to sacrifice Taiwan's security interests too much, even during periods of extremely close Sino-American ties.

The United States does not support the goal of many Nationalist Chinese to one day return to power on the mainland. Indeed, it is in the U.S. interest to deal effectively with whoever controls the mainland. China is too big and its potential too vast for Washington to ignore. As a consequence, the United States cannot be expected to sacrifice its interests in China for U.S. interests in Taiwan. Quite the contrary. U.S.

policy toward Taiwan is usually considered a part of U.S. policy toward mainland China.

At the same time, the United States will probably continue to support Taiwan's self-defense. This is because of certain basic U.S. policy predispositions:

1. The United States supports the democratization of the Chinese (mainland and Taiwan) political system.
2. The United States views peace in the Taiwan Strait as essential to East Asian stability and normal trade in the Asian Pacific.
3. The United States does not want China to become too strong as long as its government is potentially hostile to U.S. interests.
4. The United States does not want Taiwan to be controlled by a communist government in China.

There is a slight but ever-present danger of Taiwan being "sold out" by the United States. The nature of U.S.-PRC-ROC relations, however, gives Taipei ample opportunity to maneuver between the two larger countries. The need to maintain sufficient flexibility to sail these unpredictable waters is one reason Taiwan adopted a more pragmatic foreign policy in the mid-1980s. Ironically, the success of that pragmatic policy has in turn caused both Beijing and Washington to reconsider their policies toward Taiwan, a process which is ongoing.

PRC Intentions

PRC intentions to use force against Taiwan are crucial determinants of ROC security. Significantly, one of the policies accompanying Deng Xiaoping's return to power in 1978 was a change in PRC strategy from one of "liberating" Taiwan to "peaceful reunification." This policy shift was necessary to ensure that the normalization of Sino-American relations could go forward. Also, peaceful reunification supported Deng's central strategic goal of concentrating on the Four Modernizations to bring China into the ranks of the developed nations in the twentieth-first century. It seems reasonable to expect that as long as Beijing needs a peaceful international environment, maintains an open policy toward the outside world, seeks cordial relations with the United States, and concentrates on domestic economic development, powerful strategic incentives will remain for the PRC not to use force against Taiwan.

It should be noted, however, that other Chinese interests may be of even higher priority. These fundamental interests surely include the preservation and protection of Chinese territory and sovereignty. These are the precise interests threatened by Taiwan becoming an independent state. To prevent Taiwan independence, there is high probability the PRC would use force, even if such action strained relations with Washington and other Western nations for a while and postponed China's economic modernization for several years.

Chinese leaders have been quite clear in expressing their intentions on this matter. Some recent statements to this effect include:

- Politburo member Li Ruihuan was quoted in the Hong Kong newspaper *Wen Wei Po* in the spring of 1993 as saying: "Only if Taiwan doesn't push ahead with independence and create two Chinas will the mainland patiently...try to reunify Taiwan peacefully."[4]

- On March 31, 1993, Premier Li Peng and other CCP officials held a press conference following the First Session of the Eighth National People's Congress. In response to a question from the Central News Agency of Taipei in regards to Li's statement on Taiwan in his government work report that "resolute measures will be adopted when necessary," Li said: "As for the firm measures I mentioned in my government work report in relation to Taiwan, they will certainly be taken only under very special circumstances. These, for instance, entail the practice of `independence' for Taiwan, social disturbances, or interference from external hostile forces. The specific measures to be taken will depend on whatever circumstances exist."[5]

- General Secretary Jiang Zemin told *U.S. News and World Report* editor-in-chief Mortimer Zuckerman on February 23, 1993: "We stand for an early reunification by peaceful means. But we refuse to make the commitment not to use force. This is by no means directed against the people of Taiwan but aimed mainly at the proponents of `Taiwan independence' and interference from foreign forces. This position is consistent with the interests of the Taiwanese people. Activities for `Taiwan independence' on the island have increased recently. Even within the Kuomintang there are some who are publicly echoing the call for `one China, one Taiwan.' We firmly oppose `two Chinas,' `one China, one Taiwan' or `one country, two governments' in any form. We firmly oppose any attempt or act aimed at `Taiwan independence.' In the event of `Taiwan independence' or the division of China by foreign forces, we will never sit by idly. Instead, we will take decisive measures to firmly safeguard state sovereignty and territorial integrity, and preserve the fundamental interests of the entire Chinese nation, including the 20 million Taiwan compatriots."[6]

- In a meeting with a Taiwanese delegation in late October 1992, Li Ruihuan said Beijing would "use any means" to prevent Taiwan from becoming independent. He said, "We would not hesitate to shed blood....We would advance wave after wave....I know there are people in Taiwan who want to split the national territory, and there are foreigners taking part in this. I warn them not to take risks."[7]

Circumstances Leading to War

Beijing has always been explicit about the conditions under which it would use force against Taiwan. These circumstances would include:

- if Taiwan attempts to become an independent country
- if other nations attempt to separate Taiwan from China
- if there are "social disturbances" on Taiwan, presumably meaning violent confrontations between pro-unification and pro-independence advocates on the island.

After examining Chinese justifications to attack Taiwan, one recent study concluded: "Of the possible triggers for a PRC use of force against Taiwan, the most probable would be a clear indication from Taipei authorities that they intended to move toward de jure independence from mainland China. The PRC might also be tempted to intervene in the case of an entreaty from some faction on Taiwan seeking accommodation with Beijing."[8]

There are several reasons why the PRC would feel justified in using force to prevent Taiwan independence:

1. Taiwan has been claimed historically by China and is inhabited by individuals of Chinese descent.
2. Taiwan is physically close to the mainland.
3. Taiwan has vital geostrategic importance to China as a defensive shield in the Western Pacific.
4. Taiwan and the mainland are becoming increasingly intertwined economically.
5. Chinese governments are very sensitive to issues dealing with national territory and sovereignty.
6. Beijing's forty-year commitment to national reunification cannot easily be discarded by any PRC leader.

If it is assumed that there are circumstances (such as a move toward Taiwan independence) under which the PRC would use force against Taiwan, then several trends raise concern that Beijing might find it more acceptable to exercise its military option in the Taiwan Strait. These include:

- Despite increased contact across the Taiwan Strait, there is no indication that Taiwan is willing to accept China's "one country, two systems" proposal. If reunification under PRC terms is to be achieved over the next decade, some dramatic movement on the issue must take place.

- The resolution of the Taiwan issue is gaining political importance in Beijing now that the Hong Kong and Macau issues have been settled in principle.

- There is a possibility that the Taiwan issue might be caught up in a PRC power struggle once Deng Xiaoping passes from the scene. At minimum, Beijing's reunification policies after Deng are not clear; they may or may not be peaceful.

- The Tiananmen Square incident made peaceful reunification much less attractive to the people of Taiwan and to the international community in general.

- The CCP faces a difficult choice: it must reform to attract Taiwan into peaceful reunification, but such reforms might undermine the communist party's own power. The PRC leadership might conclude that unification through peaceful means is not worth the political cost.

- Taiwan's prestige in the international community is growing steadily because of its economic strength, steps toward democracy, and pragmatic diplomacy. Taipei is increasing its participation in international organizations and making some gains diplomatically. Taiwan's pragmatic diplomacy is gradually defeating the PRC strategy of isolating Taipei from the global community. This failure of strategy may lead Beijing to turn to other options to achieve reunification.

- Developments on Taiwan are very troublesome to PRC leaders. Democratization and Taiwanization have dramatically increased the possibility that the people of Taiwan will elect to move in the direction of de jure independence.

- The reduction of the Soviet, Vietnamese, and Indian threats along China's borders frees the PLA to concentrate more resources on the unresolved Taiwan issue.

- China's goal to acquire a blue water navy with long-range fighter air cover -- presumably to project power into the South China Sea -- will also enhance Beijing's ability to operate effectively in the waters around Taiwan.

- Although American naval and air units remain powerful in the Western Pacific, U.S. military reductions worldwide are seen by many in Beijing as evidence that Washington would not intervene decisively to aid Taiwan if a conflict occurred between the two Chinese sides.
- Many senior PLA officers view the United States as China's principal adversary. The PLA assessment is based on the belief that serious differences will continue to exist between the United States and China in the areas of ideology, social systems, and foreign policy.[9]
- Many Chinese analysts believe the United States is becoming weaker as a nation because of its domestic economic and political problems. One report noted, "Although the end of the Cold War has left the United States as the only superpower, its real power and position has very clearly been weakened."[10] This assessment supports the contention that the United States is unlikely to intervene in the Taiwan Strait.

In sum, although it seems unlikely that the PRC would use force against Taiwan without provocation, there is high probability that Beijing intends to use force if Taiwan's government moves toward de jure independence. Trends on Taiwan suggest that the possibility of independence is growing. Thus, the PRC threat to Taiwan must be seen as increasing rather than decreasing. Beijing's willingness to use force may also be firmer because several trends in the post-Cold War period seem to favor decisive action on the Taiwan issue.

PLA Capabilities

Ultimately, Taiwan's security is directly related to the military capabilities of its nemesis, the People's Liberation Army (PLA). The PLA is one of the world's most powerful armed forces, armed with nuclear weapons, intercontinental ballistic missiles, and at least one nuclear powered ballistic missile submarine.[11] China has over three million men and women on active duty, with well over a million in the reserves. The PLA army has over two million troops. Three Group Armies, two armored divisions, 11 infantry divisions, one artillery division, and one air defense division are assigned to the Nanjing Military Region responsible for the defense of eastern China opposite Taiwan. The PLA navy has nearly 100 submarines, including four nuclear attack boats, with an additional 54 principal surface combatants comprised of 17 destroyers and 37 frigates. The navy also has more than 200 missile patrol boats. The East Sea Fleet, headquartered in Shanghai, has two submarine, two escort, one mine warfare, and one amphibious squadrons assigned to it, with an additional 270 patrol and coastal combatants. The PLA air force has some 120 bombers, many nuclear capable and some carrying air-to-surface missiles. The air force also has about 500 ground attack fighters and about 4,000 interceptors. These aircraft can be deployed rapidly to bases opposite Taiwan, where targets can be reached in a matter of minutes.

As strong as the PLA is, there are significant military obstacles to its gaining superiority in the Taiwan Strait operational environment. These obstacles include the short range of most PLA aircraft, the rough seas often present in the Taiwan Strait, the lack of amphibious vessels to carry troops and especially heavy equipment to Taiwan, vulnerability to ROC counterattack of bases and staging areas on the mainland, the substantial defensive capabilities of the ROC armed forces, and the ever-present possibility of American military intervention.

PLA Modernization

The PLA is attempting to overcome its weaknesses through a program of rapid modernization. Military modernization has become a high national priority for the PRC, especially since the demonstration of advanced weaponry in the Persian Gulf War.

An important part of the PLA's modernization program is the acquisition of advanced military equipment, defense technology, and weapons production skill from abroad. Recent PLA acquisitions in these areas have caused grave concern in some quarters in the United States.

According to security analysts at the Strategic and Defense Studies Center of Australian National University, by the spring of 1993 the Chinese negotiated purchases of 72 Russian Su-27 Flanker long-range strike fighters and 24 MiG-31 Foxhound long-range interceptors. Beijing also made arrangements to manufacture 200 more MiG-31s in Shenyang under license. (It should be noted that U.S. government sources believed that only 24 Su-27s, plus two trainers, actually had been delivered to China by the end of 1994. There was disagreement over whether the MiG-31 deal had been consummated.)

In addition to the fighters, the Chinese were reported to be interested in buying T-72M main battle tanks, an undetermined number of A-50 airborne warning and control aircraft, and long-range early warning radar systems. The Russians may have offered China supersonic Tu-22M

Backfire long-range bombers as well. Ten Il-76 Candid heavy military transports may have also been purchased by China. In addition, the two sides have negotiated over the MiG-29 Fulcrum fighter and Su-24 Fencer ground attack fighter.

According to the Australian think tank, China recently completed an airstrip capable of handling Su-27s and docking points for frigate-sized ships on Woody Island (Lin Dao) in the Paracels in the South China Sea. Aerial refueling facilities were being built at Zhanjiang in southern China. In addition, China negotiated access to a Burmese naval base under construction on Hanggyi Island in the Bassein River. A Chinese monitoring station was also being established on Grand Coco Island in Burmese waters just north of India's Andaman Islands.[12]

During Russian President Boris Yeltsin's trip to Beijing in December 1992, Moscow agreed to help modernize some 250 Soviet-built defense plants constructed in China during the 1950s. According to Yeltsin, China bought $1.8 billion in arms from Moscow in 1992 and the Russians wanted the Chinese to buy much more. The Chinese, however, seem more interested in purchasing technology and production rights than actual hardware, a pattern similar to earlier Sino-American arms deals. The Chinese preference for technology and production rights may have slowed arms transactions, since the main motivation on the part of Russia has been the need for hard currency, which Beijing husbands judiciously. Another delaying factor in some areas of military cooperation may be Moscow's reluctance to provide China -- a potential threat to Russia -- with too much advanced equipment and technology.

Nonetheless, the *Far Eastern Economic Review* reported in September 1993 that China and Russia were discussing the joint development of a new fighter, the purchase of several conventional submarines, and the acquisition of air defense missiles. As of July 1993 China had received 26 Su-27 fighters and three Il-76 heavy military transports. Further purchases in the aerospace industry were expected, since this area was one in which the Chinese were especially weak. Items under discussion with Moscow included avionics equipment, navigational systems, aircraft engines, radar technology, and technical data for design and construction of airframes. China was expected to take delivery of another batch of 26 Su-27s by the end of 1994, but their arrival had not yet been reported by foreign observers in early 1995.

The Su-27s are especially important to the PRC since their extended operational range can provide air cover for Chinese warships as far as the Spratly Islands in the South China Sea. At present, however, there are too few aircraft for around-the-clock air superiority. As of the end of 1994, the Su-27s were not yet fully operational.[13] U.S. sources believed the plane's full integration into the PLA would take some time because of the aircraft's complexity and mission diversity.

According to other *Far Eastern Economic Review* reports, the new fighter being discussed for Sino-Russian joint development would appear before the turn of the century and would have capabilities between the MiG-29 and MiG-31. In a related sale, Russia sold China 100 Klimov/Sarkisov RD-33 turbofan engines used in the MiG-29, possibly to be fitted to China's Super 7 Fishbed fighter, an extensively modified Chinese version of the 1960s era MiG-21. Intended for export, the Super 7 was modified with U.S. and other Western help before sanctions on defense cooperation were imposed by the West in the wake of Tiananmen.[14]

Still other reports said that Moscow offered Beijing 100-150 launchers for the SA-10B Grumble/Almaz S-300 mobile medium-range air defense missile system. Each launcher has eight missiles. The cost would be approximately $1.5 billion. The S-300 has a range up to 100 kilometers and provides protection against ballistic missiles, cruise missiles, and aircraft. China bought four S-300 launchers and 60 missiles for testing. According to Russian sources, the Chinese agreed in 1992 to buy some 50 T-72 tanks and 70 BMP vehicles at a cost of $250 million.

The PRC navy has also been upgraded considerably since the mid-1980s. In recent months, the PLA has commissioned a fifth *Han*-class nuclear-powered submarine, two improved *Ming*-class diesel submarines, and the first of at least six new *Jiangwei* frigates. A new class of *Luhu* destroyers is being built, along with a new *Houang*-class of missile craft. Acquired foreign systems include coproduction of the PRC/SEMT Pielstick marine diesel engine, the SRBOC Mark 33 chaff dispenser, Mark 32 and PRC/Honeywell Mark 46 mod 2 ASW torpedoes, Whitehead ASW torpedoes, the Sea Crotale SAM, the General Electric LM-2500 naval gas turbine engine, and improvements in the Z-9A helicopter. These acquisitions have enabled China to significantly upgrade its *Luhu*-class destroyer, *Jiangwei*-class air defense frigate, new large patrol craft, and new intelligence-gathering ships.[15] Although these systems will take some time to become fully operational, they are intended to implement China's new naval strategy of "active offshore defense," which emphasizes power projection capabilities far from the coast of China.

China's interest in acquiring an aircraft carrier from Russia or the Ukraine seems to wax and wane.[16] Keen interest has been expressed, however, in Russian Kilo-class conventional submarines. China reportedly would like to buy two subs and build others itself. Newer model Kilos take about two years to build in Russia. The Kilos would considerably upgrade China's submarine fleet, mostly based on Romeo-class boats of 1950 vintage. The Kilo has a range of 9,650 kilometers and can stay at sea for 45 days.

Moscow appears to be sensitive to Asian concerns over its naval sales to China and seems reluctant to modernize the PLA navy too much. There may be some conflict of interest in this regard, however, between the Russian foreign and defense ministries, which reportedly oppose the sale of some advanced systems to China, and defense industries which want to provide jobs for their workers and to earn desperately need foreign exchange.[17]

According to congressional testimony by CIA Director R. James Woolsey in February 1993, China was obtaining missile technology from both Russia and Ukraine, "and is actively pursuing agreements [with them] covering increasingly more sensitive areas."[18] China hired about 3,000 Russian weapons experts and acquired nuclear and ballistic missile technology by offering high salaries and lavish living conditions.[19] Russian programs studied by the Chinese included the SS-25, Russia's most modern, mobile ICBM. Hundreds of Chinese experts visited Russian defense plants, and weapons designs and mathematical modeling work were sent electronically to China from Russian weapons laboratories. As Sino-Russian relations improve there is reason to expect that military cooperation will increase, although there clearly is an intrinsic limit on such assistance.

In addition to working closely with Russia, the PLA has extensive military contacts with other countries possessing advanced weapons. For example, China is known to be cooperating with Iran to acquire an aerial refueling capability to extend the range of its fighters and bombers. Israel is said to be involved in the area of advanced electronic warfare capabilities and a radar system for the PRC's F-8-II fighter under development in Shenyang. CIA Director Woolsey told Congress in early October 1993 that for more than a decade Israel sold advanced military technology to China and that its cooperation was increasing. The several billion dollars worth of technology transfers related to China's next generation of jet fighters, air-to-air missiles, and tanks. Of special interest to China were advanced tank power plants and airborne radar systems. The United States was concerned that China used its programs with Israel to obtain technology denied Beijing by Washington and other Western countries and that the PRC might export the new technology to Pakistan, Iran, and other Middle Eastern countries.[20]

U.S. military experts have warned for years that China's acquisition of advanced conventional weaponry, modern nuclear weapons, and long-range missiles is changing the PLA's orientation and capabilities from land-based defense of the Chinese mainland to force projection. The shift in Beijing's defense orientation, while not specifically made with Taiwan in mind, definitely increases the PLA's ability to utilize force against Taiwan to achieve PRC political objectives. In that sense the PLA's threat to Taiwan is increasing, although it should be viewed as more of a long-term rather than immediate threat.

For its part, Taiwan is very concerned about China's acquisition of new weapons systems, especially modern fighters. The building of new PRC aircraft, coupled with additional Su-27s, eventually could tip the air balance in China's favor, even with Taipei's purchase of F-16s from the United States and Mirage 2000-5 jets from France. Taiwan's concerns were editorialized in the *Free China Journal* of April 2, 1993. According to the editorial, the PRC had obtained

> about 60 Russian-made SU-27 jet fighters and Russian-made SA-10 air-defense missiles, which reportedly are more advanced than the U.S.-made Patriot missile. Russia has decided to sell a number of MiG-31 jet fighters to Peking. Peking has also obtained air refueling technology from Iran. On top of this, Peking has continued to develop modern weapons, including the East Wind-25 missile, with a range of 1,600 miles....For fiscal year 1994, Peking has earmarked US$7.5 billion for its military spending. That constitutes a 12.5 percent increase, or nearly twice the rate of increase for state expenditures overall.[21]

In sum, while China does not now have the capability to undertake an amphibious invasion of Taiwan or gain undisputed control of the sea and air in the Taiwan Strait, the PRC is acquiring substantial power projection forces. The effect of the PLA's modernization will not be known for some years as China assimilates advanced weapons systems purchased from Russia and other sources and produces its own modern arms with the help of recruited foreign defense experts. As the military modernization of China proceeds, the PLA threat to Taiwan will increase; but the exact time dimension of when that threat will become serious is subject to considerable debate.

U.S. Military Capabilities and Intentions

The capabilities of U.S. forces in the Pacific and Washington's intention to intervene on Taiwan's behalf if it is attacked by the PRC are vital factors in Taiwan's security.

Despite reductions elsewhere in the world, the Clinton administration said in 1993 that it would not further reduce U.S. military forces in the Western Pacific. In fact, largely because of tensions resulting from the North Korean nuclear weapons program, the administration increased to some extent U.S. military capabilities in Northeast Asia.

The 1992-1993 *Military Balance* listed the following naval deployments with the U.S. Pacific Command (USPACOM) headquartered in Hawaii:[22]

- Third Fleet (headquartered in San Diego): four carrier battle groups, four underway replenishment groups, one Amphibious Group
- Seventh Fleet (headquartered in Yokosuka, Japan): one carrier battle group, one underway replenishment group, one Amphibious Group.

In total, the Pacific Fleet had five carriers, 23 missile cruisers, seven missile destroyers, 14 destroyers, 20 missile frigates, 16 frigates, eight nuclear submarines armed with ballistic missiles, four nuclear submarines armed with non-ballistic missiles, 29 nuclear attack submarines, and 34 major amphibious ships.

The U.S. air force had 78 combat aircraft assigned to Japan and 84 combat aircraft stationed in South Korea. Guam served as a heavy bomber base. Major air force deployments were also in Alaska, Hawaii, and the West Coast. More than 26,000 U.S. army personnel were stationed in South Korea, and 21,000 Marines were in Japan. USPACOM forces can be reinforced on short notice from the European Command, the Central Command, the Southern Command, the Atlantic Command, and the Continental United States. Airlift, sealift, special operations, strategic forces, reconnaissance, early warning, and ready reserves of nearly 1.8 million are also available as needed.

U.S. military deployments in the Pacific were designed to defeat Soviet Far Eastern naval and air forces. They are also organized to wage a successful high-intensity war on the Korean peninsula. These capabilities -- the most powerful in the world -- would enable the United States to defend Taiwan from the numerous but mostly outdated PRC forces brought to bear in the Taiwan Strait. U.S. forces in the Pacific are not designed to fight a land war on the Chinese mainland, however, and it is doubtful such an attempt would ever be made. Nor would carrier battle groups want to venture too close to the Chinese mainland, where they could be threatened by PRC antiship missiles and coastal submarines. Nonetheless, despite reduction of U.S. forces in the Pacific begun under the Bush administration's 1990 *Strategic Framework* plan,[23] the United States remains the predominate military power in the Western Pacific. It is capable of projecting decisive force into the region around Taiwan. The question of U.S. intervention on Taiwan's behalf is not one of military capability, but one of political intention.

U.S. Intentions to Intervene

For the past twenty years, Washington has thought it wise to leave a degree of ambiguity in its intentions to intervene militarily in the Taiwan Strait. This has certainly been the case since the 1979 normalization of Sino-American relations. Most U.S. officials limit their public comments to affirmations of support for the Taiwan Relations Act, although private communications with PRC officials are said to be more explicit in warning against the use of force. Once out of office, however, former government officials have been more definitive about U.S. intentions, especially in regards to ensuring that Taiwan has adequate military forces for its defense. For example, former deputy secretary of defense James Lilley said in February 1993 that the 1992 F-16 sale to Taiwan was made in accordance with the U.S. promise to keep a military balance between Taipei and Beijing.[24] Also, in May 1993 former defense secretary Dick Cheney said it was in the U.S. interest to make "certain that Taiwan had sufficient defensive capability to deal with any threat."[25] And, as noted earlier, the Clinton administration has continued to affirm U.S. support for the TRA and has demonstrated its commitment to Taiwan's security through substantial arms sales, about which more will be said in the next chapter.

This consistent pattern of arms sales and promises to implement the Taiwan Relations Act suggests that, while the U.S. response to a crisis in the Taiwan Strait cannot be predetermined, there is high probability the United States would intervene militarily if the PRC attacked Taiwan without provocation. There are numerous reasons for this understated U.S. commitment to Taiwan's security, including:

- The importance of maintaining credibility for U.S. commitments elsewhere in Asia, especially in view of the dangerous situation on the Korean peninsula, the likelihood of Japan expanding its military forces if the United States loses its deterrent credibility, and the concerns of ASEAN that the United States is disengaging from the region and thereby precipitating a fundamental shift in the regional balance of power.
- A U.S. moral commitment to defend market democracies when they are attacked by communist or other non-democratic governments.
- The consistent warnings given Beijing by Washington that the United States expects the Taiwan issue to be resolved peacefully.
- Concern in the United States that if Beijing were successful in gaining control of Taiwan by force that China might become more aggressive in other parts of Asia.
- The protection of U.S. interests in maintaining peace and stability in the Western Pacific and in sustaining a favorable balance of power in East Asia.
- The precedent of previous U.S. intervention on Taiwan's behalf.
- The legal requirements outlined in the 1979 Taiwan Relations Act, which state that it is U.S. policy (1) "to consider any effort to determine the future of Taiwan by other than peaceful means...a threat to the peace and security of the Western Pacific area and of grave concern to the United States" and (2) "to maintain the capacity of the United States to resist any resort to force or other forms of coercion that would jeopardize the security, or the social or economic system, of the people of Taiwan."
- The distrust most Americans feel for the Chinese communists and the strong public and congressional support for Taiwan in Washington.

The United States does not seek a military confrontation with the PRC over Taiwan; indeed, both Washington and Beijing have sought to avoid such a confrontation since the Korean War. Nonetheless, just as many Chinese believe force may be justified to prevent Taiwan independence, so many Americans feel the United States should intervene if the PRC attacks Taiwan.

Areas of Uncertainty

One gray area -- and hence an area of uncertainty and some danger -- is the U.S. response in the event Taiwan moved formally toward independence and thereby precipitated Beijing's use of force. Since the

PRC has warned repeatedly it would "shed blood" under such circumstances, this action on Taiwan's part would be seen by many Americans as unduly provocative. Assisting Taiwan against unprovoked PRC aggression is one thing; protecting Taiwan when it unnecessarily provoked Beijing is quite another. Under these latter conditions, the modalities of U.S. intervention become much more difficult to forecast.

Fortunately for all concerned, the probability of Taiwan provoking an attack by the PRC is small. DPP leaders have said they are not so foolish as to give the PRC justification to attack the island. And, as noted earlier, the probability of Beijing attacking Taiwan without severe provocation is also quite small. Since both sides want to avoid a conflict, and U.S. policy is to encourage Beijing and Taipei to find a peaceful resolution of their differences, there appears to be only a slight chance that force will be used in the Taiwan Strait. A conflict could occur unplanned and unexpectedly, however. For instance:

- An isolated confrontation between PRC and ROC armed forces might escalate into a larger conflict. There is ample opportunity for such a clash to occur: both sides are on a high state of military alert; air and sea traffic around the East and South China Seas is extremely heavy; territorial disputes in the South China Sea remain unresolved and volatile; there is a tremendous rise in piracy, smuggling, fishing boat incidents, and airline hijacking in the Taiwan Strait region.

- Social order could break down on Taiwan, precipitating PLA intervention. Violent confrontations between pro-unification and pro-independence advocates are possible on Taiwan. Radicals from one side or the other could resort to force if they believed the ROC government was about to sell out their interests by moving decisively in the direction of either independence or early unification. In either case, an appeal for Beijing's assistance might be made by pro-unification forces. If the PRC decided to intervene, PLA and ROC forces could clash.

- The PRC might decide to signal displeasure over some development on Taiwan through a limited display of force, perhaps leading to a larger conflict. For instance, Beijing might deploy a few submarines or surface warships in the Taiwan Strait to protest Taipei's decision to drop its "one China" policy. The intent of the signal might be misinterpreted by the ROC, and the Chinese ships might be attacked. A chain of events could be initiated which would prove impossible to stop before escalating into war.

Under these and similar scenarios, there is no way of predicting how the United States would react. There would be no overt PRC aggression; there would be no provocation on the part of Taipei. Since U.S. interests would be harmed by a war between Taiwan and mainland China, Washington would try to stop the escalating violence as soon as possible. In response to the American appeal, Beijing and Taipei might de-escalate their confrontation. But there is also the possibility the Chinese might want to continue the struggle to resolve their differences once and for all. This often happens when one side in a conflict thinks it has nothing to gain by ending the war too soon, or one side believes it has gained an advantage it does not want to surrender. Moreover, as will be seen in the next chapter, a war in the Taiwan Strait would likely be one of rapid escalation and high intensity. The war's outcome might be decided before diplomacy could work its course.

In this situation of ambiguous cause and effect, U.S. policymakers might not be able to formulate an effective response -- militarily or otherwise. Unable to stop the war by political means and not wanting to intervene militarily when there was no clear PRC aggression or ROC provocation, the United States might opt to remain outside the conflict. Washington would simply be prepared to formulate a new China policy once the situation had stabilized.

In summary, the United States does have the military capability to intervene effectively on Taiwan's behalf should a war break out in the Taiwan Strait. The United States would almost certainly aid Taiwan in case of overt PRC aggression. If Taiwan provoked the PRC attack, then the U.S. response would be more problematic. If a conflict occurred unexpectedly between the two sides without clear responsibility, then U.S. policymakers might be hamstrung until it was too late to make a difference.

Conclusion

Taiwan has a complex and contradictory security environment. The factors influencing ROC security include a broad range of geographical, international, domestic, cross-straits, and U.S.-PRC-ROC dimensions, as well the military capabilities and political intentions of Taipei, Beijing, and Washington. Assessments of some of these factors suggest that the PRC threat to Taiwan is very low. Other factors suggest that the PRC threat is increasing. Overall, it appears that the present PRC threat is low but increasing. Taiwan will always require external assistance.

In terms of geographical factors, Taiwan is a large island separated from mainland China by one hundred miles of ocean. It would be difficult and very costly to blockade Taiwan effectively and almost impossible at this time for the PRC to invade and conquer the island. The offshore islands and Penghu, however, are somewhat easier objectives. Internationally, Taiwan's strong economy and status as a valuable trading partner are its chief security assets. But there is no guarantee Taiwan's economic strength would be sufficient to draw international support against a militant PRC. The only major country which might effectively support Taipei in a political or military showdown with Beijing is the United States.

Greater democracy and a prosperous economy have greatly strengthened Taiwan's security and improved its international standing. But these developments have also increased the PRC threat to Taiwan. Beijing is deeply concerned over the rise of Taiwanese nationalism. Moreover, the ROC must now be wary of becoming too dependent on mainland China for Taiwan's economic well-being.

It seems very unlikely that the PRC would use force against Taiwan except to prevent a formal move toward Taiwan independence. Such a policy decision on Taipei's part cannot be ruled out, however, given the shifting balance of political power on the island. Since the possibility of Taiwan independence is greater now than before, then the PRC threat to Taiwan is also greater. PRC intentions to stop Taiwan independence, by force if necessary, have not changed.

Taiwan must exercise great wariness to avoid having its interests sacrificed by Beijing and Washington. At the same time, the sensitivity of the Taiwan issue in Sino-American relations gives the ROC ample opportunity for maneuver.

At present, the PRC does not have all the military capabilities needed to undertake decisive military operations against Taiwan. But the PLA is modernizing its power projection forces, ostensibly for operations in the South China Sea but also in ways relevant to the Taiwan theater. The PLA will need at least a decade to assimilate and make operational advanced weapons and technology imported from Russia and other countries. The process of PLA modernization will continue well into the twenty-first century, but this does not guarantee that war will remain absent in the Taiwan Strait.

For the duration of the Clinton administration, it appears certain the United States will maintain adequate military capabilities to intervene decisively on Taiwan's behalf. However, U.S. intervention cannot be taken for granted. In case of unprovoked PRC aggression, Washington would most likely aid Taiwan militarily. If Taiwan provoked the PRC by moving toward formal independence, the U.S. response would be more difficult to predict. There are also several ambiguous situations in which the United States might not be able to formulate an effective response in time to help Taiwan in an accidental war with the PRC.

The next chapter continues this discussion of Taiwan's security by examining ROC military capabilities, its deterrent strategies, and several conflict scenarios relevant to the current security environment in East Asia.

Notes

1. Both Beijing and Taipei view the ROC occupation of the offshore islands as evidence of the KMT's continued commitment to a unified China. This commitment has required the ROC to defend the offshore islands at all costs. It also meant PRC leaders were reluctant to launch a full-scale attack against the islands because their seizure might make it easier for Taipei to drop its "one China" policy. Mao Zedong's thinking along these lines during the Quemoy crises of 1954 and 1958 is explained in Li Yuanchao, "The Politics of Artillery Shelling: A Study of the Taiwan Strait Crises," *Beijing Review*, September 7-13, 1992, pp. 32-38.

2. See Susan L. Shirk, "Chinese Views on Asia-Pacific Regional Security Cooperation," NBR *Analysis*, Vol. 5, No. 5 (December 1994).

3. ROC Defense Minister (later Premier) Hau Pei-tsun told the Legislative Yuan in December 1989: "The ROC military will not defend Taiwan in the case of independence. The ROC military will only defend the Republic of China and the ROC Constitution." *Free China Journal*, December 25, 1989, p. 2.

4. *China Post*, April 23, 1993, p. 1.

5. *Beijing Review*, April 12-18, 1993, p. 9.

6. *Beijing Review*, March 22-28, 1993, p. 9.

7. *China News*, October 31, 1992, p. 1.

8. Parris H. Chang and Martin L. Lasater, eds., *If China Crosses the Taiwan Strait: The International Response* (Lanham, MD: University Press of America, 1993), p. vii.

9. For a summary of a recent Chinese military treatise on this subject, see *New York Times*, November 16, 1993, p. A16. These scenarios fit with China's strategic doctrine of "limited and regional wars" adopted in the mid-1980s. The

doctrine emphasizes rapid reaction units characterized by mobility, flexibility, speed, and overwhelming firepower.

10. New China News Agency (Xinhua) analysis carried in various official PRC newspapers. Quoted in *China News*, August 17, 1992, p. 1.

11. PLA capabilities are taken from *The Military Balance, 1992-1993* (London: International Institute for Strategic Studies, 1992), pp. 139-140, 143-147.

12. William Branigan, "Beijing Buildup Has Asia Worried," *Washington Post*, quoted in *China Post*, April 5, 1993, p. 2.

13. *Far Eastern Economic Review*, September 2, 1993, p. 20.

14. *Far Eastern Economic Review*, October 14, 1993, p. 9. According to a January 1995 report from Hong Kong by the Japanese news agency Yomiuri Shimbun, the PRC was developing at least two new fighters with foreign assistance. One was being manufactured at the Shenyang Aircraft Corporation and was built with Russian technical assistance, particularly on the engines which were an improved version of the RD-33 used in the MiG-29. This aircraft was intended to replace the Chinese F-8 frontline fighter. The second aircraft, lighter than the MiG-29, was being manufactured at the Chengdu Aircraft Corporation with technical assistance from Israel. CNA report from Tokyo, Japan, January 9, 1995.

15. Preliminary draft by Harlan W. Jencks, "PRC Military and Security Policy in the Post-Cold War Era," paper presented to the 23rd Sino-American Conference on Contemporary China, Taipei, Taiwan, June 6-9, 1994, ms.

16. According to Yomiuri Shimbun, China's Central Military Commission recently approved a ten-year plan to build two 40,000-ton aircraft carriers, each capable of carrying forty planes, to strengthen the PLA's naval power in controversies over the South China Seas and Taiwan. CNA report from Tokyo, Japan, January 16, 1995.

17. *Far Eastern Economic Review*, July 8, 1993, pp. 24-26.

18. *Washington Post*, February 25, 1993, p. A18.

19. After the collapse of the Soviet Union, Russia's top scientists and weapons experts were not paid, and a $100 million effort led by the United States to keep track of the scientists proved ineffective. Chinese sources reported that the Russian scientists receive salaries of $2,000 a month, plus housing, car, and living expenses.

20. *New York Times*, October 13, 1993, p. A5. The *Los Angeles Times* and Reuters news agency reported in January 1995 that Israel was using American technology supplied for the cancelled Lavi fighter project to help the PRC develop a new warplane. Reuters report from Washington, D.C., January 5, 1995. See note 14 above.

21. *Free China Journal*, April 2, 1993, p. 6.

22. U.S. military forces are described in *The Military Balance, 1992-1993*, pp. 13-28.

23. *A Strategic Framework for the Asian Pacific Rim: Looking Toward the 21st Century* (Washington, D.C.: Department of Defense, 1990). The Pentagon initially planned to reduce U.S. forward deployed forces in the Pacific from around 135,000 to 120,000 by the end of 1993. Actual reductions, however, were more substantial. According to USCINCPAC Admiral Charles Larson, U.S. forward deployed forces in April 1993 were down about 25 percent to 100,000. See Charles R. Larson, "An American Umbrella for Asian Storms," *Asian Wall Street Journal*, April 16, 1993.

24. *Free China Journal*, February 26, 1993, p. 2.

25. *Free China Journal*, May 18, 1993, p. 7.

7

The PRC Threat to Taiwan

The previous chapter concluded that Beijing probably does not intend to use massive force against Taiwan unless it is necessary to prevent Taiwan independence. At present, the ROC shows no intention of declaring Taiwan an independent country, although it does seem to favor de facto "two Chinas." There is a possibility, however, of a pro-independence government coming to power on Taiwan through democratic elections. This could precipitate a military crisis in the Taiwan Strait. Also, war between Beijing and Taipei could break out accidentally. PRC leaders might also use limited force to coerce Taipei in ways short of war.

This chapter further examines the PRC threat to Taiwan by describing the military capabilities of the ROC armed forces, the ROC military modernization program, Taiwan's war-fighting strategy, the ROC formula for deterrence, and various scenarios for conflict in the Taiwan Strait.

Capabilities of ROC Armed Forces

According to the *Military Balance*, ROC armed forces in 1992 totalled about 360,000 active duty personnel, with 1,650,000 in the reserves.[1] Some 260,000 served in the army, with 1.5 million in reserves. Taiwan had over 300 M-48A5 and 150 M-48H main battle tanks and about 900 light tanks. It was well equipped with artillery, multiple rocket launchers, mortars, and antitank weapons of various kinds. Taiwan's highly mobile forces are designed to deploy in a series of formidable armored barriers to a PRC invasion of Taiwan.

The army is also responsible for Taiwan's air and shore defense. *Hsiung Feng* (Gabriel-type) surface-to-surface missiles (SSM) are deployed in strategic locations around the island, as are air defense guns and surface-to-air missiles (SAM). Of the latter, the most important are Nike Hercules, Hawk, Chaparral, and *Tien Kung* (Sky Bow) missiles. Recent versions of the Sky Bow SAM are similar to the U.S. Patriot SAM used with good effect in the 1991 Persian Gulf War against Iraqi Scud missiles.

In 1992 the ROC navy had 30,000 personnel with an additional 30,000 Marines. Its submarine fleet was minimal: two U.S. Guppy-class and two Dutch Zwaardvis-class submarines, all armed with 533mm torpedoes. Taiwan was far stronger in surface warships with 24 destroyers and 12 frigates.

Of the destroyers, eight were U.S. Gearing-class ships equipped with area SAM, antisubmarine rockets (ASROC), antisubmarine torpedoes (ASTT), and a helicopter pad for the Hughes MD-500. Six Gearing-class ASW destroyers were armed with ASROC, ASTT, helicopter pad, and *Hsiung Feng-II* antiship missiles (SSM). There were also six U.S. Sumner-class destroyers armed with ASTT, SSM, and helicopters; and four U.S. Fletcher-class destroyers armed with ASTT and SSM. The destroyers armed with SSM also carried 127mm or 76mm guns.

Of Taiwan's 12 frigates, nine were U.S. Lawrence/Crosley-class and one was the former U.S. *Rudderow*. All were armed with ASTT and 127mm guns. In addition, Taiwan had in service two recently leased U.S. Knox-class missile frigates armed with ASROC, ASTT, 127mm guns, Harpoon missiles fired from ASROC launchers, and pads for SH-2F LAMPS ASW helicopters.

In addition to these major combatants, Taiwan had 93 patrol and coastal combatants, including 52 missile patrol craft carrying *Hsiung Feng-II* antiship missiles. There were also 13 mine warfare ships, 26 amphibious craft, and 28 support and miscellaneous vessels.

The ROC air force had 70,000 personnel with 486 combat aircraft but no bombers. Taiwan's principal fighters were 214 F-5E Tigers and 142 F-104 Starfighters. The most common missiles used by the ROC air force were AGM-65A Maverick air-to-surface missiles and AIM-4D Falcon, AIM-9J/P Sidewinder, and Shafrir air-to-air missiles.

Taiwan's Military Modernization

Until the termination of U.S.-ROC diplomatic relations in 1979 and the abrogation of the 1954 U.S.-ROC Mutual Defense Treaty a year later, Taiwan relied almost exclusively on the deterrent value of the United States to protect it from PRC aggression. Equipped and trained by the U.S. military, ROC forces were expected to hold off the PLA until the United States could intervene. After the breaking of diplomatic relations, however, the credibility of the U.S. commitment -- even with the passage of the 1979 Taiwan Relations Act -- was questioned by Taipei. Taiwan began a concentrated effort to diversify sources of advanced weapons and to build an indigenous weapons production program. Areas of priority included ground, naval, and air forces, as well as air defense systems. Recent ROC acquisitions in each of these areas are noted below.[2]

Ground Forces

The modernization of ROC ground forces focused on improving heavy artillery and heavy armored weapons such as tanks and armored personnel carriers. The purpose of this modernization was to give the ROC the ability to repel any amphibious invasion of Taiwan and to establish heavily armored barriers along the routes of advance of PRC forces able to establish a beachhead on the island.

The modernization of Taiwan's ground forces mostly involved upgrading of equipment already possessed by the ROC army. Major programs included placing new cannon and power plants on M-48 heavy tanks. The army's capabilities were enhanced in early 1992 by Taiwan's purchase of 42 AH-1W Super Cobra attack gunships and 26 OH-58D Kiowa Warrior scout helicopters from the United States. The Cobras were worth $828 million and were to be shipped over the next five years. The Warriors, worth $367 million, were scheduled to arrive over the next three years. Negotiations were also underway with Bell Helicopter Textron to produce Warriors under license on Taiwan.[3]

In August 1994 the ROC army announced it had purchased 160 M-60A3 tanks from the United States at a cost of $91 million. The tanks were equipped with thermal sights. The purchase of the tanks had been delayed several months due to opposition in the parliament over arms transactions in general, opposition which also temporarily halted the purchase of a new $1 billion air defense system and the lease of 40 T-38A training planes.[4]

Naval Forces

Taiwan's efforts to develop a modern navy focused on upgrading existing destroyers and acquiring new frigates, patrol craft, submarines, antisubmarine warfare systems, and shipborne air defense systems. These systems were required to counter one of the greatest threats facing Taiwan: a naval blockade utilizing the PRC's large submarine force. Since the PLA navy is rapidly acquiring modern power projection capability, the ROC's naval modernization program will receive continued priority.

Surface Ships. One of the most important ROC modernization programs is the replacement of World War II destroyers that have made up the backbone of Taiwan's antisubmarine warfare (ASW) capabilities. A combination of purchasing, construction, and leasing of ships is achieving this goal.

In 1987 the state-owned China Shipbuilding Corporation and the U.S. Bath Ironworks company agreed to build eight modified Oliver Hazard Perry (FFG-7) frigates for $1.6 billion. The frigates, classed between a cruiser and a destroyer, are being built on Taiwan under the designation of PFG-2. Construction began in January 1990. The first ship (the *Cheng Kung*) was christened in October 1991 and entered service in May 1993. A second frigate was also launched and scheduled to enter service in 1994. Two more frigates were launched by September 1994. The six frigates, each of which takes about 40 months to complete, should be operational by the end of the decade.

The 4,300 metric-ton PFG-2 frigates are 453 feet in length and 47 feet wide. They carry two S-70C-M1 Seahawk antisubmarine helicopters and the Phalanx close-in weapons system. The second-generation missile frigates are also armed with two MK-32 triple torpedo tubes for ASW, as well as a bow-mounted missile launcher capable of firing *Hsiung Feng-II* antiship missiles at a rate of one every ten seconds. Each ship carries 40 missiles. The frigates have eight SM-1 Standard surface-to-air missile launchers. The ship's 76mm gun fires 80 rounds per minute with a range of 11 kilometers; the 40mm gun can fire 300 rounds per minute at targets eight kilometers away. In September 1994 the U.S. Department of Defense informed the Congress of its intention to sell Taiwan the MK-

45 Mod. 2 five-inch/54 caliber gun system for the PFG-2.[5] The frigates are equipped with the latest radar and radar detection equipment, and centrifugal gyros stabilize the ships in rough waters. The ROC says the mission of the PFG-2 is to patrol the Taiwan Strait.[6]

In July 1992 the ROC obtained a five-year lease for three Knox-class frigates from the U.S. navy. The lease program totalled $236.2 million, including personnel training and logistics. The frigates were placed into service in October 1993 and will be used to escort convoys and in ASW patrols. Six more Knox-class frigates will be leased between 1994 and 1995. The lease of the warships was Taiwan's first such arrangement with the United States since 1979. Taiwan might purchase the frigates as soon as the lease expires.[7]

The 3,000 metric-ton warships are equipped to handle the Light Airborne Multipurpose System (LAMPS) helicopters purchased from the United States in early 1993. The principal weapon of the frigates is the Harpoon antiship missile. In September 1993 the United States agreed to sell Taiwan 41 Harpoon missiles for the frigates. The ships are also armed with Phalanx MK-16 multiple launchers.

In August 1992 the United States announced approval of the sale of 207 SM-1 Standard naval surface-to-air missiles to be mounted on Taiwan's new frigates. The sale, totalling $126 million, included full logistic support, parts, and training.

Another major addition to the ROC surface fleet occurred in late 1991, when France approved the sale of 16 LaFayette-class frigates for $4.8 billion. The state-run Thomson-CSF and China Shipbuilding Corporation are building the 3,200 metric-ton high-speed warships for escort duty. The frigates will be shipped from France as empty hulls beginning in 1994. In May 1992 France sold Taiwan decoy launchers and optronic fire control systems for the frigates for about $54 million. In October 1993 Reuters reported that France had decided to sell Taiwan $2.6 billion worth of naval weapons for the LaFayette frigates. These included ship-to-ship Exocet missiles, Crotal and Mistral antiaircraft missiles, torpedoes, 100mm rapid-fire cannon, and electronic warfare equipment.[8]

In mid-1994 the ROC navy hoped to lease three Newport-class tank-landing ships (LSTs) from the U.S. navy at a cost of $4.7 million. The Newport-class ships displace 8,450 tons and can transport tanks, heavy vehicles, engineering equipment, and supplies too heavy for helicopters and other landing craft. The ships are equipped with two 76mm guns and a Phalanx weapons system. Although the lease was approved by the

Clinton administration as part of a proposal to transfer 17 ships to nine countries, Congress passed legislation cutting the number to only seven ships to four countries upon hearing a report from the Senate Armed Services Committee that the U.S. navy was retiring its fleet of amphibious ships too rapidly. As of September 1994 efforts were being made by the U.S. government and Taiwan to find two or three suitable mothballed Newport LSTs so as not to affect the active-duty fleet.[9]

Submarines. Taiwan's navy wants 10-12 submarines to provide a deterrent against a PRC blockade of the island.[10] At the end of 1993 the ROC had only four submarines. The two U.S.-built Guppy-class submarines transferred in 1973 were nearly fifty years old and used mostly for training. The two Dutch-built Zwaardvis-class submarines were sold to Taiwan in 1981 over strong PRC protests and were delivered by the Dutch Rotterdamse Droogdok Mij (RDM) shipyard in the late 1980s.

In early 1992 RDM sought permission to sell Taiwan ten Sea Dragon diesel-electric submarines for $4.7 billion. The 2,000-ton boats carry a crew of 60.[11] The Dutch government refused to issue an export license for the submarines, but parliament passed a resolution placing conditions on the government ban, including increased trade with the PRC and no arms sales to Taiwan by other European countries. Neither condition was met. When the United States and France sold jet fighters to Taiwan in late 1992, the Dutch parliament turned strongly in favor of the submarine sale. A key factor was the pending shutdown of the RDM submarine division due to lack of new orders.

RDM, with the support of parliament, then presented Taiwan with a proposal to build ten additional modified Zwaardvis-class submarines for around $4.5 billion. The boats would be built in Taiwan under license similar to the U.S.-Taiwan frigate construction program. The first phase of the RDM proposal would be the provision of technology and components to build four new submarines. The Dutch plan reflected the increased tendency by Western governments to use licensing programs as a way to sell Taiwan shipbuilding technology and components without direct sales of completed warships, which inevitably lead to strong PRC protests and often political or economic sanctions.

France reportedly also offered diesel-electric submarines to Taiwan. The ROC would like to purchase advanced Type-209 diesel-electric submarines from Germany, but the German government has thus far refused to sell the boats. The German subs are light-weight, about 1,300 tons, and of a size considered ideal for the shallow Taiwan Strait.[12]

ASW Helicopters and Aircraft. In October 1992 the United States sold Taiwan 12 Kaman SH-2F LAMPS-1 (Light Airborne Multi-Purpose System) ASW helicopters and 12 spare engines for $161 million. These will be deployed on the newly leased Knox-class frigates and the new *Cheng Kung*-class PFG-2 frigates. The LAMPS system is supplemented by upgraded versions of the ROC navy's Grumman S-2 Tracker maritime patrol aircraft and the Sikorsky S-70C Seahawk ASW helicopter.

Antiship Missiles. Taiwan's principal antiship missile is the *Hsiung Feng* SSM. Earlier versions of the *Hsiung Feng* derived from the Israeli Gabriel-II antiship missile, whereas the *Hsiung Feng-II* incorporates technology from the U.S. AGM-84 Harpoon. There are three models of the *Hsiung Feng-II*: air-to-ship, ship-to-ship, and surface-to-ship. Both ship-launched and air-launched versions have a range of about 100 kilometers with an active radar and imaging infrared terminal guidance seeker system. In November 1993 it was announced that test firing of the *Hsiung Feng-II* air-to-ship missile had been successfully completed.[13]

In September 1993, a few days after the release of the PRC's "White Paper on Taiwan," the United States sold Taiwan 41 Harpoon antiship missiles for $68 million. The agreement, which includes training, was the first significant U.S. arms sale to Taiwan since the F-16 sale announced in September 1992. Taiwan had been requesting the Harpoon for more than a decade.[14]

Air Force

One of the keys to Taiwan's defense is ROC air supremacy over the Taiwan Strait. If the ROC can control the skies, then a PRC amphibious invasion of Taiwan is impossible and an effective blockade of the island is prohibitively costly.

For more than fifteen years Taiwan sought to replace the backbone of its air defense system, the F-5E Tiger II, with a newer and more advanced U.S. fighter such as the F-16 Fighting Falcon, F-4C Phantom, or F-5G Tiger Shark (later designated F-20). In January 1982, however, the Reagan administration decided not to sell a new fighter to Taiwan to avoid a possible rupture in Sino-American relations. In announcing the U.S. decision the State Department said, "no sale of advanced fighter aircraft to Taiwan is required because no military need for such aircraft exists. Taiwan's defense needs can be met as they arise, and for the foreseeable future, by replacing aging aircraft now in the Taiwan inventory with comparable aircraft and by extension of the F-5E coproduction line in Taiwan."[15]

Taiwan was also unsuccessful in purchasing the Kfir fighter from Israel. In this case the principal reason was not Israeli concern over offending the PRC, but Saudi Arabia's objection to Taiwan purchasing the plane from Israel. Since the Saudis were one of the ROC's most important diplomatic friends and had promised to supply Taiwan's oil needs, Taipei did not complete the Kfir deal.

Stymied in its efforts to purchase an advanced replacement fighter from abroad, Taiwan concentrated on building its own indigenous fighter (IDF). In the post-Cold War environment of the 1990s, Taipei renewed its efforts to acquire the F-16 and the French-built Mirage 2000-5.

IDF Program. In 1981 the ROC established the Chung Shan Institute of Science and Technology to produce an indigenous fighter (IDF). Beginning in 1983 design for the IDF was assisted by General Dynamics, while Lear Siegler assisted with the avionics package and Garrett Engine company helped Taiwan develop the F-125 engine with 9,500 pounds of thrust.

The first IDF prototype, dubbed the *Ching-kuo* fighter after President Chiang Ching-kuo, appeared in 1988. Test flights were begun in 1989, but the next year the ROC decided the IDF needed a more powerful engine. Two versions were considered: a scaled-down version of the General Electric F-404 rated at 12,900 pounds of thrust and an upgraded version of Garrett's F-125 or perhaps a more advanced Garrett TFE-1088 engine.

The IDF is a sophisticated close-in air superiority fighter with some antiship capability. It has a low radar profile and can fire several kinds of missiles, including air-to-air missiles similar to the AIM-9L Sidewinder and AIM-54 Phoenix and air-to-ship missiles such as the *Hsiung Feng-II*. It is also armed with a General Electric Vulcan M-61A cannon. The IDF has a pulse Doppler fire control radar with both air and sea search modes out to about 150km and a look-down/shoot-down capability. The IDF is a day-night fighter that can attack from low or high altitudes.

Despite the purchase of the F-16 and Mirage in late 1992, Taipei decided to produce 130 *Ching-kuo* fighters. Ten standardized productions had been built as of December 1992. After thorough testing, another 120 were to be mass produced beginning in 1994 and completed by the end of the century. The ROC planned to export the IDF starting around the turn of the century at a cost of about $22-24 million each.[16]

F-16 Purchase. Taipei and Washington signed a letter of offer and acceptance (LOA) for 150 F-16s in November 1992.[17] Delivery of the first planes will occur in 1996. The F-16s offered Taiwan were the older model A and B versions, in use by the U.S. air force for over a decade. First developed in 1972, the F-16A/B models are single and two-seat aircraft respectively, with a thrust power of about 10,000 kilograms and a radius of action of about 925 kilometers. The plane has a maximum take-off weight of 16,000 kilograms, a speed in excess of Mach 2.0, and a service ceiling of over 15,000 meters. The F-16A/B is considered inferior to the Su-27, which has a thrust power of 12,500 kilograms, a maximum take-off weight of 22,000 kilograms, a top speed in excess of Mach 2.0, and a radius of action of 1,500 kilometers. The Su-27 is an all-weather, counter-air fighter, equipped with look-down/shoot-down weapons and beyond-visual-range air-to-air missiles.

The major weaknesses of the F-16A/B are its lack of updated electronic and weapons systems. The F-16C/D was designed to remedy these problems and to give the F-16 a ground attack capability. The F-16C/D, first developed in the 1980s, is equipped with beyond-visual-range air-to-air missiles, improved fire radar controls, a thrust power in excess of 12,500 kilograms, and a radius of action of 925 kilometers.

Not surprisingly, the ROC air force wanted the more advanced F-16C/D models. The United States was reluctant to do this because of the plane's offensive capabilities. A compromise was worked out with Washington whereby Taiwan would receive new F-16 MLU (Mid-Life Upgrade) aircraft similar to models scheduled to be flown by American and European air defense pilots. The F-16 MLU will be a more advanced model of the F-16A/B, with some functions identical to the F-16C/D. The cost of the 150 MLU versions of the F-16A/B is about $6 billion.

In accepting the newer models, the ROC became a partner in the F-16A/B MLU program with Belgium, Norway, Denmark, and the Netherlands. After some concern that the European countries might back out of the upgrade program and thus boost the cost to Taiwan by an additional $3.3 million per plane, Taipei confirmed in April 1993 that the four European nations would participate in the MLU program. The 680 MLU model F-16s on order will go to the United States (229), European countries (301), and Taiwan (150).[18]

In November 1992 Taiwan and the United States signed an agreement for 180 engines plus spare parts and support equipment for the F-16s, valued at about $1 billion. Pratt & Whitney, whose engines will power the F-16, contemplated in early 1993 to invest $100 million in a maintenance plant on Taiwan to service its engines.[19] In August 1994 the Defense Department announced it would sell Taiwan 80 electronic-countermeasures (ECM) pods for the F-16 at a cost of $150 million. The new pods, built by Raytheon, will probably also be installed in the IDF.[20]

A few days after President Bush's announcement of the F-16 sale, General Dynamics President Gordon England said Taiwan would get the F-16A/B and the U.S. air force's Mid-Life Upgrade program, but it would not receive the technology to build the F-16. He also ruled out the possibility of coproduction on Taiwan "at this time."[21] Nonetheless, as part of a $600 million offset agreement for parts technology, Taiwan manufacturers were allowed to produce F-16 components such as air intakes, engine access doors, ventral fins, AIM-9 rocket launchers and adapters, centerline pylons, and fuel pylons. Lockheed planned to set up a $610 million factory on Taiwan to produce components for automatic air navigation systems.[22]

In April 1993 ROC Defense Minister Sun Chen told the Legislative Yuan that Taiwan was considering the lease of older model F-16A/Bs to fill the air defense void until the newer models arrived in 1996. The ROC air force also wanted to lease T-38s training planes from Washington. The T-38 Talon carries no weapons or radar and is an earlier training version of the F-5. If leased, the planes will be used to train ROC pilots until the F-16s and Mirages arrive in order to limit flights of existing aircraft that are prone to accident.[23]

Mirage Purchase. Shortly after the announcement of the F-16 sale, Taiwan finalized the purchase of 60 Mirage 2000-5 fighters from France for $6 billion. The deal included over 1,500 Mica air-to-air missiles. The French were said to have offered Taiwan an additional 60 Mirage fighters, but Taipei declined when the United States sold the F-16. Delivery of the Mirage 2000-5 will begin in 1995. The plane will be almost identical to that used by the French air force, equipped with RDY multitarget radar and Mica air-to-air missiles.[24] The Mirage has a maximum speed in excess of Mach 2.3, a service ceiling of 18,000 meters, and a radius of action in excess of 1,800 kilometers.[25] In May 1993 it was announced that Taiwan considered the lease of 20 used Mirage 2000 for training pilots before taking delivery of the newer models.

The French Minister of Foreign Trade Gerard Longquet said in Singapore in May 1993 that Taiwan would not get technology transfers from Dassault Aviation SA, the Mirage manufacturer. He said, "technology transfers can take place in matters of civilian technology, but cannot be applied to the Mirage."[26] Meanwhile, Dassault and Taiwan continued to negotiate a joint aerospace enterprise to build civilian planes. There was also discussion over Dassault establishing a manufacturing plant on Taiwan to build parts for the Mirage.

In reaction to the French sale of the Mirage, Beijing ordered France to close its consulate in Guangzhou and banned French companies from participating in a $1 billion subway project. Pressured by French industrialists who felt they were being denied business opportunities in the PRC, Paris agreed in January 1994 to sign a communique with Beijing stating:

> [The] Chinese side reaffirms that the sale of any type of arms will bring harm to China's sovereignty, security and reunification and the Chinese Government firmly opposes it. To take account of the Chinese side's concern the French Government pledges not to authorize French enterprises to participate in arming Taiwan in the future.

The French government said that arms sales already approved for Taiwan would go forward, including the 16 LaFayette-class frigates and 60 Mirage 2000-5 fighters.[27] The French defense minister also said that the sale of armored vehicles and non-offensive military equipment would continue.[28] The communique was a blow to Taiwan's defense establishment, which had looked to France as an alternative, non-American source of modern weapons and technology. The French government's willingness to sell the Mirage was an important factor in President Bush's decision to sell the F-16 to Taiwan.

Sufficiency of Air Defense. Defense Minister Sun Chen told the ROC legislature in July 1993 that 430 jet fighters would be sufficient for Taiwan's air defense through the year 2000. These would include 150 F-16s, 60 Mirage 2000-5, 130 IDF fighters, and the 90 remaining upgraded F-5Es. He said no further purchases were planned at this time, although additional research and development on four major jet fighter projects would proceed at the Chung Shan Institute. As of mid-1993, the ROC had 120 F-104s and 220 F-5Es. Most of these aircraft were scheduled to be taken out of service in the near future as the newer fighters became operational.[29]

As with many aspects of Taiwan's security, the purchase of the F-16 and Mirage fighters ran afoul of the ROC's more democratic legislative process. Fearful that opposition in the parliament would undermine the purchase, the KMT orchestrated legislative approval. With only three members present due to a hurried roll call, the legislature approved a $12 billion special budget for the purchase of the F-16 and Mirage fighters in July 1993, cutting $56.6 million from the original proposals.[30]

Air-to-Air Missiles. To be effective, fighters must be equipped with reliable missiles, yet another area of priority for Taiwan. The Mirage deal comes with at least 1,500 Matra Mica air-to-air missiles. Taipei has discussed with Washington the purchase of the AIM-120 AMRAAM (Advanced Medium-Range Air-to-Air Missile) for use on the F-16 and perhaps the upgraded F-5E. Taiwan has developed the *Tien Chien-I* air-to-air missile, similar to the U.S. AIM-9L. The ROC is also developing the *Tien Chien-II*, a medium-range missile similar to the U.S. AIM-7 Sparrow radar-guided air-to-air missile.

Further upgrading its air defense capabilities, the ROC Defense Ministry announced in July 1992 that it had reached agreement with the United States to purchase four E-2C Hawkeye early warning aircraft for an undisclosed amount of money.[31] In March 1994 it was reported that Taiwan will take delivery in September 1995 of four Hawkeye early warning command and control aircraft valued at $760 million. The deal included logistics, personnel training, a software development lab on Taiwan, and an offset agreement worth 10 percent of the contract.[32]

Ground-Based Missile Air Defense Systems

Defense Minister Sun Chen told the Legislative Yuan in March 1993 that Taiwan faced difficulties in its air defense over the next two years because the F-16s would not be available until 1996 and the IDF would not begin mass production until 1994. He said the ROC needed to upgrade its early warning systems and antiair missile batteries.[33] Several major projects were designed to overcome this ground-based air defense weakness.

The Chung Shan Institute has designed several variations of the *Tien Kung* (Sky Bow) SAM to replace or supplement U.S. supplied Hawk and Chapparal surface-to-air missiles of 1960s and 1970s vintage. According to the Institute, the *Tien Kung-I*, which is similar to the Hawk, is capable of shooting down the Su-27.[34]

In January 1992 the Bush administration authorized Raytheon to sell advanced Patriot anti-missile guidance radar and command and control systems for incorporation into newer versions of the *Tien Kung*. Upgraded *Tien Kung* were expected by Taiwan to counter the PRC's M-9 and M-11 surface-to-surface missiles at the same level of performance as the Patriot against the Iraqi Scud missile in the Persian Gulf War.[35]

In September 1992 Raytheon and Taiwan announced they would enter a joint venture to create the Modified Air Defense System (MADS), a Patriot missile system derivative, at a cost to Taiwan of $1.3 billion. Raytheon will provide support equipment, training, technical service, and the nose end of the missile. Taiwan will produce the rear portion of the missile, including propulsion and controls, based on Raytheon design supplied for an additional $120 million. MADS will eventually replace Taiwan's current air defense system.[36] In April 1994 it was reported that 200 Patriot missiles for the defense of northern Taiwan would be purchased for more than $377 million.[37]

Reuters reported from Taipei on July 16, 1994, that Raytheon and Taiwan signed a $565 million contract, including a $170 million industrial cooperation agreement, to purchase an undisclosed number of Patriot missiles. Under the terms of the agreement, Taiwan would produce circuit boards and liquid crystal displays. Earlier in July, Raytheon announced that it had won a contract for an undisclosed sum to provide Taiwan with 100 units of its MADS based on the Patriot missile. Under the contract, Raytheon would provide MADS fire units, missiles and related hardware, as well as logistics and spare parts support, installation assistance at various sites, and training.

In October 1993 it was announced that the United States had agreed to sell Taiwan a version of the Stinger SAM to be installed on military vehicles.[38] In August 1994 Washington reportedly agreed to an initial sale of 600 Stinger missiles. There was discussion of Taiwan receiving up to 160 Avenger missile launching and control systems from Hughes Aircraft Company. Each launcher would be equipped with eight Stingers. The systems would be mounted on multipurpose vehicles and the missiles would be encoded in such a way as to not be effective against NATO aircraft.[39]

Ballistic Missiles and Nuclear Weapons

The ROC is known to be developing a ballistic missile capability both as an offensive weapon to use against mainland targets in case of war and as a deterrent to PRC use of ballistic missiles against Taiwan. Taipei conducts this research and development largely in secret because of U.S. opposition to ballistic missile proliferation. In the past the United States has prevented the sale of ballistic missile-related technology to Taiwan from various sources.

Taiwan's nuclear weapons program is also proceeding. Yen Chen-hsing, chairman of the ROC's Atomic Energy Commission, told the Legislative Yuan in December 1988 that Taiwan "absolutely" had the capability to produce nuclear weapons. He said the ROC never stopped research on nuclear arms, but it had not produced such weapons because it was a signatory of the nuclear arms nonproliferation treaty.[40] Although some analysts have noted that nuclear weapons would be effective in destroying staging areas on the mainland in case of an invasion of Taiwan, Taipei's purpose in acquiring nuclear weapons capability is almost certainly for deterring their use by Beijing.

ROC Defense Strategy

Taiwan's defense strategy can be viewed from two closely related perspectives: its war-fighting strategy and its deterrence strategy.

War-Fighting Strategy

Simply stated, Taiwan's war-fighting strategy is to maximize PLA casualties and PRC political and economic costs. To achieve this, the ROC intends to escalate any major military conflict with the PRC to high levels of intensity as quickly as possible. As Vice Admiral Ko Tun-hwa said: "Our strategy is to make the war very costly and to hang on longer than the PRC would like....A PRC blockade of Taiwan cannot remain a blockade. It will soon develop into a full-fledged war."[41]

ROC military leaders have predicted that a war with the PRC could be decided within one week. During an exhibition of army weapons produced on Taiwan in the spring of 1993, General Wu Mu-shung was asked whether the country had plans to produce additional weapons at another location in the event the PRC attacked Taiwan. His reply suggested Taiwan's total war strategy: "A war between mainland China and Taiwan would be determined in seven days. Therefore we rely on stocked [weapons and supplies]. A war between the mainland and Taiwan will be total war and will not be a conflict of slow attrition."[42]

In March 1993 Defense Minister Sun Chen said Taiwan's military defense strategy was to keep a mainland invasion prohibitively costly in terms of casualties, materials, and international image. At the same time, he said, Taiwan should be sensitive to Beijing's paranoia over Taiwan independence and not invite an attack. Sun said the ROC air force would try to keep the main battle field above the Taiwan Strait, but it would coordinate with the army to stop mainland forces from landing on Taiwan's beaches.[43]

His predecessor as defense minister, Chen Li-an, said in late October 1992 that the purchase of the Su-27 by China meant that the PRC air force was superior to the ROC air force. Nonetheless, he said, Taiwan's existing air defenses were adequate to protect Taiwan until it received the U.S. F-16s in about three years. At that time, Chen predicted, the 150 F-16s would be more than a match for Beijing's Su-27s.

Chen Li-an said Taiwan's present inventory of aircraft and missiles could repel any intruding PRC aircraft. He observed: "Any mainland Chinese aircraft, should they violate Taiwan's air, will be detected by our radar systems....We may shoot them down with our new missiles or send our fighters to intercept them in the air." He reported that the air force had recently built three new bases (presumably referring to the underground bases on the mountainous eastern side of the island) and had redeployed its missiles to ensure air supremacy.[44]

Defense Strategy and Air Requirements. According to unpublished ROC sources, Taiwan's defense strategy rests on deterrence achieved by presenting a credible war-fighting capability against a PRC attack. Taipei has no illusion of defeating the PRC in an offensive campaign. Taiwan's security depends on an ability to thwart a major PRC air-sea-land attack through offensive and defensive operations until the high costs of the war compel Beijing to call off its efforts to defeat the ROC.

Taipei understands that if the PRC were able to wage an unlimited offensive campaign the island would eventually fall. But competing military pressures on the PLA limit to some extent the war-fighting potential that can be brought to bear on Taiwan. Taiwan's defense is feasible, although many believe U.S. military intervention may be required in the final analysis. In any event, the ROC armed forces must be able to defend Taiwan under conditions of intense combat for a minimum period of several days to give the United States time to respond politically and militarily.

Taiwan's defense strategy relies heavily on qualitative advantages over the PLA, because the PRC's overwhelming quantitative superiority leaves little room for ROC error in battle. The need for qualitative superiority has increased dramatically since 1979 as the credibility of U.S.

intervention -- hence, its deterrent value -- has decreased due to the severance of diplomatic relations and the abrogation of the U.S.-ROC defense treaty. Many analysts on Taiwan doubt U.S. intervention under most conditions in the post-Cold War period.

According to some ROC scenarios, the main military threat from the PRC is a multiphase attack designed to exploit the PLA's vast quantitative superiority and to nullify Taiwan's selective qualitative advantages. In the first phase the PRC would attack Taiwan in a series of carefully timed waves of aircraft, including light bombers and fighters. The PRC objective would be to deny Taiwan air superiority over the Taiwan Strait and to take advantage of ROC air defense limitations during night and adverse weather conditions. During this first phase, night insertion of airborne troops would be carried out, as well as continuous strikes against Taiwan's airfields and supporting structures. The attacks would be timed to overburden through attrition the ROC's constantly recycling fighters. The loss-ratio would strongly favor Taiwan, but the numerical superiority of PRC aircraft would eventually wear down and then overwhelm Taiwan's fighter force. The first wave of attacks would also target naval defenses and ground-force defenses in selected landing areas on Taiwan's coast.

The second major phase of the PRC offensive would be an amphibious invasion of Taiwan utilizing the very large numbers of motorized junks and other light vessels available to Beijing. Cover provided by darkness and adverse weather would be fully utilized. The objective of this phase would be to establish a number of infantry beachheads from which troops and light armor could move out to conquer the island in the third and final phase of the PLA offensive.

During the second phase, the primary mission of the PRC air force would be to protect the landing vessels and their troops, as well as the initial beachheads. It is clear that the second and third phases of the PLA offensive would have great difficulty if the PRC had not first succeeded in establishing air superiority over the Taiwan Strait and the island of Taiwan.

In countering this threat to Taiwan's security, the importance of the ROC air force is obvious. Taipei must retain air superiority over the island and the Taiwan Strait under all conditions in which a PRC attack is possible. If this can be achieved, the PRC attack plan is rendered infeasible and Beijing is deterred.

To achieve the essential air superiority, Taiwan's fighters, while numerically inferior, must have decisive qualitative advantages over their

PLA adversaries in key areas such as aircraft and weapon system combat performance, alert status, availability of aircraft and crews, sortie rates, adequate stores and supplies, and pilot quality.

ROC military planners believe the type of defensive requirements for Taiwan fighters to achieve air superiority include:

- Avoidance of destruction on the ground. This requires advanced warning time, rapid response time, aircraft availability, high alert status, force dispersal, and combat persistence.
- Early engagement of attacking aircraft. This requires an adequate number of ROC fighters, rapid response time, high acceleration, adequate radar range, and forward aspect and radar missiles. These advanced missiles are necessary for all weather, day/night engagements at considerable distance in order to maximize the number of kills per sortie necessary if Taiwan's numerically inferior fighters can defeat the incoming massed PLA aircraft.
- Achieve high attrition ratios and kills per sortie in combat. This requires air-combat maneuverability, excellent weapon system performance, sustainability, and pilot skill.
- Ability to maintain operations while under attack. This requires aircraft availability and reliability, a high sortie rate, fast turn-around time, base survivability, and adequate logistics.
- Ability to disrupt airborne operations under all conditions. This requires fighters and weapons with all weather, day/night fighting capabilities.

In addition to these defensive operations, Taiwan's fighters need to be able to attack airfields and other facilities (mostly in Fujian Province) from which PRC aircraft would attack. ROC military sources in the mid-1980s, for example, reported that within 750 nautical miles of Taiwan the PRC had stationed 358 bombers, 2,855 fighters, 410 transport planes, 209 helicopters, and 134 other planes. Within 600 nautical miles there were 215 bombers, 100 ground-attack fighters, 1,100 interceptors, and 60 reconnaissance aircraft. At least seven major air bases were within 250 nautical miles of Taiwan, placing aircraft stationed there within five to seven minutes of their targets on the island.[45]

The ROC considers it essential that the leading edge of the PRC attack be defeated decisively with heavy enemy loses but light damage to Taiwan and its air force. Such an outcome of the first engagements would increase the probability of the conflict being terminated early. To achieve this, Taiwan needs to get the maximum number of aircraft into combat as quickly as possible and to engage the enemy as close to the mainland as possible. This requires an exceptional early warning radar system and advanced fighters with a very rapid response time, very high rates of acceleration, and long-range radar and head-on missiles.

As the battle progresses, Taiwan would assign increasing numbers of its aircraft to air-to-sea and air-to-ground operations. Many of these missions would be conducted at night or under adverse weather conditions. Thus, other requirements for Taiwan's fighters are the ability to attack multiple surface targets during each sortie, to maintain long loiter time, to possess excellent target acquisition and identification systems under all conditions, and to carry effective munitions in great quantities.

The high demands placed on fighter aircraft in Taiwan's defense strategy have been the driving force behind the ROC's relentless efforts since the late 1970s to purchase or develop replacement fighters for its inventory of outdated F-5Es and F-104s. It was not until 1992 that Taipei's efforts in this regard were successful with the purchase of the F-16 and Mirage 2000-5 and the development of the IDF. Taipei expects the introduction of these new fighters will enable Taiwan to implement its air battle strategy for the remainder of this century, despite the purchase of advanced Russian aircraft by the PRC.

In summary, the ROC is prepared to fight a high intensity conflict arising from a PRC blockade, invasion, or air attack. As will be discussed later in this chapter, it is not clear how the ROC would respond to lesser levels of force by Beijing, force designed not to defeat Taiwan in war but to coerce Taipei into accepting certain policies. ROC strategy requires ambiguity in this gray area for deterrence purposes. Beijing cannot rule out the possibility that Taipei will react with great violence to any form of coercion, thus precipitating a major conflict the mainland wants to avoid. Because of the high risks associated with any level of force used against Taiwan, this reasoning concludes, Beijing is deterred across a broad spectrum of non-peaceful action despite its more powerful armed forces.

Comprehensive Deterrence Strategy

The overall deterrence strategy of the ROC is a sophisticated and interlocking web of deterring factors involving much more than military instruments. Defense Minister Sun Chen alluded to this broader strategy in March 1993. He told the Legislative Yuan that while the mainland had enough military prowess to invade Taiwan, the ROC government was attempting to build an international environment to discourage any mainland invasion.[46]

Taiwan's comprehensive deterrence strategy discourages a PRC use of force by utilizing military, diplomatic, political, economic, cultural, social, psychological, and other instruments available to Taipei to make any PRC use of force as expensive, unlikely, and unnecessary as possible. This strategy includes certain basic elements:

1. A modern ROC armed forces kept at a high state of readiness. The maintenance of a qualitative edge over the PLA in key areas such as air superiority, air defense, ASW, and antiship capabilities is essential.
2. A credible U.S. commitment to intervene on Taiwan's behalf. Such intervention proved decisive during earlier crises over Quemoy, and the continuation of that commitment (which may be informal but must be credible) is still essential to ROC deterrence strategy today.
3. International pressure on Beijing not to use force. Through dollar diplomacy, the ROC uses its financial resources to place Taiwan in as many international relationships as possible. Economic interdependency makes it difficult for the PRC to blockade Taiwan or to use other types of force, since such actions would harm the interests of nations other than Taiwan. A similar contribution to deterrence is achieved as Taipei expands its participation in international political circles.
4. Convincing other countries not to sell advanced weapons to the PRC. This is especially true for weapon systems that can be used in the Taiwan Strait. The PRC's acquisition of the Su-27 and certain other foreign weapons systems threatens to destabilize the military balance between China and Taiwan.
5. Public adherence to a "one China" policy. Since the fundamental concern of Beijing is to prevent Taiwan from becoming an independent country, an essential part of the ROC strategy of deterrence is to hold out the expectation that China's reunification will occur eventually through peaceful means. This tactic requires expanding peaceful contact across the Taiwan Strait and ensuring that pro-independence forces do not control public policy.
6. Encouraging Beijing to adopt policies that lessen its incentives to use force against Taiwan. To this end, the ROC supports economic and political liberalization on the mainland, encourages PRC integration into the Asian-Pacific community, and applauds China's policies of opening to the outside world.

The interlocking nature of these elements of deterrence can be illustrated by examining ROC arms purchases. The most important source of foreign arms is the United States. According to the 1993 ROC white paper on foreign policy, the role of U.S. arms sales is critical in enhancing substantive relations between the two sides.[47] The document stated: "The ROC has to maintain a steady supply of arms, military materials, military technologies and spare parts necessary to preserve its security. This is one of the major concerns of the ROC's diplomatic efforts in America."

Because of Taiwan's purchasing power and status as one of the most important markets for international arms transactions, many of world's largest defense industries come to Taipei to sell advanced weapons systems. Taiwan purchases weapons not only for military and technological reasons, but also for political considerations. The purchase of foreign weapons systems usually means that Taipei has prevailed over Beijing in a confrontation of political will. The purchase of advanced systems also links Taipei and international suppliers in long-term logistic pipelines which enhance Taiwan's political relations with the selling country. Advanced arms sales also have a snowballing effect, whereby countries reluctant at first to sell weapons to Taiwan lose their inhibitions when they see other countries making similar sales. As noted by one scholar, "arms market activity is integral to Taipei's `flexible diplomacy'....A web of relationships and situations -- including arms transactions -- constitute a political-economic `situational deterrent' which renders military attack by the PRC increasingly unlikely."[48]

Whether the main purpose of Taiwan's purchase of arms abroad is to enhance its flexible diplomacy or to strengthen its military capabilities is subject to debate. University of California scholar Harlan Jencks holds to the former interpretation, while defense analyst Ronald Montaperto is convinced of the latter. Montaperto has written:

> The military instrument has emerged as the most important component of Taiwan's overall strategic posture. Although Taiwan's security policy has economic, political, and diplomatic components, at the core it is Taipei's ability to deter China from launching military operations against it that keeps Taiwan secure.
>
> In this light, Taiwan's primary goals in the international arms market involve securing the weapons systems and technologies that will enable it to preserve its qualitative military edge over China. By this means, Taiwan preserves the military balance in the Taiwan Strait and also maintains deterrence. Although Taipei regularly stretches or overlooks a point or two in order to secure military gain, it is well aware that qualitative superiority in the military sphere is what makes `flexible diplomacy' possible....

Overall, Taipei's purpose [in purchasing foreign weapons] has been to maintain the qualitative edge in military operations that facilitates continuing deterrence. By this means, competition between the two sides is in effect prevented from assuming a military character and Taiwan gains an opportunity to bring its considerable economic and political assets to bear. This nexus of the military on the one hand and the political and economic on the other is the new keystone of Taiwan's defense policy.[49]

Conflict Scenarios

There is a wide range of possible uses of force Beijing could utilize to bend Taipei's will to comply with its own.[50] These include:

- military cooperation with elements on Taiwan seeking early reunification with the mainland
- special operations forces inserted surreptitiously into Taiwan
- bombardment or invasion of Kinmen and Matsu
- attack or invasion of Penghu
- seizure of ROC-occupied islands in the South China Sea
- PLA navy harassment of ROC flag vessels or naval ships in the open sea or in the Taiwan Strait
- deployment of large numbers of armed fishing boats around Taiwan for purposes of harassment or show of force
- PLA naval deployments around Taiwan for the purpose of intimidation
- surprise PRC missile attack on key facilities on Taiwan
- use of chemical, biological, bacteriological, or nuclear weapons against Taiwan
- various levels of blockade of Taiwan
- a campaign of systematic destruction of ROC air and naval forces
- amphibious invasion of Taiwan.

With the exception of an amphibious invasion of Taiwan, the PRC has the military capability to carry out most of these missions, although several options would entail great cost to Beijing. Others, such as the use of weapons of mass destruction, seem to lack credibility given the nature of Taiwan-mainland relations.

Many analysts believe that the PRC, if it did decide to use force, would adopt an "all-or-nothing" approach (probably excluding weapons of mass destruction but including ballistic missiles with conventional warheads) that would lead to either victory or defeat. The rationale is that once force is committed, Beijing would have to be successful else risk losing Taiwan as Chinese territory. It is assumed that if Taipei thwarted the PRC attack, the movement for Taiwan independence would become irresistible and international support for Taiwan would substantially increase, particularly from the United States.

Taiwan does little to discount this type of speculation. For example, when it was reported in September 1994 that the PRC had adopted a new military action plan against Taiwan, a spokesman for the ROC's Mainland Affairs Council warned Beijing that it should take into account the possible reaction of the people of Taiwan. Should the PRC attack the island, he said, "the Republic of China might thus be forced to move toward the extreme side."[51]

Levels of Force

The PRC does not necessarily have to wage total war to prevent Taiwan from becoming an independent country, however. The PRC could use much lower levels of violence to send signals to Taipei to stop moving in the direction of independence. The danger in these carefully controlled uses of force for preventative purposes is that an accidental military exchange might lead to war between the two sides. The actual course of events in such circumstances is very difficult to predict.

There are, in other words, several different levels of force the PRC could employ in the Taiwan Strait. The levels include:

1. An "accidental" confrontation in which the two sides engage each other over some unanticipated incident.
2. A "demonstrative" use of force by Beijing to send a clear signal of warning to Taiwan to desist from some course of action.
3. A more forceful, but still limited, "preventive" use of force to stop Taiwan from pursuing some policy.
4. A limited "punitive" use of force to punish Taipei for some action.
5. A limited "interventive" use of force to influence the outcome of a social crisis on Taiwan.
6. A full-scale "aggressive" use of force to defeat the ROC and bring Taiwan under the control of Beijing.

Most Western analyses focus on potential PRC "aggressive" behavior because of the danger of wider conflict and the high costs involved. This extreme use of force, however, is least likely to occur for three principal reasons. First, no one -- Communist, Nationalist, or pro-independence advocate -- wants a full-scale war in the Taiwan Strait because of the horrendous costs to the Chinese (and Taiwanese) people. Second, the PLA currently lacks the military capability to invade and occupy Taiwan, without which other uses of force might not be sufficient to cause Taipei to capitulate. Third, U.S. intervention is most likely to occur under conditions of a direct PRC attack on Taiwan.

For purposes of deterrence, the ROC maintains that it will respond to any PRC use of force with rapid escalation to bring the conflict to a quick, decisive conclusion. This means the maximum (excluding weapons of mass destruction held in reserve to deter similar PRC weapons) use of ROC military force against a wide range of PRC targets, including military installations on the mainland itself.

Although such rapid escalation would likely occur if the PRC directly attacked Taiwan, it is less clear if Taipei would leap into full-scale war in the event of an accidental confrontation or lower levels of violence initiated by Beijing. This is especially true if Beijing's intentions to keep its use of force strictly limited were clearly understood. Presumably, Taipei possesses a flexible strategy to respond to lower levels of PRC force; but the strategy is not widely discussed since the ROC threat to escalate to total war should Beijing use any kind of force has far greater deterring value than signs of flexibility.

There is a downside to Taiwan's all-or-nothing posture, however. Because a war with the PRC is painted in such extreme terms, the threat of Beijing actually initiating a war is perceived by many as lacking credibility. Many Taiwanese, especially in the pro-independence camp, are convinced that Beijing would never use force against Taiwan because of the unacceptable costs of a full-scale war.

Another way to approach levels of violence in the Taiwan Strait is to consider how the PRC might use force to achieve different goals. These goals could include: (1) to achieve national unification, (2) to prevent Taiwan independence, and (3) to convince the international community not to recognize Taiwan as an independent nation-state. These goals are related, but they are quite different approaches to the Taiwan issue and might require different levels of force to achieve.

The first goal would be the most difficult to realize through the use of force. To compel Taiwan against its will to unify with the mainland would probably require Taiwan's defeat in a full-scale war. Under this scenario, a blockade, destruction of ROC air and naval forces, and possibly an invasion might be necessary. Anything other than the military defeat of Taiwan might not be sufficient to force Taipei to accept an unwanted unification with the communist mainland. Taiwan's resistance would be fierce. The Nationalists would be fighting to preserve the ROC and the Taiwanese would be fighting to preserve their freedom from a hostile mainland. Under these circumstances, the domestic and international environment would probably be supportive of Taiwan. U.S. intervention would be likely.

The second PRC goal -- preventing Taipei from declaring independence -- might not require the defeat of Taiwan in total war. In this situation, the domestic and international environment (at least currently) favors Beijing. A majority of Taiwan's residents do not support Taiwan independence if it means war with China. Most nations, including the United States, do not support the concept of a separate nation-state of Taiwan.

Under these conditions, the PRC might be able to use limited force, not with the intent of starting a major war with Taiwan but to warn Taipei against declaring independence. If the PRC limited its political objectives to turning Taiwan away from independence and clearly circumscribed its application of force, it is not certain the United States would intervene or even that the ROC military would support a pro-independence leadership in Taipei.

The third PRC goal of convincing the international community not to recognize an independent Taiwan would require even less use of force against Taipei. Under current conditions, the international environment strongly favors Beijing since only a few countries recognize the ROC as a sovereign state. If the PRC demonstrated its absolute opposition to Taiwan independence with a token amount of force, the international community would get the message. Unless the international climate changes appreciably, probably only a few nations would respond to Taiwan's appeal for recognition as an independent state.

How would Taipei respond to these various levels of PRC force? If China tried to force Taiwan into early reunification through military means, the ROC would almost certainly resist with the full strength of its armed forces. If Beijing sent military warning signals to Taipei not to declare independence, it would seem easier and less costly (hence more rational) for Taiwan to change its policy rather than to escalate the confrontation into a full-scale war. In the third instance of the PRC using a very limited amount of force to warn the international community not to recognize Taiwan independence, it seems unlikely Taipei would respond by escalating to total war.

Conclusion

This chapter examined several factors relevant to Taiwan's security: the current and future capabilities of the ROC armed forces, Taiwan's war-fighting strategy, Taipei's formula for deterrence, and various scenarios for use of force in the Taiwan Strait.

Taiwan's military capabilities, like those of the PRC, are rapidly improving through selected modernization programs. In the case of Taiwan, these programs are being assisted with massive infusions of foreign technology and major weapons purchases such as fighter aircraft, large naval combatants, antiship and antiair missiles, and land-based air defense systems. Taipei is determined to maintain key qualitative advantages over the PLA, but the political and economic cost is enormous.

Taiwan's defense strategy has two important aspects: a war-fighting strategy designed to exact the heaviest possible PRC casualties, and a multidimensional deterrence strategy encompassing military, political, economic, and other instruments. Taiwan's defense capabilities are strong. The greatest danger to Taiwan probably lies less in the PRC making an unprovoked attack than in political developments on Taiwan giving cause to Beijing to use force to prevent Taiwan from separating itself from China.

There are many possible scenarios for the use of force in the Taiwan Strait. The most commonly assessed are a blockade, air or naval attack, and invasion. These scenarios are the least likely to occur, however. Two reasons are the low probability of a PRC success due to Taiwan's substantive military capabilities and the strong likelihood of U.S. intervention. There are several less intense applications of force which the PRC might use against Taiwan, especially if Beijing's political objectives did not include the military defeat of the ROC or the forceful reunification of Taiwan with the mainland. Beijing might attempt to use limited force, for example, to change Taipei's mind about pursuing independence or to warn the international community not to recognize an independent Taiwan. Under these conditions of limited force and limited political objectives, the PRC might be able to avoid ROC escalation to full-scale war and U.S. military intervention. It would seem, therefore, that more U.S. attention needs to be paid to lesser forms of violence on the part of Beijing.

The risks to Beijing of pursuing any course of action utilizing force, however, are very great and probably prohibitive except under circumstances where Taiwan seemed to be moving determinedly toward independence. The PRC remains deterred, even at lower levels of force, by the increased peaceful contact across the Taiwan Strait, the PRC's concentration on economic development, the formidable strength of the ROC armed forces, and the possibility of American intervention. The likelihood of that intervention, based on an assessment of U.S. interests in Taiwan's security under the Clinton administration, will be the subject of the next chapter.

Notes

1. *The Military Balance, 1992-1993* (London: Institute of International Studies, 1992), pp. 141, 161-162. Different numbers are provided by the ROC Ministry of National Defense (MND). According to the MND, in 1993 ROC military personnel on active duty numbered 500,000. Reductions were scheduled over the next ten years to bring that number down to 400,000, or 1.7 percent of Taiwan's population. The level of 400,000 was felt to be the minimum necessary to deter the PRC. Half of the 400,000 will be army, while the navy and air force will be expanded to 100,000 each. The army had about 300,000 troops in 1993. The future size of the ROC military was determined by a size ratio with Great Britain, which has similar geography. In 1993 2.3 percent of Taiwan's population was on active duty, a high rate similar to that of Singapore and Israel. In case of war, Taiwan could mobilize about 4 million troops, including those in reserve. The downsizing of the ROC armed forces is part of an "elite troop" policy aimed at increasing combat efficiency through better training and equipment. The higher echelons will be trimmed, while the lower echelons will be reinforced. See *Free China Journal*, May 11, 1993, p. 2. For purposes of consistency and comparison with PLA forces described in Chapter 6, I have mostly used the *Military Balance* numbers in this section.

2. See also Harlan W. Jencks, "Taiwan in the International Arms Market" and the accompanying commentary by Ronald N. Montaperto, in Robert G. Sutter and William R. Johnson, eds., *Taiwan in World Affairs* (Boulder, CO: Westview Press, 1994), pp. 73-111.

3. In October 1993 the first eight Cobra and four Kiowas arrived on Taiwan. The Cobras were armed with cannons, missiles and rockets and were designed to escort ground troops and attack tanks and helicopters. The Warriors were equipped with air photo systems, night vision equipment, and laser range finders and designators to spot weapon locations, collect intelligence, support attack missions, and direct artillery fire. See *Far Eastern Economic Review*, November 19, 1993, p. 2.

4. *Free China Journal*, September 2, 1994, p. 1. See also *Washington Post*, January 23, 1994, p. A23. One reason for the Legislative Yuan's reluctance to

support the Ministry of National Defense was a well-publicized arms procurement scandal which rocked the ROC defense establishment. The scandal resulted in the transfer of several top-ranking officers and the imprisonment of several lower-ranking officers on charges of passing military secrets to defense contractors.

5. The system costs $21 million and is installed on major U.S. warships such as Aegis-class cruisers and Burke-class destroyers. CNA report from Washington, D.C., September 14, 1994.

6. *China Post*, May 8, 1993, p. 1; *Free China Journal*, May 11, 1993, p. 1.

7. *Free China Journal*, October 8, 1993, p. 1.

8. *Free China Journal*, October 22, 1993, p. 1; October 29, 1993, p. 2.

9. CNA reports from Washington, D.C., July 20, August 3, and August 24, 1994.

10. *Far Eastern Economic Review*, February 4, 1993, pp. 10-11.

11. *China News*, November 26, 1992, p. 3. The Sea Dragon was used by the Dutch navy.

12. For these and other submarine-related issues, see *Far Eastern Economic Review*, February 4, 1993, pp. 10-11.

13. *Free China Journal*, November 5, 1993, p. 2.

14. *Far Eastern Economic Review*, September 16, 1993, p. 11; *Free China Journal*, September 10, 1993, p. 1.

15. "No Sale of Advanced Aircraft to Taiwan," *Department of State Bulletin*, February 1982, p. 39. For details of the policy decision, see Martin L. Lasater, *The Taiwan Issue in Sino-American Strategic Relations* (Boulder, CO: Westview Press, 1984), pp. 178-201.

16. To export the IDF, the U.S. government would have to issue export permits because 50 percent of the plane's engine is the result of U.S. technological assistance and 60 percent of the engine's parts are sourced in the United States. *Free China Journal*, June 24, 1994, p. 8.

17. For details of the F-16 sale, see Dennis Van Vranken Hickey, *United States-Taiwan Security Ties: From Cold War to Beyond Containment* (Westport, CT: Praeger, 1994), pp. 77-93.

18. *Free China Journal*, April 16, 1993, p. 2.

19. *Free China Journal*, March 9, 1993, p. 3.

20. *Far Eastern Economic Review*, August 11, 1994, p. 13.

21. *China News*, September 5, 1992, p. 1.

22. *Free China Journal*, December 10, 1993, p. 3; June 22, 1994, p. 2.

23. *Free China Journal*, April 2, 1993, p. 2.

24. *China News*, November 26, 1992, p. 1.

25. By way of comparison, the MiG-31 has a maximum take-off weight of 41,150 kilograms, a maximum speed of Mach 2.4, service ceiling of 24,000 meters, and a radius of action of 2,100 kilometers. The F-5E has a maximum

take-off weight of 11,200 kilograms, a maximum speed of Mach 1.6, a service ceiling of nearly 16,000 meters, and a radius of action of 1,000 kilometers.

26. *Free China Journal*, June 1, 1993, p. 1.

27. *New York Times*, January 13, 1994, p. A11; *Far Eastern Economic Review*, January 27, 1994, pp. 12-14.

28. *Free China Journal*, January 21, 1994, p. 1.

29. *Free China Journal*, July 16, 1993, p. 2.

30. *Free China Journal*, July 16, 1993, p. 2.

31. *China Post*, August 1, 1992, p. 16.

32. *Free China Journal*, March 25, 1994, p. 1.

33. *China Post*, March 25, 1993, p. 16.

34. *Free China Journal*, November 5, 1993, p. 2.

35. The U.S. Department of Defense reportedly approved the sale of Patriot missiles to Taiwan in 1992. The ROC military, however, balked at the older models, saying its upgraded Sky Bow missile system was comparable to the standard Patriot. Taipei wanted the newer version of the Patriot used in the Persian Gulf. *Far Eastern Economic Review*, December 2, 1993, p. 9.

36. *Free China Journal*, March 12, 1993, p. 1.

37. *Free China Journal*, April 22, 1994, p. 1.

38. *Far Eastern Economic Review*, November 4, 1993, p. 15.

39. *Free China Journal*, August 12, 1994, p. 2.

40. *China Post*, December 8, 1988, p. 12.

41. For the ROC strategy of escalation, see the comments of Vice Admiral Ko Tun-hwa (retired vice minister of national defense and deputy chief of staff) in Martin L. Lasater, ed., *Beijing's Blockade Threat to Taiwan* (Washington, D.C.: Heritage Foundation, 1985), pp. 6-15.

42. *China Post*, March 6, 1993, p. 16.

43. *China Post*, March 25, 1993, p. 16.

44. *China News*, October 29, 1992, p. 1.

45. See Martin L. Lasater, *Taiwan: Facing Mounting Threats* (Washington, D.C.: Heritage Foundation, 1987), pp. 18-24.

46. *China Post*, March 25, 1993, p. 16.

47. *Foreign Affairs Report: Foreign Relations and Diplomatic Administration* (Taipei, Taiwan: ROC Ministry of Foreign Affairs, 1993). An English translation can be found in issues of *Free China Journal* between March 26 and May 11, 1993.

48. Harlan W. Jencks, "Taiwan in the International Arms Market," p. 99.

49. See Ronald N. Montaperto's commentary to the previously cited Jencks chapter, pp. 101, 105-106.

50. For elaboration of most of these attack scenarios, see Paul H.B. Godwin, "The Use of Military Force Against Taiwan: Potential PRC Scenarios," in Parris H. Chang and Martin L. Lasater, eds., *If China Crosses the Taiwan Strait: The International Response* (Lanham, MD: University Press of America, 1993), pp.

15-33; and Martin L. Lasater, *U.S. Interests in the New Taiwan* (Boulder, CO: Westview Press, 1993), pp. 133-169. Other books by the author discussing this subject include *Taiwan: Facing Mounting Threats*; *Beijing's Blockade Threat to Taiwan*; and *The Security of Taiwan* (Washington, D.C.: Georgetown University Press, 1982).

51. CNA report from Taipei, Taiwan, September 9, 1994.

8

U.S. Interests in the Security of Taiwan

The previous two chapters examined the current PRC threat to Taiwan, concluding that the threat may be increasing in the post-Cold War period due to the growing strength of the PLA, the greater possibility of Taiwan independence, and Chinese perceptions of U.S. reluctance to intervene on Taiwan's behalf. This chapter considers the strategic, security, political, economic, and other reasons why the United States should remain concerned with Taiwan's security in the 1990s. Also discussed are ways in which the Clinton administration can help ensure Taiwan's self-defense for the remainder of this century.

Maintaining the Balance of Power

For the past one hundred years the United States has pursued a strategy of arranging and maintaining a balance of power in Asia that is favorable to U.S. interests. This strategy has been appropriate since East Asia has sufficient resources -- if harnessed by a single hostile country or coalition of countries -- to threaten U.S. forces, allies, friends, trade, and investment in the Asian Pacific. Under modern conditions, the potential threat extends to the continental United States. Fundamental U.S. security interests dictate that Washington seek to maintain a favorable balance of power in Asia by preventing the rise of any regional hegemon.

Three Asian Pacific nations have the potential of becoming such a hegemon in the post-Cold War era: Russia, Japan, and China. Since the

United States does not intend (and lacks the resources) to dominate Asia, and since Washington cannot deny great power status to these countries, a central U.S. strategic objective is to find ways to counterbalance the power and influence of Russia, Japan, and China in Asia.

In the case of China, the United States is concerned that the PRC's modernization might one day result in China achieving its goal of playing a determining role in Asian affairs. Since the Second World War the United States has been the predominant Asian Pacific power. It is the nature of international politics that Washington should seek to deal with the challenge of China where it conflicts with American interests.

In this Sino-American competition, almost systemic in its inevitability, Taiwan plays an important role in counterbalancing the PRC. The United States does not intend to separate Taiwan from China, but it cannot easily allow the takeover of Taiwan by a potentially hostile PRC because this would tend to upset the balance of power in East Asia. A united China under a communist government would be a powerful security, political, and social threat to U.S. interests in Asia. If China were united, Beijing would be better able to attempt to expand its influence than if its leaders were focused on national unification.

If China were united through the use of force, an even more difficult situation would confront the United States. The PRC would gain momentum on using force to settle international disputes around its borders. China's neighbors would reevaluate their ties with both Beijing and Washington. In the eyes of most Asian nations, China dramatically would have increased its power while U.S. influence would have declined. This could result in adjustments in international relations in Asia undermining the currently favorable balance of power in the region. At minimum, it would put the United States in a quandary: should it abandon its leadership role in Asia to avoid confrontation with the PRC, or should it oppose Beijing and risk either war or polarization of Asia into pro-U.S. and pro-China blocs?

The present Taiwan situation makes it harder for China to exert its muscle in the region because it encumbers Beijing. It may be impossible to stop China's development and China will do what it wants anyway, but Taiwan acts as a short-term brake on PRC efforts to expand a controlling influence over Asia. The role of Taiwan as an impediment to PRC regional ambitions works to U.S. advantage at this time. The key question is whether the shorter-term benefits of U.S. support to Taiwan are worth the potential longer-term costs in damaged U.S.-PRC relations.

It seems to me that, even if the Taiwan issue were to disappear, the United States would still have to confront a resurgent China in Asia, at least under the current government in Beijing. The stronger China becomes the more in conflict will be Chinese and American interests, unless a fundamental change occurs in the PRC government or the United States elects to retract its influence from East Asia. A strong Taiwan slows China's development somewhat and encourages Beijing to moderate its domestic and foreign policies. If Beijing can resolve the Taiwan issue peacefully, this would be a very positive indicator that the United States and China could resolve other issues in a cooperative way. The objective here is not to isolate or divide China, but to encourage China's participation in regional and global affairs as a constructive partner with the United States and other Asian Pacific countries. For this reason, Taiwan plays a subtle but key role in helping to maintain a favorable balance of power in the region.

Peace and Stability in East Asia

The maintenance of peace and stability in East Asia is also a long-term, vital U.S. national security interest. Taiwan's security has been linked to East Asian peace and stability since at least June 1950, when President Truman interposed the Seventh Fleet into the Taiwan Strait. One of the best ways to understand this linkage is to consider the negative consequences of a war between the two Chinese sides.

First, there is high probability the war would not be confined to Taiwan and the Taiwan Strait. Taiwan's war-fighting strategy is to expand the conflict as widely and as rapidly as possible to maximize damage to the PRC. In addition to destruction on Taiwan, trade to Chinese ports between Shanghai and Hong Kong would be disrupted and some facilities might be attacked by ROC air and naval forces. The commercial interests of all countries trading with Taiwan, and most of those trading with mainland China, would be harmed.

Second, the likely use of PRC submarines to blockade Taiwan would pose a danger to all shipping in transit through the Bashi Channel and Taiwan Strait. These are the principal passageways through which flow the vast majority of ocean cargo moving between Northeast Asia and ports in southern China, Southeast Asia, South Asia, and the Middle East. Submarine identification of friend, foe, or neutral is enormously difficult in heavy traffic on the high seas. Similarly, most air traffic from the

United States and Northeast Asia into southern China, Taiwan, and Southeast Asia would be disrupted due to hostilities around Taiwan.

Third, a war involving the two Chinas would harm the economies of most other Asian countries. Both Taiwan and mainland China are vital export and import markets for Asian nations, and Taiwan is a vital source of investment capital. Since economic growth is a key factor in political stability in most Asian countries, the negative consequences of a war in the Taiwan Strait could extend beyond the economic sphere into areas of political and social stability.

Fourth, a conflict involving China and Taiwan would generate deep security concerns throughout Asia. Most countries in the region already harbor distrust of Chinese hegemonic ambitions. The war could lead to a major arms buildup in the region. Since many Asian countries now possess the technology, industrial capability, and financial resources to develop ballistic missiles and weapons of mass destruction, a war in the Taiwan Strait might create unprecedented proliferation problems for the United States.

Fifth, because of the long-standing U.S. commitment to protect Taiwan in the event of PRC attack, war in the Taiwan Strait would immediately focus attention on the U.S. response. Asian countries would carefully evaluate U.S. actions in terms of their own security requirements and relationships with the United States. If not handled correctly, a major crisis in the Taiwan Strait would directly challenge, if not actually threaten, the very architecture of U.S. coalition strategy in Asia.

Finally, because of firm U.S. commitments to Taiwan, a war between Beijing and Taipei could escalate into a major regional conflict involving China and the United States. The consequences of this wider war could be quite damaging to both U.S. and Chinese interests, regardless of the outcome.

Because of these and other negative consequences of a ROC-PRC war, a major U.S. goal since the Korean War has been to prevent such a conflict from occurring. The security of Taiwan continues to be intimately connected with peace and stability in East Asia today.

U.S. Credibility

In spite of the idealism of a "Pacific community," most Asian governments face problems of national security in a region traditionally characterized by intense rivalry. Each Asian nation perceives a different set of threats to its security. No Asian country -- from the smallest to the largest -- is free from anxieties caused by centuries of experience with expansionist neighbors or the intruding presence of external powers.

Since the Vietnam War the United States has played a key role in preserving a fairly stable balance of power in East and Southeast Asia. Most Asian countries would like to see the United States continue to play that role, as no major Asian power can fulfill this responsibility due to the suspicions of its neighbors. With the demise of the Soviet threat to its own security, however, the United States has reduced considerably its military presence and global commitments. President Clinton reassured Asian leaders that he will fulfill U.S. security commitments to the region, but most Asian governments doubt Washington's long-term ability or willingness to maintain a sufficient level of military force to do this. As a direct consequence of this recurring doubt, U.S. credibility in Asia is widely questioned.

Other than a North Korean attack against South Korea, the only direct challenge to U.S. security commitments in Asia is a PRC attack against Taiwan. There is very little possibility of a Russian or Chinese attack against Japan; Vietnam will not likely attack Thailand; the Philippines face no external threat; and Australia and New Zealand are not threatened by any of their neighbors. To his credit, President Clinton has done much to shore up U.S. credibility through his firm opposition to the threat of North Korean aggression. But continued U.S. efforts to ensure Taiwan's security are also viewed as important indicators of U.S. security commitments to the region.

The symbolic importance of the U.S. commitment to Taiwan's security is especially strong to countries bordering China. Most of these nations see China as a traditional threat. Because of China's huge size and the growing strength of its armed forces, Beijing's potential as a spoiler in regional affairs is very great. If the U.S. commitment to Taiwan was further weakened, Washington's credibility would be damaged and American influence reduced; at the same time, the perception of China as the dominant power of Asia would be enhanced, with inevitable shifts in political alliances. It is doubtful these adjustments in regional alignments would benefit the United States.

It should be recognized, however, that U.S. support for Taiwan must not be limited to military support. Regional countries might become disenchanted with the United States if they were to judge that obdurate U.S. military support for Taiwan led to war. The United States would win the war, but might lose the region. This concern points to the sensitivity of Asian nations to the Taiwan issue and hence the need for careful management of the issue in U.S. policy.

Protection of Democracies and U.S. Commercial Interests

Taiwan is one of the world's most successful examples of a free market economy and emerging democracy. To further its interests in nurturing market democracies in the new world order, the United States needs to protect countries like Taiwan that have made a transition from authoritarian rule to democracy. By doing so, the United States helps to stabilize the international system, further world peace, expand the community of market democracies, and secure U.S. leadership in global affairs. If the PRC were to use unprovoked force against Taiwan, Washington would be faced with a clear case of a democracy being attacked by one of world's most repressive regimes. To ignore such aggression could have severe global repercussions in much the same way that concerns were raised over Iraq's invasion of Kuwait in 1990.

Taiwan's security is also important to the United States for its own commercial interests. President Clinton has said that one of the most important national priorities of his administration is the expansion of U.S. trade and investment in Asia, the fastest growing economic region in the world. Taiwan plays a key role in the economic development of Asia, both as the region's second largest trader after Japan and as an important source of investment capital for Southeast Asia and mainland China.

U.S. economic interests would be harmed by war in the Taiwan Strait. Such a conflict would disrupt trade and investment in the region and damage the economies of nearly all Pacific Basin countries. Billions of dollars in U.S. trade with the two Chinas would be lost, and millions more in U.S. investments would be placed in jeopardy.

Consensus on U.S. China Policy

The United States has a wide range of interests in Taiwan other than security, political, and economic. These include cultural, educational, scientific, technological, sports, law enforcement, tourism, immigration, U.S. legislation such as the Taiwan Relations Act, and scores of formal agreements between the two governments negotiated by their representative organizations (AIT and CCNAA).

Contacts between the United States and Taiwan are growing annually. Their scope indicates that, in the event of an unprovoked PRC attack against Taiwan, strong political pressure would mount on Washington to intervene decisively on Taiwan's behalf. Mindful of these political realities, every U.S. administration since President Truman has assured Congress and the American people that the United States will help Taiwan maintain its self-defense capabilities.

The diplomatic turmoil for the United States generated by war in the Taiwan Strait would be matched by domestic political crisis. Many Americans would urge immediate U.S. military intervention, while others would argue for diplomacy and restraint. Because of conflicting advice and the practical need for quick response to the crisis, a war between Taiwan and China would be a political hornet's nest for any administration.

In the past, broad public support for Taiwan's security made it expedient for the U.S. government to accommodate Taiwan's vital interests when attempting to build a consensus on U.S. China policy. No China policy would be acceptable to the Congress or the American people if it did not include provisions for the sale of defensive weapons to Taiwan and statements of U.S. support for a peaceful resolution of the Taiwan issue.

In the post-Cold War period, the American public's support for Taiwan seems to be growing. Very little criticism was heard over President Bush's 1992 decision to sell F-16s to Taiwan, despite the PRC's angry reaction and the precedent of the sale; Clinton's adjustment in U.S. policy toward Taiwan in 1994 was widely criticized for being cosmetic, again despite heated blasts from Beijing. In part, this growing public support of Taiwan is due to the fact that over the past two decades, Taiwan's image has changed from that of a wartime ally and anti-communist bastion to that of a progressive, democratic state being slighted diplomatically for reasons most Americans do not fully understand.

The growth in favorable public opinion about Taiwan is reflected in the U.S. Congress, where in 1993 and 1994 numerous bills and resolutions were introduced supporting improved U.S.-Taiwan relations. Given this level of popular support for Taiwan, it would be politically difficult for any administration to be unresponsive to a PRC use of force against Taiwan. Moreover, even though American foreign policy specialists can draw the distinction between provoked and unprovoked PRC uses of force, it is not at all clear that the American public would see -- or care about -- the distinction. It is more likely the public (and many in the Congress) would see the issue in terms of a totalitarian communist state using force against a small, democratic nation that is also a close U.S. ally. As seen repeatedly in recent years, strong public opinion can have an impact on Washington's decision to use or not to use American forces in international crises.

Positive Influence on China

One of the most important U.S. interests in Taiwan's security is preserving the positive influence the ROC can have over developments in China.

Despite calls for political autonomy, Taiwan is a Chinese society with immense potential for influencing the liberalization of mainland China. Taiwan's positive influence can already be seen in southern and eastern China. Taiwanese goods and services, investment capital, technology, managers and other trained personnel are flooding into China in such numbers that over the past few years a dynamic new entity, "Greater China," has been conceptualized to describe the economic integration of Taiwan, China, and Hong Kong.

Taipei's policy of expanding contact with the mainland reinforces progressive Chinese foreign and domestic policies. Taipei cannot control the course of development on the mainland, but Taiwan (along with Singapore and Hong Kong) does play an important role in encouraging Beijing to moderate its policies in key areas of interest to the United States. These include greater openness to the outside world, cooperative relations with the West, the introduction of market incentives, and greater political liberalization.

A traditional U.S. objective in Asia has been the modernization of China along democratic and free market lines. Taiwan is one part of China that has achieved this goal, and Taiwan can contribute to the goal's eventual realization on the mainland. The ROC economy provides a powerful inducement to Beijing to adopt elements of a market economy. A less positive example is Taiwan's style of democracy, which PRC leaders must view with disgust as opposition parties disrupt the governing process and call for the island's independence. Nonetheless, the emergence of democracy within a Chinese context is an historic precedent for China's political evolution. Over time, greater political liberalization will likely occur if Beijing continues to move toward a market economy.

To the extent that PRC political reform is influenced by Taiwan, the people of China benefit and the interests of the United States are served.

Long-term U.S. interests are served by Taiwan's alternative political, economic, and social models to authoritarianism, communism, and socialism on the mainland. It is important to U.S. goals in Asia that the ROC model continue to exist. Taiwan's security is thus intimately linked to U.S. interests in a peaceful, productive, and friendly China in the future.

The U.S. Role in Taiwan's Security

The United States plays a vital role in Taiwan's security by improving the war-fighting capabilities of the ROC armed services and by strengthening Taipei's strategy of comprehensive deterrence. It is highly probable the United States will continue to play these roles because of long-term American interests in the security of Taiwan. There are, however, certain adjustments in U.S. policy which should be considered during the Clinton administration.

Strengthening ROC Armed Forces

U.S. efforts to help modernize the ROC armed forces include arms sales, technology transfers, production assistance, training, and myriad other activities required to field an effective military under modern conditions. Many of these efforts have been documented in previous chapters.

The Clinton administration's opposition to the July 1993 Murkowski amendment to the TRA, as well as the president's more accommodating policies toward China beginning later that year as part of a "reengagement" with the PRC, demonstrated Clinton's determination not to allow continued military assistance to Taiwan to interfere with Sino-American cooperation on important issues. On the other hand, Washington knows that China's strategic value to the United States has been reduced since the end of the Cold War. Accordingly, the United States no longer hesitates to sell modestly advanced weapon systems to Taiwan when these sales are justified by larger U.S. interests such as maintaining the regional balance of power.

With the end of "strategic triangle" calculations (which inclined the United States not to sell controversial weapons to Taiwan for fear of offending the PRC), decisions to sell modern arms to Taiwan became more complex. The sale of the F-16 in September 1992, for example, was influenced by many factors. There was great concern over maintaining Taiwan's capabilities to deter the Su-27s and other combat aircraft being purchased by the PRC. The need to maintain a balance of power in East Asia and a military balance in the Taiwan Strait was a key consideration. Also, it became increasingly difficult for the United States to supply spare parts for the outdated aircraft in Taiwan's inventory. The Bush administration wanted to ensure that American companies got the ROC's arms business, not French enterprises or those of other countries. The F-16 sale was meant to assist American defense industries; it was also meant to preserve strong U.S. influence over Taiwan's offensive capabilities. American electoral politics were deeply involved.

The F-16 sale illustrated the irrationality of U.S. arms sales policy under the August 1982 communique. As noted in Chapter 5, to comply with promises to reduce gradually in quantitative and qualitative terms the amount of arms sold to Taiwan, the United States adopted the "Taiwan bucket" system. The "bucket" began at a level of about $820 million in 1982 and dropped to $580 million by 1993, a $20 million average annual reduction. Despite its relevance to Taiwan's security needs, the F-16 purchase, valued at nearly $6 billion, was deliberately set aside as a one-time purchase not included in the "bucket." Earlier, U.S. defense technology transfers were exempted from the "bucket" as well.

In addition to the "bucket" mechanism, the United States adopted arbitrary guidelines not specified in the 1982 communique, such as not allowing American weapons to be sold to Taiwan for the purpose of equipping weapons platforms purchased from third countries. Thus, for example, in mid-1993 the Clinton administration would not allow Taiwan to purchase electronic combat systems and weapons integration equipment to place on the LaFayette-class frigates the ROC obtained from France.

These irrationalities in arms sales policy prompted Senator Frank Murkowski to introduce his amendment to the TRA discussed in Chapter 5. In explaining the amendment, Murkowski pointed to several billion dollars worth of U.S. business lost because of these restrictions on arms sales, restrictions which he said ran counter to the Taiwan Relations Act. According to information distributed by Senator Murkowski's office, "An aggregate of past and present defense sales lost or now at serious risk due to the `Bucket' policy reaches as high as $20 billion directly affecting

456,000 [American] jobs plus 340,000 indirect jobs." Cited as major cases in point:

- $2-3 billion lost because Taiwan could not make a larger purchase of F-16s; instead, Taipei purchased 60 Mirage fighters from France.
- $4 billion lost because the U.S. government would not allow the sale of 16 navy frigates; Taiwan was able to build seven frigates based on U.S. design and purchase the hulls of six LaFayette frigates from France worth $1.6 billion.
- $2-3 billion lost when the U.S. government refused to allow the sale of up to eight Type-209 diesel electric submarines built in the United States from German kits.[1]

The changes in U.S.-PRC-ROC relations discussed throughout this book support the contention that new guidelines for arms sales to Taiwan need to be adopted by the United States during the Clinton administration. The new guidelines should include the following basic principles:

1. Continue to adhere to the three U.S.-PRC joint communiques as a basis for cooperative Sino-American relations.
2. In compliance with the Taiwan Relations Act, sell Taiwan the weapons systems and training necessary to ensure an effective self-defense against realistic PRC threats, even if sales on occasion require the TRA to supersede the August 17 communique.
3. Where possible, sell Taipei the technology, production design, and other assistance necessary to enable Taiwan to build advanced defensive weapon systems itself.
4. Encourage Taiwan to purchase American weapons rather than arms from third countries.
5. Do not discuss with Beijing any specific arms sales to Taiwan; since arms sales are governed by U.S. law and U.S. interests, there is no need to bring Beijing into the decision-making process.[2]
6. Periodically state at the highest levels the U.S. intention to abide by the Taiwan Relations Act and to support a process of peaceful resolution of Taiwan's future.
7. Support increased contact across the Taiwan Strait, but do not become a mediator between the two Chinese sides.

These guidelines should enable the Clinton administration to sell the weapons necessary for Taiwan to sustain an effective self-defense, while maintaining cooperative relations with Beijing on mutually important issues such as the Korean peninsula, arms proliferation, human rights, and trade.

Strengthening Taiwan's Comprehensive Deterrence

Most analysts agree the probability of Beijing using massive military force in the Taiwan Strait is small. The most compelling reasons for this conclusion are:

1. The PRC is not sure it has the military capability to conquer Taiwan at reasonable cost. Taiwan's new generation of advanced weapons will increase this cost.
2. Beijing is deterred by the prospects of U.S. military intervention. U.S. forces available for intervention in the Taiwan Strait are vastly superior to those of the PRC, and Washington has a wide range of military options to make the cost of attack prohibitively high to Beijing.
3. Beijing thinks peaceful reunification is still possible. Increased exchanges across the Taiwan Strait strengthen PRC incentives not to attack Taiwan. Also, recent elections on Taiwan suggest the KMT will remain in power and that independence is not preferred by the majority of Taiwan citizens.
4. PRC leaders are committed to a long-term policy of moderate and pragmatic reform on the mainland. They believe an attack against Taiwan would harm China's modernization.

At the same time, analysts are not complacent about Taiwan's security. There are several areas of uncertainty in Taiwan's deterrence which cause concern. For instance:

1. The qualitative superiority of ROC armed forces is open to question. The PLA is modernizing in areas of utility in the Taiwan Strait and is no longer preoccupied with the Soviet threat to China's security. Also, until the end of the century, Taiwan will be weak in critical military areas such as air defense.
2. The U.S. response to a PRC use of force is difficult to predict, especially when overt aggression may not be evident or provocation on the part of Taiwan might exist. The political will of the American people to sustain overseas commitments is weak due to concerns over the domestic economy and lack of clearly defined threats to U.S. national security interests. Also, U.S. forward deployed forces in the

Western Pacific have been reduced more than 25 percent and may be reduced further in the future.

3. It is unclear whether Taipei's policies are advancing or obstructing China's unification. Beijing is very concerned that Taiwan's international position is becoming stronger through flexible diplomacy. The KMT's support for a "one China" policy is steadily eroding on Taiwan.

4. The level of support for Taiwan independence seems to be increasing both on Taiwan and abroad, even in the United States. Beijing's formulas for peaceful reunification have failed to attract Taiwan, making alternative policies more necessary. Also, the DPP and other advocates of Taiwan independence have reduced the patience of PRC leaders on the issue of Taiwan's future.

Thus, while the PRC military threat to Taiwan for the remainder of the Clinton administration seems small, enough uncertainties exist that the threat must be viewed as serious and hence threatening to U.S. interests. As the PRC white paper on Taiwan warned in August 1993, "any sovereign state is entitled to use any means it deems necessary, including military ones, to uphold its sovereignty and territorial integrity. The Chinese Government is under no obligation to undertake any commitment to any foreign power or people intending to split China as to what means it might use to handle its own domestic affairs."[3]

More difficult than determining how to respond to PRC military threats is how the United States should respond to PRC plans to isolate Taiwan diplomatically and to punish those forces which support Taiwan independence. According to Hong Kong's *South China Morning Post*, the PRC Taiwan Affairs Office recently developed a "war plan" to frustrate Taiwan's increasingly bold efforts to return to the international stage.[4] As approved by President Jiang Zemin and top PLA generals, the plan reportedly will

- focus the PRC's resources and foreign aid on "dangerous areas," those countries which may develop ties with Taiwan or whose economic relations with Taiwan may develop into political ties

- give countries concrete, material advantages to maintain ties with the mainland and sever ties with Taiwan

- increase "multi-layered contacts and exchanges" with countries recognizing the one-China principle but that continue to maintain non-official ties with Taiwan

- carefully monitor economic and political difficulties these countries may have which Taiwan might try to exploit to improve relations

- work to change the minds of countries which recognize Taiwan, are in the process of doing so, or which support Taiwan independence
- use all channels to raise conditions and brandish inducements that are mutually acceptable
- combat and condemn current efforts by Taiwan to advance independence
- offer economic incentives to Taiwan's business community so that the commercial sector will pressure Taipei to approve direct communications and other links with the mainland.

The report stated that the diplomatic-political-economic offensive against Taiwan would be accompanied by enlarged war games, presumably with Taiwan as a potential target.[5] Also reported was the deep concern Deng Xiaoping and other senior leaders were feeling over the "worsening" situation on Taiwan. Deng and Jiang were said to consider Taiwan independence one of the "four major threats" now facing the PRC.

It seems clear that China's leadership interprets political developments on Taiwan and the ROC's "flexible diplomacy" as moving Taiwan in the direction of independence. At minimum, Beijing believes Taipei is advancing a "two Chinas" policy, despite vocal support for "one China." Although some flexibility might eventually be seen on "two Chinas" (on a model similar to the "two Koreas"), the PRC is adamantly determined to stop Taiwan independence by any necessary means. Accordingly, Beijing is increasing its political and economic pressure on Taipei. The PRC is also stepping up pressure on other countries to limit Taiwan's international role. In addition to these non-military measures of intimidation, the PRC is increasing its military preparations for an assault against Taiwan should it persist to move in the direction of independence.

One question facing the United States is to what extent Beijing's non-military actions against Taiwan threaten U.S. interests. U.S. concerns about certain types of non-military threats were stated in the Taiwan Relations Act. Section 2(b) reads in part (emphasis added):

(b) It is the policy of the United States...
(3) to make clear that the United States' decision to establish diplomatic relations with the People's Republic of China rests upon the expectation that the future of Taiwan will be determined by *peaceful means*;
(4) to consider any effort to determine the future of Taiwan by *other than peaceful means, including by boycotts or embargoes*, a threat to the peace

and security of the Western Pacific area and of grave concern to the United States;...

(6) to maintain the capacity of the United States to resist any resort to force or *other forms of coercion* that would jeopardize the security, or the *social or economic system*, of the people of Taiwan.

Section 2(c) refers to U.S. human rights concerns:

> Nothing contained in this Act shall contravene the interest of the United States in human rights, especially with respect to the human rights of all the approximately eighteen million inhabitants of Taiwan. The *preservation and enhancement of the human rights of all the people on Taiwan* are hereby reaffirmed as objectives of the United States.

At what point the PRC's non-military pressure on Taiwan is interpreted by the United States as "efforts other than peaceful means" or "other forms of coercion" has not been determined. American and Chinese interests are in sharp conflict here. Washington believes that wider participation by Taiwan in some international organizations would benefit the world community. Beijing is highly restrictive in its interpretation of Taiwan's rightful place in global affairs, even threatening to boycott the 1994 Asian Games in Hiroshima, Japan, if Lee Teng-hui was allowed to attend the opening ceremony. Taiwan, on the other hand, sees itself as equal to all other nations and intends to expand its international presence as a priority goal.

It is not in the U.S. interest to support Taiwan independence, but it is in the U.S. interest to have Taiwan assume more international responsibilities. It is not in the U.S. interest to become embroiled in a war over Taiwan, but it is in the U.S. interest that the people of Taiwan have a voice in their future relationship with the mainland. It is not in the U.S. interest to become a mediator in the Taiwan Strait, but it is in the U.S. interest to encourage continued exchanges between the two Chinese sides.

Continued peace in the Taiwan Strait is of fundamental importance to the United States. Since Washington does not intend to send the Seventh Fleet to patrol the Strait and very few Americans believe the United States should compel Taiwan to unify with the PRC, the most reasonable U.S. policy is to help Taiwan maintain an effective deterrence against Beijing's military and non-military coercion. The Clinton administration can take several steps to strengthen Taiwan's comprehensive deterrence. In addition to modernizing the ROC armed forces, these steps include:

- maintain a strong, visible U.S. military presence in the Western Pacific to intervene decisively in the Taiwan Strait if necessary
- reassess the PRC threat to Taiwan and U.S. options for intervention in view of the several indirect and low intensity options available to Beijing to coerce Taipei
- use high-level meetings with the Chinese to convey the U.S. determination to implement the Taiwan Relations Act and to assist Taiwan militarily if it is attacked
- assure the PRC that the United States has no present intention of supporting an independent Taiwan separate from China
- assist Taiwan to expand its international presence through economic and other non-political organizations
- assist Taiwan to expand its international political presence when this can be done without jettisoning the "one China" principle
- develop extensive U.S.-Taiwan commercial ties, including the association of Taiwan with NAFTA
- contribute where possible to a peaceful atmosphere in the Taiwan Strait region, including the encouragement of Taipei and Beijing to continue their dialogue and cross-strait exchanges
- make clear the U.S. position on "one China" so as not to mislead the Taiwanese people about Washington's intentions to support an independent Taiwan
- issue periodic statements by high-ranking U.S. officials approving Taiwan's political and economic progress
- increase the level of contact between officials of the U.S. and Taiwan governments
- encourage Beijing's political and economic reform as positive steps toward the modernization of China
- encourage other members of the international community to (a) inform Beijing of their interests in a peaceful settlement of the Taiwan issue, (b) control arms sales to ensure a military balance in the Taiwan Strait, and (c) allow Taipei to play a meaningful role in the international community within the context of "one China."

As these steps indicate, even with the increased strength of China and budget constraints on Washington, the Clinton administration has abundant military, diplomatic, political, economic, and other means to help Taiwan maintain an effective deterrence throughout the 1990s.

Conclusion

Taiwan's security is an important element in U.S. policy toward Asia. Even in the post-Cold War environment, most U.S. considerations over Taiwan's security remain valid. These include U.S. interests in maintaining a favorable balance of power in the region, U.S. interests in maintaining peace and stability in East Asia, U.S. concerns over the long-term intentions of the PRC, and important U.S. commercial and other interests in Taiwan itself.

Developments on Taiwan since the mid-1980s have strengthened U.S. interests in Taiwan's security. In becoming more democratic, a more valuable trading partner, a greater contributor to international development, and a more willing participant in lowering tensions in the Taiwan Strait, the ROC has become a more credible and useful friend to the United States.

More than ever, it is in U.S. interests to support Taiwan in both its military modernization program and comprehensive deterrent posture. The Clinton administration has signalled on several occasions its determination to continue to implement the Taiwan Relations Act, including the sale of advanced defensive weapons to Taiwan to maintain a military balance in the Taiwan Strait. In testimony before the Senate Foreign Relations Committee in September 1994, Assistant Secretary of State Winston Lord said the Clinton administration will continue to provide material and training to Taiwan to enable it to maintain a sufficient self-defense capability. He said this was crucial not only for Taiwan but also for peace and security in the region. Lord emphasized that U.S. arms sales would continue to be consistent with both the TRA and the August 17 communique.[6]

The 1994 Taiwan policy review of the Clinton administration resulted in several positive changes in U.S.-Taiwan relations. More adjustments will be required, however, as Washington seeks to balance its interests in China and Taiwan. Rapid change in PRC-ROC relations, political evolution on Taiwan (and perhaps soon on the mainland with the passing of Deng Xiaoping), and changes in Taipei's international status create a shifting international and domestic environment that is difficult to predict, much less to stabilize. Nonetheless, despite differences with the PRC over the Taiwan issue, U.S. interests dictate that Taiwan's security remain a fundamental aspect of American policy toward Asia and the Pacific.

Notes

1. "The Taiwan Bucket-Economic Impact" and related documents supplied by the office of Senator Frank Murkowski in support of his 1993-1994 amendment to the TRA. The U.S. job loss noted in the documents was based on estimates provided by the Department of Commerce (International Trade Administration), *Contribution of Exports to US Employment, 1980-1987* (March 1989, pp. 22-24), which stated that every $1 billion in defense exports results in 22,800 man years in direct employment and 17,000 man years of indirect employment.

2. This principle is important because Beijing will attempt to use the talks to establish the principle that major U.S. weapons transfers should first be discussed with the PRC, much in the same way that Beijing has tried to establish the principle that political reform introduced in Hong Kong must first be discussed with Chinese authorities.

3. "The Taiwan Question and the Reunification of China" (Beijing, China: Taiwan Affairs Office and Information Office, State Council, August 1993), as translated in *Beijing Review*, September 6-12, 1993, pp. I-VIII.

4. Cited in CNA report from Hong Kong, September 8, 1994.

5. In August and September 1994 the PLA conducted large-scale amphibious war games around Dongshan island off the coast of southern Fujian Province and the largest-ever combined fleet exercises near Zhoushan island off the northern Zhejiang coast. The ROC chief of the general staff, General Liu Ho-chan, said Dongshan's terrain was similar to that of Taiwan's west coast and that the exercise was in preparation for an eventual attack against Taiwan. Defense Minister Sun Chen said, "This exercise takes Taiwan as its hypothetical enemy....The Chinese communists are continuously holding these kinds of small actions, so we cannot relax even for one second." Reuters report from Taipei, Taiwan, August 31, 1994; UPI report from Taipei, September 3, 1994.

6. "Statement of Assistant Secretary Winston Lord, Senate Foreign Relations Committee, Hearing on Taiwan Policy," September 27, 1994, ms.

9

Conclusion

The previous chapter described extensive U.S. interests in Taiwan's security, including peace and stability in East Asia, a favorable balance of power, U.S. credibility, protection of market democracies, commercial interests in Taiwan, and development of democratic institutions and a free market economy in China.

Several policy recommendations were also made to balance U.S. interests in diplomatic relations with the PRC and close, unofficial relations with Taiwan. These recommendations included the preservation of a "one China" policy, adherence to the three Sino-American joint communiques, expanding U.S. relations with Taiwan, and strengthening Taiwan's self-defense capabilities.

The security of Taiwan became an important U.S. interest in 1950, but that interest continues today. In the post-Cold War period many new factors have emerged in calculations of U.S. interests in Taiwan's security. These factors include political change on Taiwan, increased calls for Taiwan independence, the modernization of the PLA, Sino-American tensions over human rights and other issues, the reduction of U.S. military forces in the Western Pacific, the concentration of the American public on pressing domestic issues, and shifts in the balance of power in Asia favoring Chinese hegemony. These factors present serious challenges to U.S. policy toward Taiwan and its security.

Summary

During his first two years in office, President Bill Clinton spent considerable time focusing on Asia. Fortunately, the Asian Pacific security architecture constructed by the United States during the Cold War was not created solely in response to the Soviet threat. It served several other purposes, including the maintenance of a favorable balance of power in the region, deterrence of threats other than that of the Soviet Union, and protection of the region's political stability and economic development. Because of the utility of existing policy infrastructure, Clinton's policies toward the Asia-Pacific region were similar to those of President Bush, although President Clinton's vision of a "new Pacific community" was more coherent.

But the Asian policy environment had changed in at least two important ways: most Asian nations perceived the possibility of a fundamental shift in the regional balance of power due to a relative decline of U.S. power, and most Americans placed a much higher priority on domestic economic issues. In the first instance, Asian governments were convinced that the era of Pax Americana was coming to an end and that the United States, like other Western imperialist powers, gradually would disengage from the region. In contrast to this assessment of declining American power, Clinton gave higher priority to Asia in U.S. foreign policy because of the region's tremendous economic importance. Hence, while many Asians came to doubt U.S. commitments, the Clinton administration sought to maintain U.S. credibility by emphasizing permanent U.S. interests in the region, particularly the economic.

To this end, President Clinton assured Asian governments of his intention to maintain a strong U.S. presence in the region militarily, politically, economically, and culturally. His initial policies toward Asia included:

- a continued strong U.S. military presence in the Western Pacific
- greatly expanded efforts to combat proliferation of weapons of mass destruction and their advanced delivery systems
- new regional security dialogues involving Japan, China, Russia, and most other Asian Pacific nations
- a revived economic, political, and security partnership between the United States and Japan
- progress toward more open economies and wider free trade
- a stronger commitment to regional economic integration and greater political cooperation

- a greatly expanded role for APEC as an instrument of economic integration
- support for democracy as the political base for free markets and peaceful competition
- more vigorous support for universal standards of human rights.

Clinton said these policies would create a "new Pacific community" in which economic competition would be vigorous but free and peaceful, the diverse nations of Asia would work as equal partners to improve their individual societies, and democracy, as well as the military balance, would protect regional security.

China was key to Clinton's vision of a more integrated community in the Asian Pacific region. He accepted China as a global power and acknowledged its expanding role in regional affairs. At the same time, he insisted that Beijing abide by international standards in the areas of arms sales, the transfer of advanced weapons technology, trade, and respect for human rights.

Many of the foreign policy goals of the United States and the PRC were in sharp contrast. The United States wanted to speed the evolution of non-democratic countries into market democracies; China viewed this as U.S. hegemonism, big power politics, Western cultural imperialism, and interference in the internal affairs of sovereign states. The United States wanted to limit the expansion of nuclear and conventional forces; China saw these efforts as designed in part to maintain a favorable balance of power for the West. The Clinton administration wanted the United Nations to play a wider role in peacekeeping and peacemaking operations; China saw much of this as manipulation of the U.N. by the United States for its own purposes. The United States wanted all nations to adhere to universally accepted norms of human rights behavior; China believed human rights were the internal affair of individual states and interpreted Washington's efforts as infringement on national sovereignty.

Chinese security analysts believed the United States to be a declining power, but they also viewed Washington as the principal threat to China in the post-Cold War period because of U.S. military power and tendencies to interfere in the internal affairs of other nations. For their part, American leaders made no secret of their hope to use increased contact with the PRC to influence the transformation of China into a democratic, free market nation. PRC leaders called this long-term U.S. strategy "peaceful evolution," noting that its intent was to replace the communist system with a market democracy. Beijing needed good

relations with Washington to modernize China, but the PRC's main
objective was not good relations with the United States: it was to
increase PRC strength so that China could protect its sovereignty and
territorial integrity from countries like the United States.

President Clinton likewise understood the dual nature of Sino-
American relations. He pressured the PRC to change its policies in the
areas of missile proliferation, unfair trading practices, and human rights
abuses. At the same time, Clinton worked closely with China in areas of
mutual concern such as increased tensions on the Korean peninsula.
Early efforts to link China's MFN trading status with improvement in
human rights were soon abandoned by the administration in favor of a
pragmatic policy of "reengagement" almost identical to that of President
Bush.

Taiwan remained an "explosive issue" in Sino-American relations.
Beginning around 1986 the Republic of China adopted extensive political,
economic, and other reforms that created, in essence, a "new" Taiwan.
Most changes were in U.S. interests; and, overall, there were no
fundamental differences in U.S. and ROC policies such as those which
characterized U.S.-PRC relations.

Positive change on Taiwan necessitated improvement in U.S.-Taiwan
relations. The Clinton administration approved of Taiwan's
democratization, strong market economy, more fair trading practices, and
cooperative policies toward mainland China. While adhering to its "one
China" policy, the administration promised to honor the Taiwan Relations
Act, improve commercial relations with Taiwan, and support Taipei's
participation in GATT and certain other international organizations. The
Clinton administration also sold Taipei advanced arms and defense
technology at levels at least as high as those of the Bush administration.

In recognition of Taiwan's political and economic progress and in
response to congressional pressure to improve U.S. treatment of Taiwan,
President Clinton announced in September 1994 modest improvement in
U.S.-Taiwan relations. The "refinements" included changing the name of
Taiwan's representative organization from "Coordination Council of North
American Affairs" to "Taipei Economic and Cultural Representative
Office in the United States," and allowing senior U.S. and Taiwan
officials responsible for economic and technical matters to meet in each
other's offices. The president also reaffirmed U.S. support for Taiwan's
entrance into GATT and other international non-political organizations
and promised to continue sale of defense equipment and services in
compliance with the Taiwan Relations Act.

The Clinton administration viewed Taiwan's security as an important U.S. interest. Indeed, successive administrations since the Korean War have viewed peace in the Taiwan Strait as vital to U.S. national security objectives in East Asia. This is because fundamental U.S. interests are at stake:

- the preservation of a balance of power in Asia favorable to the United States
- the maintenance of peace and stability in the region
- the credibility of other U.S. security commitments in the Asia-Pacific region
- U.S. moral commitments to protect market democracies from hostile authoritarian regimes
- protection of U.S. commercial and other interests in both Taiwan and China
- century-old American goals of helping the Chinese people develop a democratic government and prosperous economy.

In more recent years, Taiwan has become an important moderating influence on PRC behavior. Strategically, it is in the U.S. interest that Beijing, as long as it is potentially hostile, not be united with Taiwan and thus positioned to cause greater harm to American interests in Asia.

The factors influencing Taiwan's security are many and complex. Some of these factors suggest the PRC threat to Taiwan is very low; others indicate the PRC threat is increasing; still others that the threat is fluid and uncertain. Overall, the current PRC military threat to Taiwan appears low to moderate, but the threat seems to be growing. Taiwan's security might become more tenuous if one or more of the following occurred:

- Beijing concluded that its military capabilities could overwhelm those of Taiwan.
- A movement toward de jure independence occurred on Taiwan.
- PRC leaders believed the United States was unable or unwilling to intervene on Taiwan's behalf.
- Beijing determined that a limited use of force might be successful in achieving its political objectives toward Taiwan.

A war in the Taiwan Strait would greatly harm U.S. interests. Such a conflict might not be confined to Taiwan. The commercial interests of virtually all nations trading with East Asia would be impaired.

International shipping and air traffic would be disrupted, with some loses possible due to hostilities. The East Asian economic miracle would be threatened; a major arms buildup in the region would probably occur. A further shift in the regional balance of power is probable, perhaps less favorable to the United States. The war might cause domestic political problems for the United States. There is high probability a war in the Taiwan Strait would draw China and the United States into a military confrontation.

Because a war between Taiwan and China could seriously damage U.S. interests, a major U.S. goal for the past four decades has been the prevention of such a conflict. During his administration, President Clinton can take several steps to reduce Beijing's incentives to use force against Taiwan. In terms of inducements to the PRC not to use force, the United States can continue to:

- try to convince the PRC that the peaceful resolution of the Taiwan issue is in China's long-term interest
- affirm the three Sino-American joint communiques and U.S. acknowledgement of "one China"
- contribute to a peaceful environment in the Taiwan Strait by maintaining cordial relations with both Chinese governments and by encouraging mutually beneficial exchanges across the Taiwan Strait
- more fully integrate the PRC into global economic and political systems
- cooperate with other developed nations to provide financial and other assistance to the PRC for its economic modernization
- encourage Beijing to fulfill its international responsibilities as a major power by pursuing policies of peace and moderation toward Taiwan.

To help Taiwan maintain an adequate deterrence, President Clinton can take both military and non-military steps. Militarily, the United States should assist in the modernization of the ROC armed forces and maintain U.S. readiness to intervene in the Taiwan Strait. Steps could include:

- sell Taiwan the advanced weapons and training necessary to ensure a continued military balance in the Taiwan Strait
- sell Taipei technology, production designs, and other assistance to build advanced weapons systems on Taiwan itself
- convince Taipei to purchase mostly American defensive goods and services rather than weapons from third countries

- affirm U.S. intentions to abide by the Taiwan Relations Act and state more explicitly U.S. intentions to come to Taiwan's aid if it is attacked
- maintain a U.S. military presence in the Western Pacific capable of intervening in a crisis over Taiwan.

The Clinton administration can also take non-military steps to strengthen the ROC strategy of comprehensive deterrence. These steps could include:

- communicate to Beijing the U.S. determination to support a peaceful resolution of the Taiwan issue reached between the Chinese people themselves
- assure the PRC that the United States has no plan to support an independent Taiwan state separate from mainland China
- assist Taiwan to expand its international presence through economic and other non-political organizations
- assist Taiwan to broaden its international political role within the context of "one China"
- associate Taiwan with NAFTA
- contribute to a peaceful atmosphere in the Taiwan Strait by encouraging Taipei and Beijing to continue their dialogue and exchanges
- issue statements applauding Taiwan's progress toward democracy
- increase the level of political contact between the U.S. and Taiwan governments
- encourage other members of the international community to inform Beijing of their interests in a peaceful settlement of the Taiwan issue, to control arms sales to ensure a balance of power in the Taiwan Strait, and to support Taipei's efforts to play a more meaningful role in the international community.

Taken together, these steps establish an implicit linkage between PRC peaceful approaches to the Taiwan issue and U.S. cooperation with China's modernization. These steps also enhance ROC security by strengthening Taiwan's deterrence. Finally, the steps are designed to improve Taiwan's standing in the world community while adhering to a "one China" policy.

The purpose of U.S. policy is not to divide Taiwan and China, but to persuade Beijing not to use force against Taiwan. This requires a carefully balanced U.S. policy so that U.S. interests in both China and Taiwan can be protected and served. It is in the U.S. interest to preserve this balanced policy, but doing so has become more difficult in recent years. The policy dilemma for the United States is that Washington may be nearing the end of its ability to play both sides. The United States may have to make difficult choices in the future regarding Taiwan's security.

Critical Factors

Two of the factors contributing to this difficulty are the threat of low intensity conflict in the Taiwan Strait and the rise of Taiwanese nationalism.

Low Intensity Conflict

U.S. air and naval forces in the Pacific are adequate to handle any major PRC military operation against Taiwan. The U.S. military is not equipped to respond effectively to certain forms of low intensity force designed to pressure or coerce Taipei. There is a wide range of such options available to Beijing, including assassination, terrorism, "fifth column" activities, sabotage, riots, and other special operations. Demonstrations of PRC military force in the Taiwan Strait or South China Sea, designed to frighten but not harm Taiwan, also fall into this category.

The United States cannot protect Taiwan from these types of force, nor is the U.S. threat of intervention credible under these circumstances. For low intensity threats, the ROC will have to depend on its own resources. Whether PRC uses of limited force would be successful in accomplishing China's political objectives would be determined less by the military capabilities of Beijing, Taipei, and Washington than by the political will of Taiwan.

Theoretically, this gives Beijing an opportunity to force Taipei to accommodate PRC wishes. It is certainly within PRC capabilities to mount these kinds of operations. On the other hand, such low levels of force might not be effective in compelling Taipei to accede to Beijing's demands. Indeed, such action might further alienate the Taiwanese people, harden the ROC position on reunification, and result in economic sanctions from Washington or increased U.S. arms sales to Taiwan.

Thus, while the military risks in low intensity operations are minimal, the political risks are high.

Nonetheless, by mid-1994 there was evidence that Beijing had decided to adopt elements of this "harder" strategy. Its new "war plan" increased political and economic pressure on Taiwan and its international supporters, and accelerated PLA military posturing. In August-September 1994 the PLA flexed its muscles by holding large naval and combined forces exercises in the Taiwan Strait region with Taiwan as its supposed enemy. The exercises were interpreted as a warning to Taiwan over its international aspirations and to Washington over further upgrading relations with Taiwan. If Beijing continues to increase its pressure on Taiwan, it will become more difficult for the United States to pursue a balanced policy toward the PRC and Taiwan.

Taiwanese Nationalism

One of the most complex factors to evaluate in Taiwan's new security environment is the impact of Taiwanese nationalism on the probability of U.S. military intervention in the event of a PRC attack. No one knows whether the growth of Taiwan's self-identity and desire for self-determination will lead eventually to a declaration of independence from China. But the possibility exists, and the democratization of the decision-making process on Taiwan has greatly increased its probability.

If in response to public demand the Taiwan government formally declared the island an independent nation-state, Beijing would probably respond with force. Most likely, the PRC would attempt to enforce a naval blockade of Taiwan, seek to establish air supremacy over the Taiwan Strait, and prepare to invade Taiwan if necessary. Various other overt and covert operations would probably be undertaken simultaneously.

Under these circumstances, there would be agonized debate in Washington over an appropriate response. On the one hand, Taiwan had provoked the PRC by declaring independence. On the other hand, the Taiwan people had exercised their right of self-determination against a hostile communist government. The president might decide to intervene, or he might not on the grounds that American security commitments do not extend to Taiwan when Taipei provokes an attack.

If the president refused to intervene, American politics could become decisive. There is high probability the Congress and the American people would believe Taiwan's bid for independence was justified. If this were the case, then political pressure would mount quickly on the administration to prevent Taiwan from being overwhelmed by the Chinese communists. CNN and major television networks would contribute to this pressure by showing footage of Taiwan's plight. The president would risk being labeled as responsible for having "lost China" a second time. The degree of public condemnation could make the president's re-election (or that of his party's next candidate) difficult. A considerable number of congressional seats held by the president's party might also be lost. The president could not escape the pressure by postponing a decision until the crisis was resolved. To do too little would be almost as politically damaging as to do nothing. Faced with a deteriorating domestic political situation, the president might order American intervention to stop the fighting, despite his initial reluctance to do so. Numerous options -- such as deploying one or more carrier battle groups, ASW assets, or AWACS -- would be available to the president to maximize Taiwan's defense capabilities while minimizing U.S. loses.

This illustrates a crucial point. Although the president is commander-in-chief, one key to U.S. intervention is support for Taiwan by the Congress and the American people. The PRC works closely with the Executive Branch of the U.S. government to ensure continuity in Sino-American diplomatic relations. But the Republic of China has spent millions of dollars and thousands of man-hours to cultivate a positive image in the Congress and with the American public. This strategy has served Taiwan's interests very well, since the Congress repeatedly has protected Taiwan from those ready to sacrifice ROC interests to further U.S. relations with the PRC.

But pro-independence advocates on Taiwan should not assume that Congress or the American people would support an independent Taiwan in the same way they have supported the security of the ROC. Some overlap in support would exist, but it might not be sufficient to tip the scale in favor of U.S. military intervention to support Taiwan independence. At minimum, the movement toward Taiwan independence clouds American perceptions and makes it more difficult to pursue a balanced policy toward Beijing and Taipei.

Implications for U.S. China Policy

There is growing evidence that U.S. China policy may be overtaken by events on Taiwan. Democratization has released pent-up emotions of

Taiwanese nationalism. This is reflected in the strong showing of the Democratic Progressive Party in elections since 1989 and in the deepening divisions within the KMT over the ROC's "one China" policy. The lack of KMT consensus on "one China" contributes to a loss of credibility for those arguing for eventual reunification. Indeed, those on Taiwan supporting China's unification are often ridiculed for being unrealistic and sometimes even called "traitors." Fewer and fewer Taiwan residents -- wherever their families' ancestral home -- have a sense of identification with the mainland. Their home is Taiwan.

Until the late 1980s, the sense of nationalism on Taiwan was restrained because of authoritarian KMT rule. But this has changed dramatically in recent years. The mainlanders in the KMT no longer control the political process. Now free to choose their own destiny, the majority Taiwanese population (especially younger generations, regardless of their parent's provincial origin) see few advantages in being part of China, especially when the much larger mainland is perceived as being repressive, corrupt, backward, and arrogant. The residents of Hong Kong have no choice but to return to the "embrace of the motherland" in 1997. The people of Taiwan believe they do have a choice in the matter.

Economic success and political progress are increasing public demands on Taiwan that their government play a more active role in international affairs. Repeated diplomatic setbacks due to PRC opposition have contributed to a widening sense of frustration with the ROC government's "one China" policy. Many on Taiwan view this policy as responsible for Taipei's diplomatic isolation since it forces other countries into an "either them or us" choice which the PRC usually wins. More people are willing to take significant risks to enhance Taiwan's international role. After all, they say, what do we have to lose?

A growing number of Taiwan foreign policy specialists are convinced that Taiwan can separate successfully from China. Several arguments are used:

- The PRC will never attack Taiwan because Chinese leaders are more concerned about China's economic modernization.
- Since the PRC will not use force if Taiwan declares independence, other nations will feel confident to recognize Taipei diplomatically.
- If the PRC does attack, it lacks the amphibious capability to invade Taiwan.
- The United States, even if it is initially reluctant to do so, will eventually come to Taiwan's aid if it is attacked by the PRC.

- Even if the United States does not intervene, Taiwan can withstand a blockade and defeat a PRC amphibious assault.
- Once having demonstrated its ability to withstand a PRC attack, Taiwan will win diplomatic recognition from other countries.
- Thus, whether the PRC attacks or does not attack, most nations will recognize Taiwan as an independent country if the Taiwan people decide to move in that direction.

As these arguments have become more widely accepted on Taiwan, there is a growing tendency to reject warnings from Beijing that it might use force if Taiwan moves in the direction of independence. Indeed, PRC warnings fuel sentiment in favor of "two Chinas" and Taiwan independence. Thus, while Taiwanese nationalism does not equate to Taiwan independence, the question of Taiwan's future relationship with China has become a much more urgent public policy issue in Taipei, Beijing, and Washington.

One result of the democratization and Taiwanization of ROC politics is that an increasing number of people actively oppose unification with the mainland under any circumstances. In response to this growing public opposition to unification, the KMT party and ROC government are gradually modifying their "one China" policy. Lip-service is paid to unification as an eventual goal, but practical steps are taken to secure Taiwan's immediate autonomy as a separate international political entity with equal rights and responsibilities with other nation-states.

PRC leaders view these developments on Taiwan with deep concern. As China's central government, Beijing must protect Chinese territorial integrity. Evidenced by the PRC's handling of political reform in Hong Kong, China is not inclined to allow economic considerations, public opinion, or world opinion to overshadow the importance of political control over Chinese territory. Moreover, the PRC is intent on increasing its national power to play a larger and more definitive role in regional and global affairs. If Taiwan "slipped away," China's prestige and influence would be weakened, Beijing's credibility as a major power would be undermined, and Chinese leaders would suffer an historic loss of national face. These costs are too high for China to bear, unless forced by weakness to do so.

From the U.S. perspective, there is a great deal the PRC can do to further reform its system to make reunification more palatable to the people of Taiwan. Also, Beijing can improve its reunification terms to make them more attractive to Taipei. Although such policy changes would be welcomed by Washington and Taipei, they carry political risks for the Chinese communist leadership. Beijing also realizes that the DPP and a segment of Taiwan's population might not passively accept any form of reunification.

If the Chinese Communist Party is unable or unwilling to adopt the necessary reforms for peaceful reunification, or if the people of Taiwan decide they want to separate from the mainland regardless of PRC proposals, Beijing will probably conclude that only a use of force will prevent Taiwan from becoming an independent country. China's leaders might be further inclined to reach this conclusion if they believed the correlation of forces in East Asia favored their position. Favorable conditions might include:

- U.S. forces were stretched too thin for effective intervention.
- U.S. political attention was diverted elsewhere, either domestically or toward some other international crisis.
- There was lack of political will in the U.S. government to intervene on Taiwan's behalf.
- Taiwan's armed forces were not strong enough to defend the island.
- Taiwan's will to resist PRC pressure was weakened due to internal divisions.
- PLA forces were sufficiently strong to undertake successful military operations against Taiwan.

The possibility that the ROC might move away from its "one China" policy and that the PRC might rethink its commitment not to use force in the Taiwan Strait strike at the very heart of U.S. interests and policies in East Asia. The Clinton administration should be concerned that this possibility is growing. As a consequence, the United States may find that managing the Taiwan issue will become more difficult over the next decade.

Given this emerging challenge, President Clinton's policy toward China should include the following elements:

1. Use China's concern over the Taiwan independence movement to encourage more rapid and far-reaching political, economic, and social reform on the mainland.
2. Maintain cordial relations with the PRC, including MFN and high-level dialogue on global, regional, and bilateral issues.
3. Encourage Beijing to make greater concessions to Taiwan in PRC proposals for reunification.

4. Reassure Beijing that the United States does not seek to separate Taiwan from China, nor does the United States intend to violate the principles contained in the three communiques.

5. Assure Beijing and Taipei that the United States will not play a role in mediating their differences, but that it will support a peaceful process and outcome negotiated between the two sides.

6. Maintain a close dialogue with the DPP to (a) gain insight into opposition objectives, plans, and strategy; (b) inform DPP leaders and opinion makers on U.S. views of the realities of international politics and U.S. interests; and (c) exert a moderating influence on DPP actions insofar as these impact U.S. interests.

7. Maintain wide contacts among the various factions of the KMT, armed forces, and other centers of power on Taiwan to achieve the same purposes.

8. Continue to upgrade Taiwan's defense capabilities to enhance deterrence in the Taiwan Strait. Arms sales should be adjusted upward because of (a) the drawdown of U.S. forces in the Pacific, (b) the PRC's force modernization and more aggressive posture in East Asia, and (c) Beijing's uneasiness over political transformation on Taiwan.

9. Be more supportive of Taiwan's participation in international organizations as a means to (a) pacify the growing sense of Taiwanese nationalism, (b) strengthen the ROC government's argument that moderate policies are working, (c) add international incentives for Beijing not to use force against Taiwan, and (d) demonstrate U.S. approval of Taipei's efforts to internationalize and liberalize its economy and to push forward with democratic reform.

10. Lift unnecessary restrictions on exchange visits by U.S. and Taiwan government officials, including those with political and defense portfolios.

It is inevitable that any move to modify U.S. policy toward Taiwan, even those as modest as the Clinton administration's "refinement" in 1994, will be viewed with suspicion in Beijing and encourage the DPP to press harder for Taiwan independence. However, developments on Taiwan are generating pressures that need to be managed and channeled in ways not damaging to U.S. interests. At the same time, efforts must be made to prevent the PRC from misreading strategic changes in Asia and concluding that some use of force in the Taiwan Strait is a viable option.

For the United States to advocate or support Taiwan independence would result in long-term Chinese condemnation and poison Sino-American relations for many years. This policy would not be wise unless: (a) Beijing explicitly or implicitly approved of Taiwan's independence, (b) the PRC became an enemy of the United States, or (c) the Chinese state disintegrated. At the same time, however, the United States should be consistent with its own moral principles and not seek to prevent Taiwan independence if that is the democratic choice of the people of Taiwan. As to whether the United States should defend an independent Taiwan or formally recognize it as an independent country, these are matters so dependent upon circumstances that little good would be served by additional speculation.

Conclusion

Since 1979 the United States has been able to serve its interests in China and Taiwan through a policy characterized by three interlocking principles:

1. adherence to a "one China" policy acknowledging China's claim that Taiwan is Chinese territory
2. a pragmatic "dual track" approach of maintaining diplomatic relations with the People's Republic of China and informal but friendly relations with Taiwan
3. insistence that the Taiwan issue be settled peacefully by the Chinese themselves.

The success of this policy has been conditioned on its acceptance by Beijing and Taipei, both of whom saw their fundamental interests protected in the U.S. formulation. If both Chinese sides would agree to "two Chinas" (unlikely, but theoretically possible), the United States could change its policy to one of dual recognition. The United States could even recognize the independence of Taiwan, if both Chinese sides agreed.

However, the United States cannot so easily drop its insistence that the Taiwan issue be settled peacefully. There are fundamental U.S. interests in Taiwan's security that extend beyond China and Taiwan. Because of these broader interests in preserving peace and stability in East Asia as a whole, the United States must deter the PRC from attacking Taiwan and must provide Taipei with adequate defensive weapons.

The continued U.S. involvement in Taiwan's security makes a peaceful and honorable settlement of the Taiwan issue possible over time.

To weaken the U.S. involvement in Taiwan's security would add to the likelihood of force being used in the Taiwan Strait, particularly in an era of rising Taiwanese nationalism. The maintenance of peace in the Taiwan Strait is thus a cornerstone of U.S. policy toward China and toward East Asia as a whole. It is for this reason that Taiwan's security should remain of great concern to the United States under the Clinton administration and for the remainder of this century.

Bibliography

Bader, William B. and Jeffrey T. Bergner. *The Taiwan Relations Act: A Decade of Implementation.* Indianapolis: Hudson Institute, 1989.

Barnett, A. Doak. *The FX Decision.* Washington: Brookings Institution, 1981.

_____. *U.S. Arms Sales: The China-Taiwan Tangle.* Washington: Brookings Institution, 1982.

Bonds, Ray. *The Chinese War Machine.* London: Salamander Books Ltd., 1979.

Borthwick, Mark. *Pacific Century: The Emergence of Modern Pacific Asia.* Boulder: Westview, 1992.

Bullard, Monte R. *China's Political-Military Evolution.* Boulder: Westview, 1985.

Bullock, Mary Brown and Robert S. Litwak, eds. *The United States and the Pacific Basin: Changing Economic and Security Relationships.* Washington: Woodrow Wilson Center Press, 1991.

Bunge, Frederica M. and Rinn-sup Shinn. *China: A Country Study.* Washington: American University, 1981.

Chaffee, Frederick H. *Area Handbook for the Republic of China.* Washington: American University, 1969.

Chang, Gordon H. *Friends and Enemies: The United States, China, and the Soviet Union.* Stanford: Stanford University Press, 1990.

Chang, Jaw-ling Joanne. *United States-China Normalization: An Evaluation of Foreign Policy Decision Making.* Baltimore: University of Maryland School of Law, 1986.

Chang, Parris H. and Martin L. Lasater, eds. *If China Crosses the Taiwan Strait: The International Response.* Lanham: University Press of America, 1993.

Chen, Jie. *Ideology in U.S. Foreign Policy: Case Studies in U.S. China Policy.* Westport: Praeger, 1992.

Cheng, Tun-jen and Stephan Haggard. *Political Change in Taiwan.* Boulder: Lynne Rienner Publishers, 1992.

China: U.S. Policy Since 1945. Washington: Congressional Quarterly, Inc., 1980.

Ching, Frank. *Hong Kong and China: For Better or For Worse.* New York: China Council of the Asia Society and the Foreign Policy Association, 1985.

Chiu, Hungdah. *Constitutional Development and Reform in the Republic of China on Taiwan.* Baltimore: University of Maryland School of Law, 1993.

_____. *Koo-Wang Talks and the Prospect of Building Constructive and Stable Relations Across the Taiwan Straits.* Baltimore: University of Maryland School of Law, 1993.

Chu, Yun-han. *Crafting Democracy in Taiwan.* Taipei: Institute for National Policy Research, 1992.

_____, ed. *The Role of Taiwan in International Economic Organizations.* Taipei: Institute for National Policy Research, 1990.

Clough, Ralph N. *Island China.* Cambridge: Harvard University Press, 1978.

_____. *Reaching Across the Taiwan Strait.* Boulder: Westview Press, 1993.

Cohen, Warren I. and Akira Iriye, eds. *The Great Powers in East Asia: 1953-1960.* New York: Columbia University Press, 1990.

Copper, John F. *Taiwan: Nation-State or Province?* Boulder: Westview, 1990.

_____. *China Diplomacy: The Washington-Taipei-Beijing Triangle.* Boulder: Westview, 1992.

_____. *Historical Dictionary of Taiwan.* Metuchen: Scarecrow Press, 1993.

_____. *Taiwan's 1991 and 1992 Non-Supplemental Elections.* Lanham: University Press of America, 1994.

Damrosch, Lori Fisler. *The Taiwan Relations Act After Ten Years.* Baltimore: University of Maryland School of Law, 1990.

Downen, Robert L. *To Bridge the Taiwan Strait.* Washington: Council for Social and Economic Studies, 1984.

Fairbank, John K. *The United States and China.* Cambridge: Harvard University Press, 1979.

Fang, Lizhi. *Bringing Down the Great Wall.* New York: W.W. Norton & Company, 1990.

Folte, Paul Humes. *Swords Into Plowshares? Defense Industry Reform in the PRC.* Boulder: Westview, 1992.

Fu, Jen-ken. *Taiwan and the Geopolitics of the Asian-American Dilemma.* Westport: Praeger, 1992.

Furuya, Keiji. *Chiang Kai-shek: His Life and Times.* New York: St. John's University Press, 1981.

Garver, John W. *China's Decision for Rapprochement with the United States, 1968-1971.* Boulder: Westview, 1982.

Gelber, Harry G. *Technology, Defense, and External Relations in China, 1975-1978.* Boulder: Westview, 1979.

Gilbert, Stephen P. *Northeast Asia in U.S. Foreign Policy.* Beverly Hills: Sage Publications, 1979.

_____, ed. *Security in Northeast Asia: Approaching the Pacific Century.* Boulder: Westview, 1988.

_____ and William M. Carpenter, eds. *America and Island China: A Documentary History.* Lanham: University Press of America, 1989.

Gill, R. Bates. *Chinese Arms Transfers: Purposes, Patterns, and Prospects in the New World Order.* Westport: Praeger, 1992.

_____. *The Challenge of Chinese Arms Proliferation: U.S. Policy for the 1990s.* Carlisle Barracks: U.S. Army War College, 1993.

Godwin, Paul H.B. *The Chinese Defense Establishment: Continuity and Change in the 1980s.* Boulder: Westview, 1983.

_____. *Development of the Chinese Armed Forces.* Maxwell Air Force Base: Air University Press, 1988.

Gold, Thomas. *State and Society in the Taiwan Miracle.* Armonk: M.E. Sharpe, 1985.

Goldwater, Barry M. *China and the Abrogation of Treaties.* Washington: Heritage Foundation, 1978.

Gregor, A. James. *The China Connection.* Stanford: Hoover Institution, 1986.

_____ and Maria Hsia Chang. *The Republic of China and U.S. Policy.* Washington: Ethics and Public Policy Center, 1983.

_____ and Andrew B. Zimmerman. *Ideology and Development: Sun Yat-sen and the Economic History of Taiwan.* Berkeley: University of California Press, 1981.

Harding, Harry. *A Fragile Relationship: The United States and China Since 1972.* Washington: Brookings Institution, 1992.

_____ and Yuan Ming, eds. *Sino-American Relations 1945-1955: A Joint Reassessment of a Critical Decade.* Wilmington: Scholarly Resources, Inc., 1989.

Dennis Van Vranken Hickey. *United States-Taiwan Security Ties: From Cold War to Beyond Containment.* Westport: Praeger, 1994.

Hinton, Harold C. *Communist China in World Politics.* Boston: Houghton Mifflin Co., 1966.

_____. *Peking-Washington.* Beverly Hills: Sage Publications, 1976.

_____. *The Sino-Soviet Confrontation.* New York: National Strategy Information Center, 1976.

_____. *The China Sea.* New York: National Strategy Information Center, 1980. •

Hsiung, James C. *Contemporary Republic of China: The Taiwan Experience 1950-1980.* New York: American Association for Chinese Studies, 1981.

Jencks, Harlan W. *From Muskets to Missiles: Politics and Professionalism in the Chinese Army, 1945-1981.* Boulder: Westview, 1982.

Joffe, Ellis. *The Chinese Army After Mao.* Cambridge: Harvard University Press, 1987.

Kintner, William R. *A Matter of Two Chinas.* Philadelphia: Foreign Policy Research Institute, 1979.

Klintworth, Gary. *China's Modernization: The Strategic Implications for the Asia-Pacific Region.* Canberra: Australian Government Publishing Service, 1989.

Kuo, Shirley W.Y. *The Taiwan Economy in Transition.* Boulder: Westview, 1983.

_____, Gustav Ranis, and John C.H. Fei. *The Taiwan Success Story.* Boulder: Westview, 1981.

Lasater, Martin L. *The Security of Taiwan.* Washington: Georgetown University Press, 1982.

_____. *The Taiwan Issue in Sino-American Strategic Relations.* Boulder: Westview, 1984.

_____. *Taiwan: Facing Mounting Threats.* Washington: Heritage Foundation, 1987.

_____. *Policy in Evolution: The U.S. Role in China's Reunification.* Boulder: Westview, 1988.

_____. *A Step Toward Democracy: The December 1989 Elections in Taiwan, Republic of China.* Lanham: University Press of America, 1990.

_____. *U.S. Interests in the New Taiwan.* Boulder: Westview, 1993.

_____, ed. *Beijing's Blockade Threat to Taiwan.* Washington: Heritage Foundation, 1985.

Lee, Lai To. *The Reunification of China: PRC-Taiwan Relations in Flux.* New York: Praeger, 1991.

Leng, Shao Chuan. *Chiang Ching-kuo's Leadership in the Development of the Republic of China on Taiwan.* Lanham: University Press of America, 1993.

Li, Chin-ch'uan. *Sparking a Fire: The Press and the Ferment of Democratic Change in Taiwan.* New York: Columbia University Press, 1993.

Li, Kwoh-ting. *The Evolution of Policy Behind Taiwan's Development Success.* New Haven: Yale University Press, 1988.

Lin, Chong-pin. *China's Nuclear Weapons Strategy: Tradition Within Evolution.* Lexington: Lexington Books, 1988.

Moody, Peter R. *Political Change on Taiwan: A Study of Ruling Party Adaptability.* New York: Praeger, 1992.

Mosher, Steven W. *China Misperceived: American Illusions and Chinese Reality.* New York: Harper Collins, 1990.

_____, ed. *The United States and the Republic of China: Democratic Friends, Strategic Allies, and Economic Partners.* New Brunswick: Transaction Publishers, 1989.

Nelson, Harvey. *Power and Insecurity: Beijing, Moscow, and Washington 1949-1988.* Boulder: Lynne Rienner Publishers, 1989.

Pollack, Jonathan D. and James A. Winnefeld. *U.S. Strategic Alternatives in a Changing Pacific.* Santa Monica: Rand Corporation, 1990.

Rabushka, Alvin. *The New China: Comparative Economic Development in Mainland China, Taiwan and Hong Kong.* Boulder: Westview, 1987.

Ranis, Gustav, ed. *Taiwan: From Developing to Mature Economy*. Boulder: Westview, 1992.

Robinson, Thomas W., ed. *Democracy and Development in East Asia: Taiwan, South Korea, and the Philippines*. Lanham: University Press of America, 1991.

Scalapino, Robert. *The Last Leninists: The Uncertain Future of Asia's Communist States*. Washington: Center for Strategic and International Studies, 1992.

Segal, Gerald. *Defending China*. London: Oxford University Press, 1985.

Shambaugh, David. *Beautiful Imperialist: China Perceives America, 1972-1990*. Princeton: Princeton University Press, 1992.

Shen, James. *The U.S. and Free China*. Washington: Acropolis Books, 1983.

Simon, Denis Fred and Michael Y.M. Kau, eds. *Taiwan: Beyond the Economic Miracle*. Armonk: M.E. Sharpe, 1992.

Simon, Sheldon. *The Future of Asia-Pacific Collaboration*. Lexington: Lexington Books, 1988.

Snyder, Edwin K., A. James Gregor, and Maria Hsia Chang. *The Taiwan Relations Act and the Defense of the ROC*. Berkeley: University of California Press, 1980.

Solomon, Richard H. *Chinese Political Negotiating Behavior: A Briefing Analysis*. Santa Monica: Rand Corporation, 1985.

Spence, Jonathan. *To Change China: Western Advisers in China, 1620-1960*. New York: Penguin Books, 1980.

_____. *In Search of Modern China*. New York: Norton, 1990.

Sutter, Robert G. *Taiwan: Entering the 21st Century*. Lanham: University Press of America, 1988.

_____ and William R. Johnson, eds. *Taiwan in World Affairs*. Boulder: Westview, 1994.

Swanson, Bruce. *Eighth Voyage of the Dragon*. Annapolis: Naval Institute Press, 1982.

Tan, Qingshan. *The Making of U.S. China Policy: From Normalization to the Post-Cold War Era*. Boulder: Lynne Rienner Publishers, 1992.

Tien, Hung-mao. *The Great Transition: Political and Social Change in the Republic of China*. Stanford: Stanford University Press, 1989.

Tow, William T. *Encountering the Dominant Player: U.S. Extended Deterrence Strategy in the Asia-Pacific*. New York: Columbia University Press, 1991.

_____, ed. *Building Sino-American Relations: An Analysis for the 1990s*. New York: Paragon House, 1991.

Tsai, Wen-hui. *In Making China Modernized: Comparative Modernization Between Mainland China and Taiwan*. Baltimore: University of Maryland School of Law, 1993.

Tucker, Nancy Bernkopf. *Taiwan, Hong Kong and the United States, 1945-1992*. New York: Twayne, 1994.

U.S. Department of Defense. *A Strategic Framework for the Asian Pacific Rim: Looking Toward the 21st Century.* Washington: U.S. Government Printing Office, 1990.

Wheeler, Jimmy W. and Perry L. Wood. *Beyond Recrimination: Perspectives on U.S.-Taiwan Trade Tensions.* Indianapolis: Hudson Institute, 1987.

Winckler, Edwin A. and Susan Greenhalgh, eds. *Contending Approaches to the Political Economy of Taiwan.* Armonk: M.E. Sharpe, 1988.

Wolff, Lester L. and David L. Simon. *Legislative History of the Taiwan Relations Act.* New York: American Association for Chinese Studies, 1982.

World Bank. *The East Asian Miracle: Economic Growth and Public Policy.* New York: Oxford University Press, 1993.

Wortzel, Larry M., ed. *China's Military Modernization: International Implications.* New York: Greenwood Press, 1988.

Wu, Yuan-li. *Becoming an Industrialized Nation: ROC's Development on Taiwan.* New York: Praeger, 1985.

Yu, George T. *China in Transition: Economic, Political, and Social Developments.* Lanham: University Press of America, 1993.

Zhan, Jun. *Ending the Chinese Civil War: Power, Commerce, and Conciliation Between Beijing and Taipei.* New York: St. Martin's Press, 1993.

Zhao, Quansheng and Robert G. Sutter, eds. *Politics of Divided Nations: China, Korea, Germany and Vietnam.* Baltimore: University of Maryland School of Law, 1991.

About the Book and Author

The increased military power of China since the close of the Cold War has forced the United States to reconsider its security policy toward Taiwan. In this volume, Martin Lasater explores the many new factors that are now influencing U.S. calculations of one of its more enduring and important security interests in Asia. He considers such security concerns as the reduction of U.S. military forces in the western Pacific, a new arms race in the Taiwan Strait, Sino-American tensions over human rights and arms proliferation issues, increased calls for Taiwan's independence, the Clinton administration's concentration on domestic issues, and the shifting balance of power in the Asia Pacific—especially the PRC's growing influence. Considering the difficult issues President Clinton must weigh, Lasater provides a timely analysis of Taiwan's security in the 1990s within the broader context of Sino-American relations.

Martin L. Lasater is a specialist on East Asia.

Index